MASS CONTROL:

Engineering
Human
Consciousness

Jim Keith

Mass Control: Engineering Human Consciousness

Published by
Adventures Unlimited Press
Kempton, Illinois 60946 USA

www.adventuresunlimitedpress.com

ISBN 1-931882-21-5

Printed on acid free paper in the United States of America

10 9 8 7 6 5 4

For the Inhabitants of Planet 9

After the publication of my book *Mind Control, World Control*, I was contacted by many persons with new information on the subject of human control, both researchers in the field as well as some persons who believe that they have been the subject of abuse by intelligence and other agencies. The necessity for an update and an expansion of my earlier research became apparent. This book is the result.

As always, I was greatly assisted by my personal friends, network of fellow researchers, and readership. Special thanks are due my family who continue to tolerate my odd hours and bohemian brain-style, and to my publishers, to whom I owe much gratitude.

"What luck for rulers that men do not think." —Adolf Hitler

CONTENTS

CHAPTER 1

ORIGINS OF CONTROL

Agents of the world's elite have been long engaged in a war on the populace of Earth. Greed is the motivation for this war, a greed so pervasive that it encompasses the planet and all of the beings on it, but in recent times a philosophy has been used to justify that greed. It is the philosophy of mass control, that ultimately aims at dictating every aspect of human life—even remolding man's perception of reality and himself.

Although the lust for control can be discerned since the beginning of recorded history, a nexus of particular importance arose in Germany in the latter half of the 19th century. As the country increased in military and industrial might, becoming the strongest power in Europe, a revolution simultaneously took place in German philosophic and scientific thought that paradoxically would spread through the world to create positive technological change as well as to birth innumerable toxic children. According to one source:

"The sudden change from relative political weakness to world power and from economic insecurity to prosperity proved to be a great strain on the German character and public life. The spread of materialistic philosophy of life was world-wide in this age, and the idolatry of power was not confined to Germany, but its corrosive effect was particularly strong in a country that was not inured to power."[1]

One aspect of this transformation, this "idolatry of power" was a negative transformation of the psychological sciences. In the late 19th century, earlier more humanistic approaches to understanding mankind were replaced by a scientific philosophy that would be employed less as a measure for the understanding of man than as a justification for a new feudalism and a mechanism of pure control.

The materialist overhauling of psychology was in great part ushered in by the work of the German psychologist Wilhelm Maximilian Wundt. Wundt was a professor of philosophy at the University of Leipzig, and in 1875 established the world's first psychological laboratory there, a move that would eventually turn the world of more humanistic-oriented psychology on its head. Interesting, but Wundt's grandfather is documented as having been a member of the Illuminati secret society, making it not unreasonable to imagine that *herr* professor may also have been a member of that group.

Wundt, in reflection of a powerful materialistic groundswell in German thought that began with Schopenhauer at the beginning of the 19th century and that was to be later epitomized by Karl Marx, rejected in cavalier fashion the notion that man might have a soul or deeper significance than the merely physical, that he was in fact anything more than an animal. Following this line of reasoning, an approach that came to be known in psychology as Structuralism, Wundt insisted that all psychological studies should depend entirely on the study of body reactions. The truth of man, Wundt insisted, could be determined solely through mechanistic means: measurement, analysis, and dissection of bodies. After Wundt had thoroughly infused the psychological sciences with his materialist approach, many scientists—and the members of the ruling class that employed them—believed that they were justified in treating human beings as if they were pieces of meat, and as an overall plan of action, proceeded to do so.

The materialist psychological doctrine spread rapidly with at least twenty-four laboratories established by Wundt's students between the years 1883 and 1893, with more of the German's acolytes fanning out to infiltrate related fields, such as education. Wundt's materialistic approach would infect the thinking of most of the influential psychologists, psychiatrists, educators, and social planners who would follow in the 20th century.[2]

One man who marched to Wundt's dirge was the Russian, Ivan Petrovich Pavlov. Pavlov conducted a wide-ranging research into techniques of control, primarily using dogs for his experimentation. In the now-famous experiment, Pavlov fed his dogs, stimulating salivation, while at the same time ringing a bell. After doing this many times, Pavlov was able to stimulate salivation in reaction to the sound of the bell alone. Other of Pavlov's experiments involved rewarding dogs with petting, or punishing them with pain. Using these kinds of approaches, Pavlov developed his theory of the conditioned reflex, demonstrating that animals are motivated by patterns of conditioned response, and that conditioning can be artificially induced. The results of Pavlov's experiments did not escape the social planners of his day, nor those who would follow.

Notes:
1.   "Germany—History Since 1850," *Encyclopedia Americana*. New York: Americana Corporation, 1963
2.   Lionni, Paolo. *The Leipzig Connection*. Sheridan, Oregon: Delphian Press, 1988; "Germany—History Since 1850"; Wood, Samuel and Ellen Green. *The World of Psychology*, third edition, at www.prenticehall.ca/wood; Weiten, Wayne. "A New Science is Born: The Contributions of Wundt and Hall," *Psychology: Themes and Variations*. 3rd edition, at http://psychology.wadsworth.com/book

CHAPTER 2

PERFECTING INHUMANITY

A time-dishonored approach to the manipulation of mankind is through the philosophy and techniques of eugenics. This is the attempted 'perfecting' of humanity through genetic means: selective breeding, sterilization, biological manipulation, and even murder for those considered unfit.

The study of eugenics has its beginning in Germany, sometime after the mid-19th century mark, stimulated by *volkish* concerns for Aryan racial purity. Rudolf Virchow, pathologist and politician, began a study of national ethnic statistics in 1871, convinced that the majority of Germans would prove to be of relatively pure Nordic descent. The results of his studies proved otherwise. According to Virchow, the obvious solution was to set about Nordicizing the debased German stock.[1]

The popularity of eugenics theories was given a jumpstart in England by Francis Galton, a cousin of Charles Darwin. In 1869 Galton published his book *Hereditary Genius*, that Cornell University anthropology professor Davydd Greenwood has called "an impassioned brief for hereditary aristocracy that became the first modern document of the modern eugenics movement." Galton was the man who launched the 'nature vs. nurture' debate that quietly rages today, arguing for the domination of innate rather than acquired human abilities. It was Galton's opinion that the human race could be improved by selective breeding and the extermination of the unfit. Galton once said that he hoped that eugenics would become "the religion of the future." In the latter part of the century, with endeavors like the Human Genome Project that seeks to map the entirety of human DNA, his hope seems to be moving toward fulfillment.

Galton's theories were influenced in part by his examination of the family trees of eminent stuffed shirts in England. He noted that most persons of accomplishment were related to each other—an aristocratic theory of intelligence— thus theoretically putting the aristocracy on a genetic pedestal and rationalizing a stratified society, or caste system, in Britain and the world.

Even the name of the subject betrays something of its orientation. Galton derived the word eugenics from the Greek *'eugenes'* meaning 'well born.' This aggrandizement of the privileged class was one of the reasons why eugenics research found ready support from the monied in both America and Europe; it justified their disdain for and parasitism of "the masses."[2]

Chairs in Eugenics and Eugenics in Working Society were established at the University College in London in 1904, with the Galton Laboratory for National Eugenics founded in 1907. In 1905, in the United States, the Rockefellers and Carnegies constructed the Eugenics Records Office at Cold Springs Harbor, New York, where genetic research (none dare call it eugenics) is still being done in 1999.[3]

In 1912 the first International Congress of Eugenics was convened at the University of London, presided over by its president, who also happened to be Charles Darwin's son. Vice Presidents of the Congress included the First Lord of the Admiralty, Winston Churchill; M. von Gruber, Professor of Hygiene at Munich University; Dr. Alfred Ploetz, President of the International Society for Race Hygiene; Charles W. Eliot, President Emeritus of Harvard, and the inventor of the telephone, Alexander Graham Bell.

The second International Congress of Eugenics was held in 1921, sponsored by U.S. Secretary of Commerce Herbert Hoover and the presidents of Clark University, Smith College, and the Carnegie Institution. Other prominent supporters of eugenics of the period—who will loom large in the history of control to follow—included many members of the American Eastern establishment, particularly of the Eastern Establishment Dulles and Harriman families.

From 1907 to 1960 more than 100,000 persons were eugenically sterilized in over thirty states in the United States. It is unlikely that the well-known and horrific Nazi approach to eugenics, brutally carried out in laboratories and concentration camps during World War II and reportedly claiming hundreds of thousands of victims, would have taken place without eugenics theory having been earlier popularized by British and American scientists and media, and funded by American and British money interests.[4]

German eugenics studies were organized and bankrolled by the family-run Rockefeller Foundation and its allies in medicine, industry, and politics, with large grants provided to the Kaiser Wilhelm Institute for Psychiatry and the Kaiser Wilhelm Institute for Anthropology, Eugenics, and Human Heredity, in Munich. The latter facility was run by the fascist Swiss psychiatrist Ernst Rudin and his underlings Otmar Verschuer and Franz J. Kallmann. In 1932, Ernst Rudin was named president of the worldwide Eugenics Federation. Rockefeller funding for eugenics research in Germany would continue during World War II, the stated justification being that the war should not impede scientific research.

The Kaiser Wilhelm Institute's eugenics studies were initially endowed by Gustav Krupp von Bohlen und Halbach, the head of the Krupp munitions monolith, and James Loeb, of the Kuhn-Loeb banking family. Loeb's relatives, the Warburgs, were banking partners of William Rockefeller, and both families were responsible for setting up the American Harriman family—also movers and shakers in eugenics—in business.[5]

Although we know little about what took place in German laboratories researching mind control and brainwashing during this period, there are some hints. In 1933, the German Reichstag building was burned. In the time-honored tradition of "the patsy," a Dutchman, a mental patient named Marinus Van der Lubbe, was arrested and charged with the crime. Psychiatric reports called Van der Lubbe an unstable but happy man, who lived as a vagabond and entertained notions of changing the world. In court, however, Van der Lubbe seemed nothing of the sort, appearing almost completely apathetic, responding dully to questions. On the forty-second day of the trial, Van der Lubbe suddenly made a remarkable change. Now he began excitedly talking about "inner voices" that commanded him. He demanded that he be put to death, and then just as suddenly slumped back into apathy. Van der Lubbe was convicted by the court and executed. Subsequent events made it clear, however, that it was members of the Nazi party itself who had burned the Reichstag. It is not outside the realm of possibility that Van der Lubbe had been brainwashed to take the fall, as many other patsies have been programmed to do in the years that have ensued.[6]

After Hitler took control in Germany, Rudin's organizational structure was internalized as part of the Nazi political machine. Rudin was appointed head of the Nazi Racial Hygiene Society, with he and his staff joining the Task Force on Heredity, chaired by Himmler, the group that was to institute the infamous Nazi sterilization laws.

One of Rudin's employees was Josef Mengele, also known as "the Angel of Death," who was to become the medical commandant of Auschwitz and perform his own horrific experimentation upon inmates of the camp.

In 1936, the direct predecessor of the CIA's more famous MKULTRA mind control operation was launched at the New York State Psychiatric Institute, funded by the Freemasonic Scottish Rite Northern Supreme Council, and supervised by Dr. Nolan D.C. Lewis, the Masonic Field Representative of Research on Dementia Praecox. The program was directed by Winfred Overhulser, a prominent Freemason and the superintendent of St. Elizabeth's Hospital in Washington, D.C, where much CIA mind control experimentation would later take place. In 1943, Overhulser went on to become the chairman of the "truth drug" committee for the OSS, among the earliest mind control research programs instituted by American intelligence.

In 1936, Ernst Rudin's assistant Dr. Franz Kallmann, after being exposed in Germany as being half-Jewish, emigrated to America where he established the Medical Genetics Department of the New York State Psychiatric Institute, an operation also funded by the Scottish Rite.

In the preface to his Masonic-funded study of schizophrenics, Kallmann wrote that schizophrenics were a "source of maladjusted crooks...and the lowest types of criminal offenders. Even the faithful believers in liberty...would be happier without those." He added, "I am reluctant to admit the necessity for different eugenics programs for democratic and fascistic communities... There are neither biological nor sociological differences between a democratic and a totalitarian schizophrenic."[7]

After World War II, Otmar Vershuer—who had procured funds for Mengele's experimentation at Auschwitz—was hired by the Rockefeller-funded Bureau of Human Heredity in Denmark, and Rudin, Vershuer, and Kallmann participated in founding the still-active American Society of Human Genetics. Kallman was elected director of the organization and would hold that position until 1965. The American Society of Human Genetics is primarily responsible for the current $3 billion Human Genome Project—headquartered at Cold Springs Harbor, the historical center of American eugenics study that is in the forefront of the news today.

The relation of eugenics to British psychiatry bears examination. The primary controlling body for psychiatry in England is the British National Association for Mental Health (NAMH), formed in 1944, and initially run by the mentally-unstable Montagu Norman, previously of the Bank of England. The group originally met at Norman's London home, where he and Nazi Economics Minister Hjalmar Schacht had met in the 1930s to arrange financing for Hitler.

NAMH is a renaming and public relations sanitization of the National Councils of Mental Hygiene, earlier one of the primary proponents for eugenics programs worldwide, and a group that broadly collaborated with Nazi eugenics practitioners prior to World War II. It can be seen that the current British psychiatric establishment proceeds in a direct line from the earlier eugenics establishment, much the same as the majority of movers and shapers in American politics have come from eugenics pro-active families. In 1948, NAMH joined forces with the United Nations and the Tavistock Institute, a long term collaboration between British military intelligence and psychiatry. NAMH and Tavistock convened an International Congress of Mental Health at the Ministry of Health in London. A World Federation of Mental Health was formed there to coordinate planetary psychological operations. The head of the World Federation was chosen: Brigadier General Dr. John Rawlings Reese, who was also the head of Tavistock. Co-director was Frank Fremont-Smith, the chief medical officer of the Macy Foundation, an organization that was later to be a primary funding source for the CIA's MKULTRA mind control projects. Vice presidents of NAMH included Tavistock psychiatrist and eugenics activist Professor Cyril Burt; Dr. Hugh Crichton-Miller, a founder of Tavistock; psychiatrist Sir David Henderson, author of *Psychiatry and Race Betterment*; Lord Thomas Jeeves Horder, the president of the Eugenics Society of Great Britain and the Family Planning Association; pro-Nazi psychiatrist Carl G. Jung, who was also the psychiatrist for the Dulles family; Dr. Winfred Overhulser, representative of the Scottish Rite Masons; and Dr. Alfred Frank Tredgold, of the British Ministry of Health's Committee on Sterilization.

Although eugenics organizations and activists sought deep cover after the defeat of Hitler, something of the stench of the death camps clinging to the subject, the same programs to weed out the "inferiors" from mankind would continue, with the same personnel or their successors in charge of the programs. Working out of the family offices of the Rockefellers in the United States, the Eugenics Society now metamorphosized into the Society for the Study of Social Biology.[8]

Although it has been a carefully guarded secret by the watchdogs of the mainstream media, eugenics programs were never discontinued worldwide, with involuntary sterilization programs continuing in many countries to this day. Information has only recently surfaced that sterilization programs for those considered to be unfit because of genetics or behavior continued to exist in Scandinavia and in France until the 1970s. At the same time, massive involuntary sterilization programs continue to be implemented in the third world.

Eugenics practice has continued is Australia, where more than one thousand "intellectually disabled" women have been illegally sterilized since 1991. The Human Rights and Equal Opportunity Commission discovered that 1,043 sterilization operations—only 17 of them approved by the court, as mandated by Australian law—had been performed. The number of such operations may in fact have been "several times" as high, since only operations performed using medical insurance were registered.[9]

In 1974 Federal District Court Judge Gerhard Gesell estimated that 'over the last few years' between 100,000 and 150,000 low-income persons had been sterilized under federally funded programs in the United States. Gesell stated 'an indefinite number' of those sterilized were 'improperly coerced' into accepting sterilization.[10]

One of the prime target groups for sterilization in the United States has been the Native American population. According to Ruthann Evanoff, in an article titled "Reproductive Rights and Occupational Health" states that, "Overall, at least twenty-five percent of the Native women of childbearing age have been sterilized, although the total population numbers less than one million. Recent reports estimate that the percentage sterilized in one tribe alone, the Northern Cheyenne, is eighty percent."[11]

An oft-cited justification for current eugenics practice is the elimination of violence in society. At this time millions of dollars are being spent on research into the control of violence through genetic means. In 1992, a report was produced jointly by the National Academy of Science and the National Research Council, titled "Understanding and Preventing Violence." Among the groups funding the report were the Centers for Disease Control, the U.S. Justice Department, and the National Science Foundation. The report suggested that more studies should be done on "biological and genetic factors in violent crime," and suggested that the higher crime rates among black males might come from a genetic predisposition.[12]

In England, concerns are similar. The Department of Health has recently commissioned research into a "delinquency gene" called "Fragile X." According to the *London Sunday Times,* it is believed by some scientists that one in every 259 women carry the defective Fragile X, which causes a lack of brain protein, resulting in anti-social behavior. Health officials are planning to engage in mass screenings so that women who carry the defective gene can be alerted and induced to abort their children.[13]

Notes:
1. Hillel and Henry. *Of Pure Blood.* New York: Pocket Books, 1975
2. Tweedy, Michael, "Francis Galton: The Man and his Science," *University of Calgary Course Notes*; Reilly, Phillip R. "A Look Back at Eugenics," *The Gene Letter*, Volume 1, issue 3, at www.geneletter.org/ ; Lapon, Lenny. *Mass Murderers in White Coats (From Harvard to Buchenwald: A Chronology of Psychiatry and Eugenics)*; Kuhl, Stefan. *The Nazi Connection*—Eugenics, American Racism, and German National Socialism. New York: Oxford University Press, 1994
3. Chaitkin, Anton, "British Psychiatry: From Eugenics to Assassination," *EIR*, October 7, 1994.
4. Lapon
5. Chaitkin
6. Meerloo, Joost A.M. *The Rape of the Mind: The Psychology of Thought Control*, Menticide, and Brainwashing. New York: World Publishing Company, 1956
7. Chaitkin
8. Chaitkin; Reisman, Phd., Judith A. *Kinsey: Crimes and Consequences.* Arlington, Virginia: The Institute for Media Education, Inc., 1998; "Editorial: Ernst Rudin, 1874-1952," American Journal of Medical Genetics, Volume 67, number 4; Chaitkin, Anton, "Population Control, Nazis, and the U.N.!"
9. "More Than 1,000 OZ Girls/Young Women Illegally Sterilized" by Michael Perry, December 15, 1997, Reuters news service
10. Mehler, Barry, "In Genes We Trust: When Science Bows to Racism," Center for the Study of Psychiatry and Psychology, *The Public Eye*, March 1995
11. Evanoff, Ruthann, "Reproductive Rights sna Occupational Health," *WIN* magazine, undated clipping

12. "Recent FDA Decision Highlights Ethical Issues in Drug Research On Children," Peter R. Breggin, M.D., otherwise unattributed clipping
13. Neill, Patricia, "Mass Testing for 'Delinquency' Gene,' Parascope, at www.parascope.com/main.htm

CHAPTER 3

DUMBING US TO DEATH

A n ideological Fifth Column subverted American education in the early days of the twentieth century, with the leader of the movement Daniel Coit Gilman, the first president of Johns Hopkins University and the Carnegie Institute. Gilman studied at the University of Berlin in 1854-55, at the same time that Wilhelm Wundt taught there. After Gilman, Wundt's materialist spin on the subjects of the mind and soul—or lack thereof—would dominate the thinking of the most influential of American educators. The result was that children would soon after be viewed as something akin to lab rats, to be put through mazes, their characters molded at the whims of the "educational" totalitarians.

Another form of Germanic thinking informed Gilman's views: he was a member of the Skull & Bones society. Skull & Bones is a highly secret, ritualistic society based at Yale University that has been called "The most powerful organization in America."

Incredibly, Skull & Bones may be a front for that most mysterious of secret societies, the Illuminati. The German organization from which Skull & Bones obtained its charter appeared within a year after the outlawing of Adam Weishaupt's group in Bavaria and, additionally, an inscription found in the *sanctum sanctorum* of the Bonesmen at Yale is nearly identical in wording to that of a ceremony cited in

Proofs of a Conspiracy, an early condemnation of the Illuminati by Robison. Like the Illuminati, Skull & Bones initiates refer to the group as "the Order."[1]

Since the formation of Skull & Bones about 2,500 persons have been inducted into the secret group, with a small group of Eastern Establishment families forming the core of the group. These families include the Allen, Bundy, Gilman, Perkins, Wadsworth, Phelps, and Lord families. Other families who rose to wealth in the 18th and 19th century have been added to this group, including the Harriman, Davison, Rockefeller, Payne, Pillsbury, and Weyerhauser families. A third group—not Bonesmen—have acted as intermediaries between Skull & Bones and the financial hub of London. This group includes the Warburg, Schiff, Guggenheim, and Meyer families.

Undoubtedly the most important influence that Skull & Bones has had on the world is through the world of politics. Since the turn of the century the direction of American statecraft has been largely steered by prominent Bonesmen from the Harriman, Bundy, Taft, Stimson, Bush, and other families, although I do not recommend that you hold our breath waiting for the establishment media to avail you of this fact.

According to accounts of the time, members of Skull & Bones took over the administration of Yale University in the late 1800s while Daniel Coit Gilman was employed there, and it is reported that all presidents of Yale since that time have been either Bonesmen or closely affiliated with the group.

Yale and Skull & Bones have provided fertile recruiting grounds for American intelligence agencies, with an in-house club for Bonesmen existing in the CIA, according to *Covert Action Information Bulletin*. The term "spook," CIA jargon applied to spies, in fact was a Yale expression designating a member of a campus secret society.[2]

After becoming head of Johns Hopkins University, Daniel Coit Gilman hired another Wundt-trained specialist who not-coincidentally happened to be a Bonesman. This was G. Stanley Hall, who took over the psychological lab at the university. Hall also founded the American Psychological Association and the *American Journal of Psychology*, and mentored the career of Fabian Socialist and New World educator John Dewey.

Dewey, who went on to become the most influential teacher of this century, also studied under George Sylvester Morris, an Hegelian philosopher who had taken his doctorate at the University of Berlin under the same teachers as Gilman. Dewey was among the first to promote school as a mechanism for the creation of a Socialist world order, and as a forum for enforcing "conformity" of the masses rather than as a place to learn the three 'R's. In 1899 Dewey said, "Children who know how to think for themselves spoil the harmony of the collective society which is coming where everyone is interdependent."

One reason for the success of Dewey's "progressive education" is that it was backed to the hilt by Rockefeller and Carnegie money. Dewey for many years was the honorary president of the National Education Association, founded in 1857. The group was founded as a lobbying organization for teachers but soon aligned itself behind a scarlet psychopolitical banner of "progressive education"—a delightful-sounding term that conceals the brainwashing *modus operandi* pioneered by the Soviets. By the turn of the century the NEA was working in full support of Dewey's plans, advocating the dumbing down of the masses into a malleable unit, as well as a one world Fabian Socialist view. A 1934 NEA report avowed, "A dying laissez-faire must be completely destroyed and all of us, including the 'owners,' must be subjected to a large degree of social control."

This one-worldly view persists in current NEA literature, but it has been recontextualized in recent times as a "liberal" viewpoint. The group now issues the following *pronunciamento* in its NEA journal: "The teacher ...can do much to prepare the hearts and minds of children for global understanding and cooperation... At the very top of all the agencies which will assure the coming of world government must stand the school, the teacher, and the organized profession."[3]

Another American student of Wundt was James McKeen Cattell, who was Wundt's assistant in Leipzig in the years 1883-86. Cattell was also deeply influenced by Francis Galton, the founder of eugenics. In 1891 Cattell took over the psychology department at Columbia University, and spent the rest of his life disseminating Wundtian/eugenics doctrine through an abundance of magazines and reference works he edited and wrote.[4]

These and other materialist Wundtians and Fabian one-worlders, funded by the Rockefellers, the Carnegies, and others intent on the suppression and pacification of the populace of the world, completely remade the face of American education in the twentieth century. The agenda that they pursued has culminated in the all-too-familiar situation of American education today in which the majority of persons graduated from high school are functionally illiterate and ill-prepared for doing anything else than saying "yes" to Big Brother and his telescreens.

From the standpoint of the social controllers there are many advantages to keeping the populace stupid, not the least being that the less intelligent a person is, the more susceptible he is to exterior control.

Currently, one of the primary thrusts in American educational brainwashing goes by a variety of names, including Mastery Learning, World Class Education, Common Core of Learning, and Outcome Based Education, but which is most commonly referred to as Goals 2000. Written into law by Bill Clinton in 1994, Rockefeller monies have launched literally hundreds of books into the educational market pushing Goals 2000. Promoted by the National Education Association, the literature describes Goals 2000 as "an Academic/ Behavior Modification Plan based on control theory/reality therapy." The simple purpose of Goals 2000 is populace control and promotion of the totalitarian world order.

Instead of teaching children the academic skills that most parents favor, Goals 2000 and its educational offshoots emphasize "life adjustment skills," family-life education," and "environmental stewardship." Academic study is de-emphasized while "cooperative" attitudes are mandated, including attitudes which significantly seem to bolster a eugenics agenda in the mind of the child, such as the attempted normalizing of homosexuality and playboyism, and abortion as a form of birth control. Providing a hint of what the future of American 'education' is going to be like is a Goals 2000 program that has been adopted in forty states: the "Parents as Teachers" (PAT) program. It is a program that would be more aptly termed the "Teachers as Parents" program. Under this plan children are given a personal computer code number by which they can be tracked for the entirety of their life, and a "parent educator" visits the homes of students a minimum of eight times a year to see that Mom and Dad are giving Junior his tranquilizers and doing their bit in programming a good little robot.

Another offshoot of Goals 2000 is 'the Oregon Option,' which was signed into being on December 5, 1994 by the entire Clinton cabinet and members of the Oregon Congressional delegation. This program was developed by the administrations of former Oregon governors Mark Hatfield and Neil Goldschmidt, and was drafted under the direction of Goldschmidt, a member of the Trilateral Commission. Persons backing the plan include members of the Council on Foreign Relations, the World Bank, the Carnegie Foundation, and the RAND Corporation. One of the main thrusts of the Oregon Option is to seamlessly transition children from school into the industrial workforce, with apprenticeships provided by large corporations.

Again, under the Oregon Option all children conceived in Oregon are entered into a huge database. All expectant parents will be required to attend parenting classes. Once the child is attending school, home visits will be undertaken by school teachers and administrators to determine if the family is fit for rearing the child. Those families deemed to be unfit, or offering "developmental neglect," can be ripped asunder, with children shunted into foster homes or state-run facilities.[5]

Furthering the goals of the social planners, perhaps the most destructive current trend of the educational establishment is the wholesale drugging of students. Drugs, especially amphetamines and Ritalin, are commonly used to dose schoolchildren throughout America. Ritalin is a highly dangerous stimulant that is, according to the U.S. Drug Enforcement Administration, more addictive than cocaine. It also has a wide variety of other negative side effects, including nausea, insomnia, the inhibition of growth, nervous tics, and potential brain damage.

A current estimate of the number of U.S. schoolchildren being drugged with Ritalin is three to five percent, or in excess of two million kids! Since most of the children to whom the drug is given are male, it has been estimated that 10 to 12 percent of all male school children in the U.S. between the ages of six and fourteen are being zombified with Ritalin.

This drugging is being done because of alleged brain malfunctions that cause the children to be "hyperkinetic" or "hyperactive." In most cases the children have been diagnosed by their teachers, almost none of whom who have the medical credentials to do such an assessment.

The main problems that drugs are supposedly used to handle are classed as Attention Deficit Disorder (ADD), and Attention Deficit Hyperactivity Disorder (ADHD). These conditions have in fact never been proven to exist outside of the imagination of medicos and sociatrists, but instead are catchalls that include a wide variety of common childhood problems including inability to concentrate, nervousness, fidgeting, interrupting people, and disciplinary problems. No consistent brain abnormalities have been demonstrated to be linked to ADD or ADHD, although brain disorders including cortical atrophy have been shown to have been caused in some cases by long term treatment with Ritalin and other drugs commonly-prescribed for children.

The symptoms that 'educators' are treating with drugs may in fact have nothing to do with congenital brain defects, as they have argued, but with a number of other less mysterious factors including:

—Poor nutrition, fostered by parents either too poor, irresponsible, or dumbed down themselves to provide decent food for their kids; encouraged by a criminal food production industry more intent on moving cheap, sugar-coated, chemically-dyed, pesticide-poisoned swill than in providing healthy food. Sugar, pesticides, and chemical additives may be a key factor in causing what is termed ADD and ADHD.

—Television and other media. Kids are estimated to watch six hours per day of an electronic medium deliberately designed to foster a short attention span, with quick three-to-five second visual cuts purposely stimulating the kind of artificial agitation that induces a child to respond to commercials. Is it any wonder that these kids have a short attention span?

—Another negative aspect of the pop media is the abundance of sexual and violent images disseminated via TV, movies, hyper-violent video games like *Mortal Kombat*, and music with violent/sexual 'gangsta' ghetto rap. There are many studies showing that when television is introduced to a community that violent acts double over the course of a few years.

As an example of the character of current media that is aimed at children, while waiting in an office recently I was surprised to find a depiction of full female nudity when I picked up a "Batman" comic for the first time in many years. Far be it from me to put down female nudity, but such images are certain to provide a potent distraction to children entering puberty, as well as to encourage a eugenics-friendly "Playboyism," of the kind advocated by Hugh Hefner, himself an admitted acolyte of eugenicist Alfred Kinsey.

—Families who have taken the Dr. Spock or New Age amalgam to heart are another source of problems in childhood discipline. For a kid whose role model is Tupac, Ice-T, KISS, or Marilyn Manson, and whose fantasies are fed by the quick-cut, toxified kink of M-TV, 'Time out' is not going to be an effective disciplinary action.

—Little parental contact with kids at all. The prevailing economy, regardless of the praises of Rapegate Bill, is designed so that both parents usually have to slave full time, leaving very few moments for contact with the kids. The situation of the single parent family is usually worse.

—Finally, there is a problem with the nature of public schooling itself, which does not challenge children to learn or to think creatively, but instead indoctrinates them to conform to their prison-like surroundings. I personally would not like to endure again the circumstances of regimentation and immobilization—sitting at an uncomfortable desk with hands folded and mouth clamped shut for hours every day—that children are forced to put up with in public schools. I would also not relish again being forced to drag my eyes over and memorize deadly-dull texts that no sane adult would ever read if given a choice in the matter. In circumstances like these, it is no surprise that any child with an ounce of wit or energy would rebel and begin to longingly ogle his father's gun cabinet.[6]

These are some of the real causes of ADD and ADHD in school, symptoms for which children are being treated with Ritalin and other addictive drugs. A dramatic example of the results of drugging children may have been played out on April 20, 1999, in Littleton, Colorado, when two young men in black trench coats systematically killed 12 of their schoolmates, and then themselves. Eric Harris, one of the shooters, had been turned down from joining the Marines a scant five days prior when they were informed that he was being prescribed the psychiatric antidepressant drug fluvoxamine maleate, or Luvox, a chemical relative of Ritalin. The American Journal of Psychiatry reports that "Our observations confirm the efficacy of fluvoxamine [Luvox] in the treatment of depression but suggest that this drug can induce mania in some patients when it is given at a normal dose." The coroner's report showed that Harris had therapeutic levels of Luvox in his bloodstream at the time of the shooting, and friends of Harris state that the young man was attempting to quit using the drug in the days prior to the shooting.[7]

There is no indication that the drugging of children is going to diminish in the near future. Quite the contrary. In an address by James Basco at the National School Boards Association, he said, "In my crystal ball, I see that the teacher of the 21st century will not be trained in schools of education as we know them today but rather will be trained in a school which is an amalgam of contemporary schools of education, medicine and pharmacy. A considerable portion of the teacher's training will be devoted to understanding physiology and psychopharmacology, which will equip the teacher to administer drugs which affect learning and learning-related behaviors."[8]

Nor should we be surprised. Since the advent of "progressive education" schools have not been intended to educate, but simply to regiment.

Notes:
1. Sutton, Antony C. *America's Secret Establishment*. Billings, Montana: Liberty House Press, 1986; Lionni, Paolo. *The Leipzig Connection*. Sheridan, Oregon: Delphian Press, 1988; Millegan, Kris, "The Order of the Skull & Bones," *Parascope*, at www.parscope.com/main.htm; Robison, John. *Proofs of a Conspiracy*. Los Angeles: Western Islands, 1967
2. Goldstein and Steinberg, "George Bush, Skull & Bones and the New World Order: A New American View," International Edition White Paper; Millegan, Kris, "The Order of the Skull & Bones," *Parascope* at www.parascope.com/main.htm
3. Samuelson, Eric, "A Brief Chronology of Collectivism," October 1997; Sutton; Lionni; Stormer, John. *None Dare Call It Treason...25 Years Later*. Liberty Bell Press: Florrisant, Missouri, 1992; Allen, Gary. *The Rockefeller File*. Seal Beach, California: '76 Press, 1976
4. Sutton; Lionni
5. "Sinister Oregon Plan Underway to Control Children & Families," Paul Richmond—*Sightings* at www.sightings.com
6. Scanlon, Dana S., "Menticide Against the Children of America," *The New Federalist*, May 13, 1996
7. Weller, Robert, "25 May Be Dead in School Shooting," Associated Press, April 20, 1999; *American Journal of Psychiatry*, September, 1991; KCNC News 4, Denver, Colorado, May 4, 1999; Reuters news service, May 6, 1999
8. Basco, James, cited in Packard, Vance. *The People Shapers*. New York: Bantam Books, 1977

CHAPTER 4

TAVISTOCK

One prominent locus of world control—its influence spreading through the media, the scientific establishment, corporations, governments, and the military—is the Tavistock Institute. Tavistock, a collaborative effort of British military intelligence and the psychiatric establishment, was created in 1921 reportedly on the orders of members of the Royal Institute of International Affairs (also known as Chatham House). The RIIA is an arm of the British Rhodes Round Table group, founded by British imperialist and Freemason Cecil Rhodes. The Round Table, functioning through a myriad of offshoots, has been this century's most effective proponent for the creation of a one world government. Tavistock relies on grants for its operations from the Rockefellers, Carnegies, the British Home Office, and large anonymous grants.

Initially run by British military intelligence officer Major John Rawlings, from its inception Tavistock was intended as a coordinating center for planetary social control using "psychological shock troops," a term coined by Reese. These shock troops in white lab coats have fanned out across the planet, infiltrating organizations in order to implement policies deemed productive by the organization's strategists.

At core Tavistock consists of Freemasonic British intelligence agents collaborating with the hydra heads of world psychiatry to achieve two goals:

(1) A one world order where the nation state has been abolished and a single totalitarian control center established. (2) The simultaneous psychological control of the world or, using their term, "socictry." Even the official literature of Tavistock is candid in admitting its broad world mind control orientation.[1]

In 1932 German psychologist Kurt Lewin, one of the creators of the American OSS intelligence network, precursor to the CIA—took over the steering of Tavistock from Reese. Lewin was an early proponent of the use of trauma for reprogramming both individuals and societies, his *modus operandi* possibly more than merely an analog of the Freemasonic dictum *"Ordo Ab Chao,"* meaning "order out of chaos."

Lewin's theory was the origin and definition of the concept of *Future Shock,* written by Tavistock-associated Alvin Toffler, although Toffler promotes the idea that current cultural deconstruction and leveling is an accident. It is not.

This Tavistock signature approach, this "Future Shock" deprogramming of the subject to a vegetative state through torture and trauma, for subsequent reprogramming—is the recurring methodology for world mind control as well as cultural programming in the 20th century.

Dr. William Sargent of the Tavistock Institute, reported to have been at the time working in the CIA's MKULTRA mind control program, in his 1957 book *Battle for the Mind— A Physiology of Coversion and Brain-Washing* elaborated on Lewin's theories by stating:

"Various beliefs can be implanted in many people after brain function has been sufficiently disturbed by accidentally or deliberately induced fear, anger, or excitement. Of the results caused by such disturbances, the most common one is temporarily impaired judgement and heightened suggestibility. Its various group manifestations are sometimes classed under the heading of 'herd instinct,' and appear most spectacularly in wartime, during severe epidemics, and in all similar periods of common danger, which increase anxiety and so individual and mass suggestibility."

During World War II, Tavistock ran the British Psychological Warfare Directorate, and the group maintained its military orientation after the war. Tavistock agents have penetrated American intelligence agencies, psychiatric institutions, industry, media, and political organisms, firmly guiding those bodies in alignment with the purposes of the Tavistock controllers.[2]

Spreading out from Tavistock, agents have been present at the creation of institutional centers such as the Stanford Research Institute's Center for Advanced Behavioral Sciences, the Sloan School at MIT, the Wharton School of Finance and Business Administration at the University of Pennsylvania, the Institute for Social Research at the University of Michigan, and other locations. The Tavistock network has also influenced and penetrated such groups as Esalen, the RAND Corporation, the Hudson Institute, and the Heritage Foundation.

A key thrust of Tavistock has been accomplished by the National Training Laboratories, sponsoring group "encounter" or "sensitivity" programs involved in breaking down an individual's personality and reconstructing it along lines agreeable to the group—a microcosmic intervention intended to gradually bring about the macrocosm of the New World Order. It is estimated that millions of persons have been put through this type of "processing," including most of America's corporate leaders and officials from the State Department, the Navy, the Department of Education, and the National Education Association.

Although touted as a tool for personal and organizational liberation, sensitivity programs are also an effective tool for control along the lines the group leader desires, as has been effectively demonstrated through the use of similar methods in cultic groups such as those of Charles Manson and Jim Jones.[3]

Tavistock is invariably portrayed in its literature as being a non-political organism, but the lie is apparent. As an example, one recent Tavistock project is SMARTCARDS, a pilot program done in collaboration with Manchester Metropolitan University on behalf of the European Commission.

This project for putting a person's work history and skills including academic accreditation onto a single ID card is being carried out in Europe and America, and is intended to gradually facilitate the creation of a universally-policed and regulated world economic system.[4]

Notes:
1. Dicks, Henry Victor. *Fifty Years of the Tavistock Clinic.* London, England: Routledge & K. Paul, 1970; Wolfe, L., "The Tavistock roots of the 'Aquarian Conspiracy'," *EIR*, June 5, 1987; Coleman, Dr. John. *Conspirator's Hierarchy: The Story of the Committee of 300.* Carson City, Nevada: America West Publishers, 1992; "Tavistock—The Best Kept Secret in America" at tavinstitute.org/index.htm
2. Chaitkin, Anton, "British Psychiatry: From Eugenics to Assassination," *EIR*, October 7, 1994; Steinberg, Jeffrey, "'Anticipatory democracy': Britain's Tavistock Institute brainwashed Newt." *EIR*, January 12, 1996
3. "Will You Allow Your Child to Be Spiritually Molested?," *The New Federalist*
4. EDRU, Educational Development and Review Unit white paper of the Tavistock Institute

CHAPTER 5

INJECTING IDEOLOGY

W e are only being told what they want us to know. Probably the most effective method of control ever discovered is simple information management. This technique consists of withholding information, disseminating lies (disinformation) or providing misdirection so that we cannot fully comprehend the reality that we deal with, and the forces that shape our lives. These deceptive views are projected to the populace through various communications media, but primarily by television, radio, motion pictures, newspapers, magazines, and the Internet.

A gauge of elitist thinking on the topic of media control is provided in the work of Edward Bernays, a close friend of New World Order mastermind H.G. Wells. Bernays wrote *Crystallizing Public Opinion* (1928), *Propaganda* (1928), and *The Engineering of Consent* (1955). In *Propaganda*, Bernays wrote:

"As civilization becomes more complex, and as the need for invisible government has been increasingly demonstrated, the technical means have been invented and developed by which public opinion may be regimented. With printing press and newspaper, the telephone, telegraph, radio and airplanes, ideas can be spread rapidly, and even simultaneously, across the whole of America.

"We are governed, our minds are molded, our tastes formed, our ideas suggested, largely by men we have never heard of. What ever attitude one chooses to take toward this condition, it remains a fact that in almost every act of our daily lives, whether in the sphere of politics or business, our social conduct or our ethical thinking, we are dominated by a relatively small number of persons, a trifling fraction of our hundred and twenty million, who understand the mental processes and social patterns of the masses. It is they who pull the wires which control the public mind, and who harness social forces and contrive new ways to bind and guide the world."

Far from disapproving of this manipulation, Bernays felt that it was vital for the masses to be controlled by propaganda:

"The conscious and intelligent manipulation of organized habits and opinions of the masses is an important element in a democratic society. Those who manipulate this unseen mechanism of society constitute an invisible government which is the true ruling power in our country."

Bernays also participated in the crafting of American psychological warfare programs. It is hardly surprising that he was put in charge of the CBS communications network in its early days.

The single factor that most enables control of the media and its use as a tool of propaganda is monopolistic ownership. Ninety-eight percent of the 1,700 daily newspapers in America are owned by fewer than 15 corporations, with Time, Inc. taking in about 40% of the total revenues. The three major TV networks, ABC, CBS, and NBC still have the majority of the television watching audience.[1]

Monopolistic ownership is reinforced through additional interlocking controls and failsafe systems. These include the membership of media bosses and workers in such conclaves as the Council on Foreign Relations; Skull & Bones; the Trilateral Commission; and the Bilderbergers, among other groups. Many of the members of these organizations hold memberships in other related elitist social, political, and business groups, insuring coherent action amongst these ruling classmates. Membership in one or more of these groups is virtually required to obtain *entree* to the highest levels of success in the Western world.

One is reminded of the statement of ex-CIA director William Colby, although he was speaking specifically of the American intelligence community:

"Socially as well as professionally they cliqued together, forming a sealed fraternity. They ate together at their own special favorite restaurants; they partied almost only among themselves; their families drifted to each other, so their defenses did not always have to be up. In this way they increasingly separated themselves from the ordinary world and developed a rather skewed view of that world. Their own dedicated double life became the proper norm, and they looked down on the life of the rest of the citizenry."[2]

According to author G. William Domhoff in *The Higher Circles*:

"[T]he power elite have created and developed that wonderful field of public relations on an incredible scale. Some of the early practitioners of this art helped scrub up the images of the 'Robber Barons' families; others specialized in the corporate image and the corporate conscience. Functionally speaking, the public relations departments of large corporations, in conjunction with the giant public relations firms that service many corporations, have become the early warning system of the upper class, picking up and countering the slightest remark or publication that makes funny lines on their sensitive radar. Thanks to them public opinion is well-monitored, with an assist of course from the alert social scientists in certain university institutes financed by the big corporations and foundations. Wayward opinions, once detected, are duly corrected by a barrage of printed matter and public pronouncements..."[3]

Intelligence agency penetration of the media began at the same time as the forming of the American media conglomerates in the first half of this century. One of the first and most successful control operations of the media was launched in 1919 with the creation of RCA by Westinghouse, Morgan Guaranty and Trust, General Electric, and the United Fruit Company. In 1929 David Sarnoff, a close associate of Tavistock, was appointed head of RCA. Shortly afterward, British Intelligence set up the "Black Chamber" intelligence operation in the RCA building in New York, under the direction of Sir William Stephenson (Code name: "Intrepid") and General Marlborough Churchill, a relative of Winston Churchill. General Churchill would later be instrumental in founding the Macy Organization, which would be used as a funding conduit for CIA MKULTRA mind control operations. All three major American television networks were offspring of RCA.[4]

The information war entered a new realm of effectiveness in the 1930s when the Rockefeller Foundation launched "secret psychological war projects" to shape public opinion. According to Christopher Simpson, author of *Science of Coercion*:

"[They were] a remarkably tight circle of men and women who shared several important conceptions about mass communications research. They regarded mass communication as a tool for social management and as a weapon in social conflict, and they expressed common assumptions concerning the usefulness of quantitative research—particularly experimental and quasi-experimental effects research, opinion surveys, and quantitative content analysis as a means of illuminating what communication 'is' and improving its application to social management."[5]

At about the same time that the Rockefeller's media manipulation programs went into overdrive, the Office of Strategic Services and the Office of War Information began recruiting "the best and the brightest" from American intelligentsia for initiation into the ranks of spookdom, as well as inserting their agents into powerful positions in the mass media, in politics, and in the universities. A survey of Office of War Information alumni working in the media in the early 1950s included:

"The publishers of *Time*, *Look*, *Fortune* and several dailies; editors of such magazines as *Holiday*, *Coronet*, *Parade*, and the *Saturday Review*, editors of the *Denver Post*, New Orleans *Times-Picayune*, and others; the heads of the Viking Press, Harper & Brothers, and Farr, Strauss and Young; two Hollywood Oscar winners; a two-time Pulitzer prize winner; the board chairman of CBS and a dozen key network executives; President Eisenhower's chief speech writer; the editor of *Reader's Digest* international editions; at least six partners of large advertising agencies; and a dozen noted social scientists...chief of the U.S. government's overt psychological warfare effort from 1950 to 1952 and later dean of the Columbia Graduate School of Journalism and founder of the *Columbia Journalism Review.*"[6]

During the 1950s American mass media interlocked directly with the CIA, the Agency feeding information to journalists in exchange for their own intelligence developed domestically and abroad. Reporters were employed by the CIA to deliver communiqués as well as money to contacts, and to tow the Agency line in their own dispatches. The CIA even ran a training program teaching reporting skills to agents.

It is virtually impossible to determine the exact number of American journalists who are currently on the CIA or other intelligence agency payrolls—much less who are informally slipped information—but in 1977 Carl Bernstein, in an article for *Rolling Stone*, guessed the number at that time to be about 400.

—Bernstein noted a longstanding relationship of the Agency with the CBS network, and former CIA director Allen Dulles' friendship with CBS' president, CFR member William Paley. The president of CBS News from 1954 to 1961, CFR member Sig Mickelson, acted as Paley's liaison with the CIA, using a direct telephone line that bypassed the network switchboard and connected directly with the Agency. The chief directors and news anchors of CBS have also been CIA-connected, according to Bernstein.

The journalist wrote that, "Over the years the [CBS] network provided cover for CIA employees, including at least one well-known foreign correspondent and several stringers; it supplied outtakes of news film to the CIA; established a formal channel of communications between the Washington bureau chief and the agency, and allowed reports by CBS correspondents...to be routinely monitored by the CIA."

—*The New York Times* and its publisher, CFR member Arthur Hays Sulzberger, frequently liased with the CIA, providing cover for at least ten CIA agents during the 1950s and 60s.

—The publisher of *The Washington Post*, CFR member Katherine Graham, was close friends with CIA directors Dulles and Casey, and employed a number of reporters who worked with the CIA.

—Henry Luce, the founder of *Time* and *Life,* was a friend of CIA Director Allen Dulles, and looked the other way when some of his reporters attended CIA briefings. C.D. Jackson, a leading exec at *Time-Life* lived a double life as a mover and shaker in American psychological warfare efforts.

—According to CIA files, ABC news was used as a cover by agents during the 1960s.

—Bernstein also noted the following news organizations as having also provided cover for CIA agents: the *New York Herald-Tribune*, the *Saturday Evening Post*, Scripps-Howard Newspapers, Hearst Newspapers, the Associated Press, United Press International, the Mutual Broadcasting System, Reuters and the *Miami Herald*.

—Another means of CIA control over the media is through outright ownership. The *New York Times* in 1997 reported that the CIA owned more than fifty radio stations, wire services, magazines, and newspapers, with the majority of them being overseas. Many foreign news agencies were also infiltrated with CIA agents, and more than one thousand books that had been subsidized or produced outright by the CIA had been put in print by American publishers. Given these extensive involvements, would it be too much to venture that the American media, that bastion of freedom and independence, holds CIA credentials?[7]

—Another means of influencing public opinion has been through the Advertising Council, a tax-exempt non-governmental agency whose membership is heavily weighted with members of the Council on Foreign Relations. Among the projects that the Advertising Council has furthered are ones aimed at the creation of a one world government, including "World Peace Through World Law" and various "public service announcements" promoting the United Nations.

A technique for influencing public opinion is polling organizations which have demonstrably been shown to slant their public opinion questions in order to achieve desired results, but which may also be engaged in outright deception and alteration of statistics in the service of whomever is paying them. During the recent bloody American intervention in Yugoslavia public opinion pollsters placed approval of the war by the public at 73 percent, while an informal poll that I and some friends conducted determined exactly the opposite, that only one-third of Americans supported the bombing. I know that we are not lying.

Probably the most infamous example of media manipulation took place after the assassination of American President John F. Kennedy. A CIA memorandum dated April 1, 1967 was issued on the use of Agency "assets" in the media in "Countering Criticism of the Warren Report" on the assassination of John F. Kennedy, a murder that many researchers have in fact laid at the doorstep of American intelligence itself. Among the ways to "answer and refute" those critical of the Warren Whitewash the CIA suggested, were a variety of ploys including saying that a critic's research was faulty, that they had a financial interest in writing negatively on the Warren Report, and that "Conspiracy on the large scale often suggested would be impossible to conceal." Of course, this was in the horse-and-buggy days before the expediency of calling someone a "conspiracy nut" existed.[8]

Within the last year another example of media manipulation may have saved President Bill Clinton from impeachment, due to an incident that has come to be known as "Rapegate." During the impeachment trial of Clinton, Juanita Broaddrick, referred to as "Jane Doe #5" in the Starr Report, was interviewed at length by NBC correspondent Lisa Meyers. Broaddrick alleged that in 1981 Bill Clinton had raped her in an Arkansas motel room when she had been working for his campaign for governorship. This is not an incredible allegation, since Clinton has been accused of rape and forcing his sexual attentions on women on numerous occasions in the past, the first time that we know of during his studies at Oxford University in England in the 1960s. There were several reliable witnesses to corroborate Broaddrick's story, including a nurse who treated her for injuries inflicted during the alleged rape. NBC completed the interview with Broaddrick prior to the end of the impeachment trial, but the network suppressed airing the story until the trial was over, after the story had been picked up by the *Wall Street Journal*, and other media outlets. Thus Congress and the American public were prevented from making a fully informed decision about the suitability of Clinton as president.

Media management does not always have to be so dramatic. Simple distraction—the "circuses" part of the historic "bread and circuses" formula—is another effective technique. The dissemination of entertainment—"popular culture"—and useless factoids has channeled public attention away from far more important issues such as poverty, human rights abuses, the equitable distribution of the wealth of the world, true political representation for the vast majority of humans— and media control by the elite. This is one of the main functions of the television, which is in essence a propaganda box spewing out the "positive" drug-like reinforcements of sex, violence, and simulated social interaction.

As an example of distraction by the media, the political struggle of black Americans for economic and political wellbeing has been effectively derailed by the safe-to-the-Establishment energetics of "gangsta rap" culture, drugs, and sports, preparing black youth to take their place in the world as drug addicts and latterday Steppin' Fetchits struggling in grinding McPoverty.

Journalist John Swinton—one of the most respected of the breed at the time—described the situation succinctly when he gave a toast at the New York Press Club in 1953. Swinton said,

"There is no such thing at this date of the world's history, in America, as an independent press. You know it and I know it. There is not one of you who dares to write your honest opinions and if you did, you know beforehand that it would never appear in print. I am paid weekly for keeping my honest opinion out of the paper I am connected with. Others of you are paid similar salaries for similar things, and any of you would be so foolish as to write honest opinions would be out on the streets looking for another job. If I allowed my honest opinions to appear in one issue of my paper, before twenty-four hours my occupation would be gone.

"The business of journalists is to destroy the truth, to lie outright, to pervert, to vilify, to fawn at the feet of mammon, and to sell his country and his race for his daily bread. You know it and I know it, and what folly is this toasting an independent press?

"We are the tools of rich men behind the scenes. We are jumping jacks, they pull the strings and we dance. Our talents, our possibilities and our lives are all the property of other men. We are intellectual prostitutes."

Another media strategy employed in the latter half of the 20th century is subliminally embedded messages. There are a number of methods by which subliminals can be injected into a communication. In electronic media these include the use of sub-audible sounds, backwards masking, tachistiscopic flashes, image associations, and other techniques. Print media primarily utilizes embedded messages, image association, and symbolism.[9]

Some verified examples of media subliminals are:

—In 1956 the British Broadcasting Company transmitted a subliminal message during the course of a regularly-scheduled television program. When the program was over, viewers were queried whether they had noticed anything unusual about the program. Only a few persons responded, and still fewer able to identify the subliminal message that had been broadcast. This, of course, is not an indication that the subliminal was unsuccessful; the viewer is not supposed to be able to perceive consciously what the message is, only be influenced subconsciously.[10]

—In September of 1957, American advertising executive James Vicary told a gathering of journalists that subliminal advertising had been successfully tested. For a period of six weeks, subliminal messages to drink Coca-Cola and to eat popcorn had been shown to 45,699 patrons at a movie theater. The projected subliminals had been brief in duration, 1/3000th of a second, and had been projected every five seconds during the airing of motion pictures. It was reported that popcorn sales rose almost sixty percent, while Coca Cola sales increased almost twenty percent.[11]

—At about the same time as Vicary's announcement, the Los Angeles television station KTLA announced that they would be commencing with subliminal broadcasts. In order to quell public concerns, the station indicated that programs bearing subliminal messages would be announced prior to airing, and that they would only carry non-commercial subliminals, at least initially. The general manager of the station, Lew Arnold, said, "We'll flash on something like 'Join the Army' or 'Give to the March of Dimes.' The next step would be to promote our own shows. Then—and I have a feeling this is a long way off—we might go into the commercial end of it." According to a press release from the station, however, the subliminals were reportedly cancelled without having commenced.[12]

—Also in 1957, radio station WTWO in Bangor, Maine began running subliminal messages in station promo announcements. The content was, "If you have seen this message, write WTWO," and it was flashed thousands of times for 1/80th of a second during a one-month period. The experiment was considered unsuccessful, so the station reported, since there was no increase in mail.[13]

—On January 19, 1958, an undisclosed subliminal message was flashed across the television screens 352 times during a CBC-TV network program. A spokesperson for the CBC said that the experiment was inconclusive.[14]

—Also in 1958, sub-audial "phantom spots" were broadcast during radio programs. Broadcasting stations that ran such spots included stations WCCO in Minneapolis; WAAF in Chicago; KLTI in Longview, Texas; KOL in Seattle; and KYA in San Francisco.[15]

—In 1958 researchers in the media and sociology departments of Indiana University ran subliminal experiments on both closed-circuit television and broadcasts of WTTV, in

Bloomington, Indiana. Indiana University crops up surprisingly frequently in research into mass control, and was the home base for sexologist Alfred Kinsey, who will be profiled in the next chapter, as well as a recruiting grounds for death evangelist Jim Jones.[16]

The effect of subliminal motivational techniques did not escape American intelligence agencies. It is documented that the CIA, for one, looked into the use of subliminals beginning in 1958. A partially declassified CIA document dated January 17, 1958 stated "it may be that subliminal projection can be utilized in such a way as to feature a visual suggestion such as 'Obey [deleted from original document]." Martin A. Lee, writing in *High Times* magazine, quotes an anonymous CIA agent as saying, "some thought was given to whether or not we could affect political outcomes by using subliminal perception on things like radio and TV."[17]

—According to a statement of the Federal Communications Commission, shortly before Christmas in 1973 American television viewers complained about the insertion of a message of almost instantaneous duration saying "Get it" in an advertisement.[18]

—In 1994 a viewer of Channel 11 in Rome, Georgia, saw a rapid flash of light while viewing reruns of the *Batman* television series. Since he had been recording the show on his VCR, he freeze framed the moment of the flash, only to find out that a scene of protestors with "Keep Abortion Legal" signs had been inserted into the program.[19]

—In 1997 in Japan more than 700 children went to the hospital after viewing the popular cartoon series *Pokemon*. The children experienced convulsions and in at least one case stopped breathing, supposedly because of a scene twenty minutes into the cartoon that triggered "photosensitive epilepsy" with strobing lights. According to one report, "Tokyo doctors...described the effect of the scene as similar to hypnosis."

There is another possibility other than epileptic seizures that may have affected the children, that may not have occurred to many. Russian Major I. Chernishev, writing in the military journal *Orienteer* in February, 1997, referred to experimentation by the Japanese in "noiseless cassettes." Chernishev claimed that the Japanese had developed techniques for patterning messages at infra-low frequencies over music, messages that could be used for mind control. A related technique was described by the Russian Dr. Victor Solntsev, of the Baumann Technical Institute in Moscow. In a Russian military publication Solntsev described a computer virus termed Virus 666. The virus is displayed visually in every 25th frame on a visual display including television or computer, and supposedly broadcasts colors that put the viewer into an hypnotic trance. If exposure is continued, it can result in arrhythmia of the heart. This is not simply Solntsev's fantasy, but has been spoken of by other Russian scientists. It is suggested that Virus 666 can be used to subliminally influence a viewer's thinking and perceptions.[20]

Another secret subliminal technique is described by an informant of the author who chooses to remain anonymous. He wrote, on April 14, 1999:

"I went back to college for the summer to work on my Media degree (I had hoped for awhile to get into TV and film production—and become a movie director). Anyway, I happened upon some of the TV technicians there discussing a rumor that they had heard about a new subliminal process that was being called Fractional Framing. And, as I was into TV technology at the time, I joined their brief discussion to just find out more, for curiosity's sake.

"As they described it, Fractional Framing is very similar to the regular movie subliminal cut. In the subliminal cut, a whole frame of the film is removed and replaced with an ad or an order. And, though you cannot see it with your eye, it affects your subconscious and you end up craving the thing advertised or doing what was ordered. However, for Fractional Framing, rather than taking out a whole frame on the TV screen, all they do is replace a few of the five hundred lines on the TV screen (which makes it harder to detect). But, it appears to be just as effective!

"Being interested in subliminals, which we had discussed in my various Media classes, I asked if there was any proof of these rumors. One of the technicians insisted that he had heard it that it had been experimented with on the public at KIRO TV channel 7 in Seattle."

As in subliminal broadcasting, at this time the great majority of the information that we receive from major media is designed to keep us confused, entrapped, and to motivate us without our knowledge. As Professor Noam Chomsky wrote, in *Chronicles of Dissent*:

"Our system works much differently and much more effectively [than the Communist system]. It's a privatized system of propaganda, including the media, journals of opinion and in general including the broad participation of the articulate intelligentsia, the educated part of the population. The more articulate element of those groups, the ones who have access to the media, including the intellectual journals, and who essentially control the educational apparatus, should properly be referred to as a class of 'commisars.' That's their essential function: to design, propagate and create a system of doctrines and beliefs which will undermine independent thought and prevent understanding and analysis of institutional structures and their functions."

At times the controllers themselves are even willing to admit the manipulation, as David Rockefeller did, when addressing the Trilateral Commission in June of 1991:

"We are grateful to *The Washington Post, The New York Times, Time Magazine,* and other great publications whose directors have attended our meetings and respected their promises of discretion for almost forty years. It would have been impossible for us to develop our plan for the world if we had been subject to the bright lights of publicity during those years. But the world is now more sophisticated and prepared to march toward world government. The supranational sovereignty of an intellectual elite and world bankers is surely preferable to the national autodeterminism practiced in past centuries."[21]

Surely. But media was never a singly effective enough tool for you, Mr. Rockefeller, nor for the other rulers of this world. You have sought other means for control.

Notes:
1. Bagdikian, Ben, "The 50, 26, 20... Corporations That Own Our Media," *Extra!*, June 1987
2. Colby, William (with Peter Forbath). *Honorable Men: My Life in the CIA*. New York: Simon and Schuster, 1978
3. Domhoff, G. William. *The Higher Circles*. New York: Vintage Books, 1970
4. Coleman, Dr. John. *Conspirator's Hierarchy: The Story of the Committee of 300*. Carson City, Nevada: America West Publishers, 1992; Chaitkin, Anton, "British Psychiatry: From Eugenics to Assassination," *EIR*, October 7, 1994
5. Simpson, Christopher. *Science of Coercion: Communication Research & Psychological Warfare*, 1945-1960. New York: Oxford University Press, 1994
6. ibid.
7. Overbeck, Ashley, "Spooky News: A Report on CIA Infiltration and Manipulation of the Mass Media," *Parascope* at wwww.parascope.com/main.htm; "Journalism and the CIA: The Mighty Wurlitzer," *NameBase Newsline* No. 17, April-June 1997
8. Constantine, Alex. *Virtual Government, CIA Mind Control Operations in America*. Venice, California: Feral House, 1997
9. Parkes, Eric, "Subliminal Stimuli: Sleep, Obey, Sex," *MindNet Journal*, Vol. 1, No. 52, at visitation.com/mindnet/MN16A.HTM
10. "Subliminal Projection," 1977, Information bulletin of the Federal Communications Commission
11. *Human Rights Law Journal*, "Freedom of the Mind as an International Human Rights Issue," Vol. 3, No. 1-4
12. Elliston, Jon, "The Subliminal Scares," *Parascope* at www.parascope.com/main.htm
13. "Subliminal Projection"
14. ibid.
15. ibid.
16. ibid.
17. Gafford, Richard, "The Operational Use of Subliminal Perception," *Studies in Intelligence*, Spring 1958 (CIA's previously classified journal); Lee, Martin A., "The CIA's Subliminal Seduction,' *High Times*, February 1980.
18. "Subliminal Projection"
19. "TV Station Zaps Viewers with Subliminal Abortion Message!," *Paranoia*, Winter 1994/1995
20. Thomas, Timothy L. "The Mind Has No Firewall," *Parameters*, Spring, 1998, U.S. Army War College Quarterly; http://conspire.lycos.com/curren39.html
21. "The Invisible Hand of the Media," *World Internet News* Distributary Source, http://thewinds.org/index.html

CHAPTER 6

SUBVERTING SEX

Another loyal foot soldier in the program for the subjugation of the masses was Rockefeller-funded Alfred C. Kinsey, the co-author of the influential *Sexual Behavior in the Human Male*, and other volumes. One technique of eugenics and control that is little acknowledged is the destruction of traditional morality, and the normalizing of deviancy.

Kinsey studied at the Bussey Institution at Harvard in the 1920s—at the time a hotbed of eugenics research—then moved on to teach at Indiana University, where his work in cultural deconstruction would ultimately succeed in decimating American sexual mores, help to fragment the American family, and leave the population still more vulnerable to reproductive, cultural, familial, and mind programming.

Kinsey, always portrayed in the press as a wholesome *Leave it to Beaver* style family man, was, "one of the scholarly eugenicists of pre-W.W.II," according to biographer James Jones, and recommended that a portion of the "lower classes" should be sterilized to foster a more robust gene pool. Among Kinsey's intimates was Dr. Ewen Cameron, the infamous Canadian mind control doctor, who will be treated in a later chapter. In many ways what took place at Kinsey's research laboratory is highly reminiscent of what was going on at intelligence agency psychiatric labs at the same time.

Another of Kinsey's influences was Dr. Hermann Muller, a colleague at Indiana University. Muller, who had begun receiving Rockefeller-funding from the National Research Council in 1925, received a Guggenheim grant in 1932 to pursue his work in the genetics department of the Rockefeller-funded Kaiser Wilhelm Brain Research Institute in Berlin. Muller studied under Ernst Rudin, who was to become the head of the Nazi Racial Hygiene Society. One of the benefits of Rudin's policy for the extermination of hereditary undesirables was that it provided a continual harvesting of fresh brains for the Kaiser Wilhelm Institute's brain research division.[1]

According to Roderick Gorney in his book, *The Human Agenda*:

"The more radical method of genetic intervention is called 'positive eugenics.' This is a more ambitious and controversial proposal, championed, among others, by the late Hermann Muller, who [advocated] selective breeding...to eliminate the defects...[and] to increase the number of people with 'superior' qualities. One way to accomplish this would be to establish sperm (and eventually egg) banks in which the reproductive cells of individuals with the exceptional health, intelligence, or special talent could be preserved. These could then be used by people who want to produce children with better endowment than would result from their own genes. Some have objected that people would not willingly agree to substitute the sex cells and characteristics of others for their own. Muller rejects 'the stultifying assumption that people would have to be forced, rather than be inspired, to engage in any effective kind of genetic betterment.' He points out that...seemingly 'normal couples'...would elect to use this means of having at least a part of their family..."

Another of Kinsey's apparent influences was the occultist Aleister Crowley, whose Thelema Abbey Kinsey visited shortly before his death in 1955. Although it has not been established that Kinsey used Crowley as a research source in his books, they shared mutual friends and acquaintances such as filmmaker Kenneth Anger, American Nazi George Sylvester Viereck, and Frenchman Rene Guyon.[2]

Kenneth Anger has said that:

"Kinsey was obsessed with obtaining the Great Beast's [Crowley's] day-to-day sex diaries... To obtain grant monies and maintain the support of the university, Kinsey needed the excuse of research to validate his twenty-four-hours-a-day obsession with sex. However, Prok's [Kinsey's nickname] battle cry of 'Do your best and let other people react as they will' seemed a variation on Crowley's 'Do what thou wilt' maxim." If in fact such was the case, I wonder how the American public would have reacted to find out that the highly respected Kinsey was a disciple of the Great Beast?[3]

Kinsey's most effective weapon for psychological warfare was his Rockefeller-funded study of American sexuality, the most famous volume being his vaunted study, *Sexual Behavior in the Human Male*, published in 1948. Upon release of the book, 200,000 copies were sold in two months, primarily due to the championing of the volume by American media and the Rockefellers.[4]

According to Rene Wormser, legal counsel for the Reece Committee investigating tax-exempt foundations in 1954:

"The Rockefeller Foundation's statement filed with the Committee explained its connection with the Kinsey studies in this way. In 1931 it 'became interested in systematic support for studies in sexual physiology and behavior'... Its work in these areas was chiefly in connection with the 'committee for research in problems of sex of The National Research Council,' to which, by 1954, the Foundation had granted $1,755,000 in annual grants running from $75,000 to $240,000. Beginning about 1941, a considerable portion of these funds was supplied to Dr. Kinsey's studies, and one grant was made direct to Dr. Kinsey... The work of the NRC produced some results of truly noteworthy importance... [However] the much-publicized 'bestseller' Kinsey studies base an advocacy of criminal and social reform on the very unscientific material which Dr. Kinsey had collected and permitted to be widely disseminated."[5]

According to Judith A. Reisman, Ph.D., the author of *Kinsey: Crimes & Consequences*:

"Kinsey's quantitative research and his numbers, were a perfect fit for Rockefeller to utilize the mass media to 'shape public attitudes and conduct.' Attitudes were changed through mass communications, which caused a rejection of chastity, self control and moral public governance, as well as increased illicit sexual conduct. 'Social management' of this sort was nothing less for Rockefeller than changing America's way of life, by among other things altering what Kinsey would call 'breeding patterns' along an evolutionary or animalistic view of human sexual conduct."[6]

The main problem with Kinsey's "quantitative research and his numbers" is that they were radically skewed in order to achieve his own purposes. Researchers into Kinsey's methods—which purportedly catalogue normal sexuality in America—have noted that he loaded the ranks of his test subjects with an inordinately high number of persons imprisoned for sex deviancy, prostitutes, and child molesters—criminals estimated by one researcher as providing as high as one third of his overall subjects. Kinsey entered them into his database as normal examples of the population.

In addition, Kinsey relied heavily on volunteers. Six years before the publication of Kinsey's volume, psychologist Abraham Maslow had pointed out that, "any study in which data are obtained from volunteers will always have a preponderance of [aggressive] high dominance people and therefore will show a falsely high percentage of non-virginity, masturbation, promiscuity, homosexuality, etc. in the population."[7]

Kinsey Institute Director Paul Gebhard described Kinsey's approach:

"At the Indiana State Farm we had no plan of sampling—we simply sought out sex offenders and, after a time, avoided the more common types of offense (e.g. statutory rape) and directed our efforts toward the rarer types... In the early stages of the research, when much interviewing was being done at Indiana correctional institutions, Dr. Kinsey did not view the inmates as a discrete group that should be differentiated from people outside; instead he looked upon the institutions as reservoirs of potential interviewees, literally captive subjects. This viewpoint resulted in there being no differentiation in our 1948 volume between persons with and without prison experience...the great majority of the prison group was collected omnivorously without any sampling plan—we simply interviewed all who volunteered and when this supply of subjects was exhausted we solicited other inmates essentially at random... Kinsey...never...[kept] a record of refusal rates—the proportion of those who were asked for an interview but who refused."[8]

Kinsey's manipulation extended to his choice of staff. His assistants in his studies were selected from young students, both male and female, who were required prior to coming on board to provide their sexual histories. Another requirement was that they be filmed in explicit sexual movies (ostensibly for research) in Kinsey's attic.

Psychologist Wardell Pomeroy, who worked with Kinsey, reports that, "The public would have been astounded and disbelieving to know the names of the eminent scientists who appeared at the Institute from time to time to examine our work and talk with Kinsey, and who volunteered before they left to be photographed in some kind of sexual activity."[9]

Kinsey's research included observation of child sexuality, the manual and oral stimulation of children's genitals, and the timing of child orgasms with stopwatches.

According to Reisman, "The Kinsey Report claims at least '317 pre-adolescents' were sexually experimented upon by 'older adults,' and confirmation of at least 2,035 child experimental subjects were later admitted in 1980 by Gebhard and Pomeroy as reported in *Ethical Issues in Sex Therapy*."[10]

Part of Kinsey's collection of sex films included films of children in sex acts, and adult-with-child sex. Kinsey Institute Director Paul Gebhard wrote, in 1981:

"Since sexual experimentation with human infants and children is illegal, we have had to depend upon other sources of data. Some of these were parents, mostly college educated, who observed their children and kept notes for us. A few were nursery school owners or teachers. Others were homosexual males interested in older, but still pre-pubertal children. One was a man who had numerous sexual contacts with male and female infants and children and, being of a scientific bent, kept detailed records of each encounter. Some of these sources have added to their written or verbal reports photographs and, in a few instances, cinema... The techniques involved adult-child contacts—chiefly manual or oral."[11]

Gebhard, with a candor rare among social engineers, many years after his collaboration with Kinsey admitted that: "We [were]...amoral at best and criminal at worst. Examples of amorality are our refusal to inform a wife that her husband has...an active venereal disease, and our refusal to tell parents that their child is involved in seriously deviant behavior. An example of criminality is our refusal to cooperate with authorities in apprehending a pedophile we had interviewed who was being sought for a [child] sex murder."[12]

Taken as a description of American sexuality, the information in the Kinsey volume was damning in the extreme. It reported that 95 percent of American males had violated sex laws serious enough to put them in jail, 85 percent had had premarital sex, 69 percent had used prostitutes, 45 percent were adulterers, as high as 37 percent had experienced orgasm in a homosexual act, and that 17 percent had had sex with an animal. In these post-Kinsey days this information is not that shocking, in fact is almost believable, but in 1948 it fell upon the public like a bombshell.

According to reports of the time, the *Kinsey Report* "shocked" and "dumbfounded" the nation in 1948. The reason for this was simple: Americans knew that the information he had catalogued did not fit with their own perceptions of sexual morals and behavior. Kinsey's statistics were wrong, and they remain wrong. Recent studies of American sexuality show that even in this era of "liberated" sexuality, figures of homosexuality, deviancy, and promiscuity do not approach the figures broadcast by Kinsey. One recent study by the National Opinion Research Center at the University of Chicago showed that 83% of Americans had sex with one person or did not have sex in the preceding year, with half of those polled having had only one sex partner in the previous five years.[13]

Reisman reports:

"Over the past fifty years, enormous changes in law, medicine, science, and education have been wrought by Kinsey's data which was Kinsey's 'grand scheme' from the beginning. The reason for a massive and extensive legal, educational, and political effort to continue the deception and suppress efforts to bring the full truth out in the open, is due to the enormity of the multidisciplinary sex edifice in the United States and extending today worldwide through the United Nations. This edifice stands four square upon the foundation of the false authority of Alfred Kinsey's science, yet billions in government-funded programs dealing with sex, gender and human reproduction are advanced based upon the Kinsey false authority."[14]

One spearhead launched by the Kinsey Institute was an "encounter" group called Sexual Attitude Technique, which trained at least 60,000 people beginning in the early 1980s. Writing in *Esquire* magazine, George Leonard reported his SAR experience:

"The sensory overload culminated on Saturday night in a multi-media event called the F-korama...in the darkness...images of human beings—and sometimes even animals—engaging in every conceivable sexual act, accompanied by wails, squeals, moans, shouts and the first movement of the Tchaikovsky Violin Concerto. Some seventeen simultaneous moving pictures... Over a period of several hours, there came a moment when the four images on the wall were of a gay male couple, a straight couple, a lesbian couple, and a bestial group. The subjects were nude... I felt myself becoming disoriented...was she kissing a man or a woman? I struggled to force the acts I was watching into their proper boxes...and now I couldn't remember which was which. Wasn't I supposed to make these discriminations? I searched for clues. There were none. I began to feel uncomfortable. Soon I realized that to avoid vertigo and nausea I would have to give up the attempt to discriminate and simply surrender to the experience... The differences for which lives have been ruined, were not only trivial, but invisible. By the end... Nothing was shocking... But nothing was sacred either. But as I drove home, I began to get a slightly uneasy feeling. It was almost as if I had been conned...by my own conditioned response of taking the most liberated position...whatever my deeper feelings...love had not been mentioned a single time during the entire weekend."[15]

Another of Kinsey's accomplishments was to force the courts, through dint of the "normalcy" of what had hitherto been thought of as perverse, to lessen penalties for illegal sex acts, and to normalize homosexuality in the military.

With Kinsey, American mores were almost completely warped, to the point where almost any sexual act is now acceptable. Wife swapping, easy divorce, swinging, the depiction of sex acts in the media, homosexuality, and sadomasochism are promoted as the norm.

As with most actions of the social engineers, there are a number of reasons for this.

—One is the creation of what has been called a "sensate" society, satiated with sex, drugs, and TV (the modern form of "bread and circuses," so that no challenge is ever mounted to the controllers by a numbed electorate.

—Another reason for this is the decoupling of sex from procreation, thus making the instituting of sterilization and birth control policies including abortion more easily instituted upon the "masses."

—Another purpose is the destruction of the nuclear family, opening the door for greater societal intervention and manipulation.

Although it is dangerous to point out in this era of Ellen-degenerated "sexual liberation," the forces that spawned the fascist New World Order as well as eugenics have also historically been the first wave of assault for the destruction of traditional values regarding sex. This approach was exemplified by the Nazis, for whom, according to Pearl Buck, "Love was old-fashioned, sex was modern. It was the Nazis who restored the 'right to love' in their propaganda."[16]

The war against sexual sanity—and for mass control—continues today.

Notes:
1. Reisman, Phd., Judith A. *Kinsey: Crimes and Consequences*. Arlington, Virginia: The Institute for Media Education, Inc., 1998; Chaitkin, Anton, "British Psychiatry: From Eugenics to Assassination," *EIR*, October 7, 1994; Jones, James. *Kinsey: A Public/Private Life*. New York: W.W. Norton, 1997; Abrams, Kevin E., "Kinsey, Rockefeller and the Nazi Doctors," *Alberta Report*, June 29, 1998]
2. Reisman
3. Landis, Bill. *Anger*. New York: Harper Collins, 1995, cited in Reisman
4. Reisman
5. Wormser, Rene. *Foundations*. New York: The Devin-Adair Company, 1958, cited in Reisman
6. Reisman
7. Maslow, Abraham, "Test for Dominance-Feeling (Self-Esteem) in College Women," 1940, cited in Reisman
8. Gebhard, Gagnon, Pomeroy, Christenson. *Sex Offenders*. New York: Bantam Books, 1965, cited in Reisman
9. Pomeroy, Wardell. *Dr. Kinsey and the Institute for Sex Research*. New York: Harper & Row, New York, 1972, cited in Reisman; Reisman
10. Reisman
11. Letter of Paul Gebhard, Kinsey Institute Director, to Judith Reisman, dated March 11, 1981
12. Masters, Johnson and Kolodny, Ed. *Ethical Issues in Sex Therapy and Research*, Reproductive Biology Research Foundation, Conference. Boston: Little, Brown and Company, 1977
13. Reisman; Lively and Abrams. *The Pink Swastika*. Keiser, Oregon: Founders Publishing Corporation, 1997
14. Reisman
15. Leonard, George, "The End of Sex," *Esquire*, December, 1982, cited in Reisman
16. Buck, Pearl, cited in de Jonge, Alex. *The Weimar Chronicle: Prelude to Hitler*. New York: New American Library, 1978

CHAPTER 7

THE CIA AND CONTROL

A study of control must draw a tight focus on the programs of American intelligence agencies. General William "Wild Bill" Donovan in 1940 is believed to have been the first person to call attention to the need for an American psychological warfare division. Thus is explained the beginning of the Office of the Coordinator of Strategic Services (COI), that became the Office of Strategic Services (OSS) in 1942. The COI from its inception was a black operation run by Donovan, with little governmental scrutiny applied to the way it used its funds.

There may have been another influence on Donovan other than the simple perception of the need for spying. According to John Marks in *The Search for the Manchurian Candidate*, "Clandestine lobbying by British agents in the United States led directly to President Franklin Roosevelt's creation of the organization that became OSS in 1942… Learning at the feet of the British who made available their expertise, if not all their secrets, Donovan put together an organization where nothing had existed before."

After the formation of the OSS, research was launched into the discovery of a "truth drug" for use during interrogation, as well as into what would later be termed the "Manchurian Candidate": hypnotically programmed agents and assassins, the popular coinage derived from the 1959 fiction book of the same name.

The OSS, run by Donovan, was terminated in 1945, with American intelligence operations taken over by Allen Dulles and the Central Intelligence Agency (CIA). The CIA's Office of Scientific Intelligence continued research into mind manipulation, with an early emphasis on drug research. Early phases involved reviewing the drug-related work of a number of hospitals around the country for results which could be applied to covert operations.[1]

Although responsibility for the mind control programs that were launched in America in the early 1950s has been placed at the doorstep of the CIA, this attribution ignores earlier sources. These programs were the visible edge of a wave that had begun much earlier, with the British, American, and Nazi eugenics/ psychiatric/New World Order combination, propelled by Rockefeller and Round Table funding, with the most prominent agents of this group in America being the Eastern Establishment's Harrimans and Dulleses.

Skull & Bonesman W. Averell Harriman's family had promoted eugenics causes since the turn of the century. Harriman was also a major supporter—through his controlling interest in Union Bank—of Hitler's rise to power in Germany. In 1951 Harriman was named director of the Mutual Security Agency, elevating him to an influential position in shepherding the American/British military intelligence alliance. Harriman and his business partners Allen and John Foster Dulles, also from a pro-eugenics background, were largely responsible for the increase of American efforts in the area of covert and psychological warfare operations, as well as for promoting the Fabian one-world orientation that was the *raison d'être* of the Council on Foreign Relations.[2]

Allen Dulles, the first director of the CIA, was in many ways the penultimate political insider. His family was an influential early supporter of international eugenics movements and had strong financial connections with the Nazis. The Dulleses were intermarried with the Prevosts and Mallets of Switzerland, who in collaboration with the British royals, had been European spymasters for hundreds of years and, it is said, instrumental in injecting the Scottish Rite of Masonry into the United States.

Perhaps most important to their rise to power was that at the end of World War I, Allen and John Foster Dulles were recruited by the infamous one worlder "Colonel" Edward House (who in fact bore no military rank), and during the Paris peace conference the brothers were informally inducted into the Rhodes Round Table group. The Dulles brothers were responsible for starting the American branch, the Council on Foreign Relations, with funding coming from the Rockefellers, the Morgans, Bernard Baruch, Paul Warburg, and others.

In 1920 Allen Dulles was appointed First Secretary of the American Embassy in Berlin and, perhaps because of his family connections, took over American intelligence in the strategically key country of Switzerland. Dulles was chief of station in Berne, Switzerland in the early 1940s, at the time that the effects of LSD were purportedly discovered by Dr. Albert Hoffman, working for Sandoz laboratories. At the same time mind control experimentation using mescaline and other drugs were being used on inmates of the Dachau concentration camp, a scant 200 miles away.

Allen's brother, John Foster Dulles, became the chief executive of the influential Sullivan and Cromwell law firm, that represented the notorious I.G. Farben during the rise of the Nazis. I.G. Farben, run until 1937 by the Warburg family, banking partners with the Rockefellers, along with Rockefeller's Standard Oil of New Jersey, were merged in hundreds of transnational cartels. They were in essence the same firm. After World War II, the president of Standard-Germany, Emil Helfferich, testified that Standard Oil funds had been used to pay the wages of SS overseers at Auschwitz.

CIA mind control experimentation emerged full-blown under Project BLUEBIRD in 1947, that sought an "exploitable alteration of personality," through testing a wide variety of drugs, under the supervision of Security operator Morse Allen. At the same time the U.S. Navy was doing its own drug experimentation under Project CHATTER, a project that sought a "truth drug." In 1950, LSD was used on suspected double agents and North Korean prisoners of war under the auspices of BLUEBIRD, and Morse Allen requested of his boss Paul Gaynor that the CIA acquire what was termed an 'electro-sleep' machine that had been built at a Richmond, Virginia hospital.

Basic to the financing of mind control projects, Nelson Rockefeller merged three federal corporations into the Department of Health, Education and Welfare, and HEW and its sub-agency the National Institute of Mental Health were used to fund ARTICHOKE and other early CIA mind control projects. Other agencies involved in research into people manipulation at the time included the Defense Department, the National Science Foundation, the Veteran's Administration, the Department of Labor, the Department of Health, Education and Welfare, the National Institute of Mental Health, and the Law Enforcement Assistance Administration.

Funding conduits for control operations run by the CIA and other agencies were and have been numerous, octopus-like. The Rockefellers and Allen Dulles established the Society for the Investigation of Human Ecology at Stanford which channelled funds for this type of research. Other organizations that provided cash for CIA mind control operations included the Macy Foundation and the Geshickter Fund, named after MKULTRA contractor Charles Geshickter. Another channel was the H. Smith Richardson Foundation, formed in the late 1959s by Bonesman Eugene Stetson, assistant manager for Prescott Bush at Brown Brothers Harriman, one of the largest private banks in the world at the time.[3]

The following is a listing of early major CIA mind control experimentation with brief descriptions, as documented in the Congressional record in 1977, by the Subcommittee on Health and Scientific Research of the Committee on Human Resources:

MKDELTA: This was apparently the first project established by the CIA in October, 1952, for the use of biochemicals in clandestine operations. It may never have been implemented operationally.

MKULTRA: This was a successor project to MKDELTA established in April, 1953, and terminating some time in the late 1960s, probably after 1966. This program considered various means of controlling human behavior. Drugs were only one aspect of this activity.

MKNAOMI: This project began in the 1950s and was terminated in 1969. This may have been a successor to MKDELTA. Its purpose was to stockpile severely incapacitating and lethal materials, and to develop gadgetry for the dissemination of these materials.

MKSEARCH: This was apparently a successor project to MKULTRA, which began in 1965 and was terminated in 1973. The objective of the project was to develop a capability to manipulate human behavior in a predictable manner through the use of drugs.

MKCHICKWIT: This was apparently a part of the MKSEARCH program. Its objective was to identify new drug developments in Europe and Asia and to obtain information and samples.

MKOFTEN: This was also apparently a part of the MKSEARCH project. Its objective was to test the behavioral and toxicological effects of certain drugs on animals and humans.

In the Top Secret "Memorandum for Chief, Medical Staff, PROJECT ARTICHOKE [deleted in original document], Evaluation of I & S Role, January 25, 1952," the question was posed, "Can we get control of an individual to the point where he will do our bidding against his will and even against such fundamental laws of nature such [sic] as self-preservation?

In a moment of candor as he spoke before Princeton alumni in 1953, CIA Director Allen Dulles spoke about two fronts in the "battle for men's minds." He said the first front in America was indoctrination, both through censorship as well as public relations techniques, and a second, vital and more specialized front, was individual "brainwashing" and "brain changing."[4]

Using the justification that Communist mind control programs were more advanced than those of their American counterpart programs, MKULTRA was authorized three days after Dulles' peptalk. Created as an adjunct to the ARTI-

CHOKE program, $300,000 initially funded this highly secret, compartmented umbrella program researching mind control. The great majority of MKULTRA programs were 'black' or undocumented programs about which little has ever been revealed. What is documented of MKULTRA, however, is horrific enough to provide scripts for a hundred grisly horror films—and to provide credibility to the monstrous stories about mind control programs that surface to this day.

The primary administrator for CIA mind control programs was Sidney Gottlieb, who had a doctorate in biochemistry from CalTech. At age 33 he headed up the Agency's technical services division, presiding over MKULTRA and its minimum of 149 subsets conducted in universities, hospitals, prisons, and military institutions across the country, as he would until 1973. The Strangelovian Gottlieb compensated for a club foot and a severe stammer by being an avid folk dancer, demonstrating new steps before his co-workers after his return from foreign lands.

An excerpt from a characteristic Gottlieb memo follows:

11 May 1953
MEMORANDUM FOR THE RECORD SUBJECT: Visit to Project [deleted]
1. On this day the writer spent the day observing experiments (Mr. [deleted] has already submitted his proposal to the [deleted])
2. The general picture of the present status of the project is one of a carefully planned series of five major experiments. Most of the year has been spent in screening and standardizing a large group of subjects (approximately 100) and the months between now and September 1 should yield much data, so that these five experiments should be completed by September 1. The five experiments are; (N stands for the total number of subjects involved in the experiment.)
Experiment 1 - N-18 Hypnotically induced anxieties to be completed by September 1.
Experiment 2 - N-24 Hypnotically increasing ability to learn and recall complex written matter, to be completed by September 1.

Experiment 3 - N-3 Polygraph response under Hypnosis, to be completed by June 15.

Experiment 4 - N-24 Hypnotically increasing ability to observe and recall a complex arrangement of physical objects.

Experiment 5 - N-100 Relationship of personality to susceptibility to hypnosis.

3. The work for next year (September 1, 1953 to June 1, 1954) will concentrate on:

Experiment 6 - The Morse code problem, with the emphasis on relatively lower I.Q. subjects then found on University volunteers.

[deleted material]

Experiment 7 - Recall of hypnotically acquired information by very specific signals.

[deleted] will submit detailed research plans on all experiments not yet submitted.

Among other experiments authorized by Gottlieb were those of Dr. Harris Isbell, who ran the Center for Addiction Research in Lexington, Kentucky. Using black heroin addicts as research fodder, Isbell tested more than eight hundred psychoactive chemicals, shipped to him directly from Gottlieb. In one experiment Isbell kept seven addicts stoned on quadruple normal dosages of LSD without interruption for 77 days, jolting them with electroshock to wake them when they fell asleep. In another experiment Isbell strapped nine men to gurneys, inserted rectal thermometers, shot them up with massive hits of psilocybin, shined lights in their eyes to check pupil dilation, and pounded on their joints to test nervous system response. The subjects of Isbell's torture garden were paid off with heroin fixes.

In 1952 Gottlieb collaborated with government drug agent George White, setting him up in Operation Midnight Climax. Safehouses decorated to resemble bordellos were set up in both New York and San Francisco, where men would be lured by prostitutes and then dosed with LSD without their knowledge. In most cases, the victims were given LSD-spiked drinks, but in at least one instance LSD gas was sprayed into a restroom before the john entered the john. The ever-curious White observed the unsuspecting victims through a mirror, while sitting on a portable toilet sipping gibsons. As with most accounts of CIA testing, one suspects that more was going on than was documented. My own suspicion is that White's ultimate mission was to obtain compromising information on crime figures and perhaps politicians in an ancient-by-then drugging and prostitution ruse.[5]

Other participants in MKULTRA and programs that followed were recruited from approximately five thousand Nazis brought from Germany immediately after World War II through the clandestine Project PAPERCLIP. These included:

—Karl Tauboeck, a Nazi expert on sterilization drugs and a chief plant chemist at I.G. Farben.

—Theodore Wagner-Jauregg, Kurt Rarh, and Hans Turnit, who continued their wartime research on super poisons like Sarin and Tabun.

—SS Brigadier General Walter Schieber, a specialist in chemical warfare and nerve gas.

—Dr. Huburtus Strughold, who worked in MKULTRA as well as at NASA. According to a report by the *Jewish Telegraphic Agency* in 1995:

"The sadistic Nazi background of a late German scientist has resulted in plans to remove his name from a U.S. Air Force library. In 1993, soon after the scientist's background was first uncovered, his portrait was removed from a mural of medical heroes at Ohio State University. Scientist Huburtus Strughold, who died in 1986, was secretly brought to the United States in 1945 to work on the space program, even though he was sought for prosecution in Nuremberg. The library at the School of Aerospace Medicine at Brooks Air Force Base in Texas had been named to honor Strughold, who helped develop the pressure suits used by astronauts as well as the U.S. space capsule. As the head of Nazi Germany's Air Force Institute for Aviation Medicine, Strughold participated in a 1942 conference that discussed 'experiments' on human beings. The experiments included subjecting Dachau concentration camp inmates to torture and death."[6]

Curiously, another MKULTRA faction consisted of representatives of the Scottish Rite of Masonry, which had sponsored research into eugenics, psychiatry, and mind control since at least the 1930s. MKULTRA doctor Robert Hanna Felix was director of psychiatric research for the Scottish Rite of Freemasonry, and the director of the National Institute of Mental Health. Felix was the immediate senior of Dr. Harris Isbell, already noted in relation to MKULTRA. Another prominent Freemason involved in MKULTRA was Dr. Paul Hoch, financed by the Army Chemical Center. A member of the American Eugenics Society, Hoch was co-director with Nazi eugenicist Franz Kallman in research at Columbia University's New York State Psychiatric Institute.

Other participants in mind control programs were garden variety American fascists and sadists who saw intelligence agency work as being the perfect milieu for fulfilling their own murderous desires.[7]

Among the areas investigated during MKULTRA were: brain surgery including lobotomy; the use of electrical and chemical shock; the effects of stress on human beings, including hunger, fear, fatigue, duress, and torture; narcoanalysis; handwriting analysis; ultrasonic, subsonic, and vibrational disorientation and control; interrogation techniques; drugs that induced speech and amnesia, sensory deprivation and "electrosleep"; radiation; genetic research including gene splicing and the creation of mutations; ESP; various forms of brainwashing; personality assessment; concussions produced by remote control; brain implants and electrodes; the use of prostitutes as agents; hormonal and glandular products; gases; poisons; drug agents that could be sprayed; and drugs, including LSD, amphetamines, morphine, nicotine, ether, psychedelic mushrooms, barbiturates, heroin, cocaine, and marijuana. At least four of the MKULTRA programs were specifically conducted on children. This is the vast sub-structure of MKULTRA experimentation that has for the greater part been successfully concealed by the Agency.[8]

One early MKULTRA experiment had agents driving a 1953 Mercury through the streets of New York City, an altered tailpipe belching an unspecified gas that was probably laced with LSD. LSD was also sprayed in the New York subways, with the results undocumented in extant paperwork, and an unspecified gas sprayed and dissipated off the Golden Gate Bridge in San Francisco. The CIA was only too aware that it was engaged in illegal research, and cautioned its employees about secrecy. In 1957 CIA Inspector General Lyman issued an internal memo warning that "precautions must be taken not only to protect the operations from exposure to enemy forces, but also to conceal these activities from the American public in general. The knowledge that the Agency is engaged in unethical and illicit activities would have serious repercussions in political and diplomatic circles and would be detrimental to the accomplishment."[9]

One of those "unethical and illicit activities" may have been the elimination of the black American entertainer and political activist Paul Robeson. Aside from his involvement in the struggle for black rights in the U.S., Robeson had also campaigned for the colonial independence movement abroad as led by men like Jomo Kenyatta and Jawharlal Nehru. In the spring of 1961, three weeks before the CIA's Bay of Pigs fiasco, Robeson travelled to Moscow where he had meetings and interviews and gave speeches. The next stop on Robeson's itinerary was to be Cuba, where he was scheduled meet Fidel Castro, then he planned to head back to the United States to continue his commitment to civil rights activism.

Robeson, according to the people who were with him in Russia, "was in unusually good spirits." After a surprise party at his Moscow hotel, Robeson suddenly felt possessed by extreme paranoia. He went off by himself and tried to kill himself by cutting his wrists. Robeson was admitted to the Priory hospital in London where, within 36 hours, he was given the first of 54 electro-convulsive shock sessions that he would eventually receive. Robeson was never to fully recover from the sudden "paranoiac" bout or from the electroshock.

Now, in 1999, Robeson's son has presented formal appeals to British, American and Russian intelligence agencies for the release of classified materials relating to his father's visit to Moscow and his subsequent medical treatment. He

believes that the symptoms that his father exhibited suggest
he was poisoned by the CIA with the psychoactive chemical
BZ in order to halt the entertainer's visit to Havana, and to
nullify him as a force in the civil rights movement. Robeson
Jr. cites the fact that there had been previous attempts on his
father's life, as well as the fact that two of the doctors who
treated him in London were linked to MKULTRA.[10]

MKULTRA was administratively reformed as MK-
SEARCH in 1963, running until 1973. Among the MKULTRA
subprojects that were carried over was one on the paranor-
mal and the use of ESP for espionage. This project was said
to have been discontinued in 1973, but is documented as having continued until 1984.[11]

In 1977 a Senate Select Committee on Intelligence was
convened to gaze into the darkness that was MKULTRA.
According to Senator Edward Kennedy, testifying before the
committee:

"Perhaps most disturbing of all was the fact that the extent of experimentation on human subjects was unknown. The
records of all these activities were destroyed in January 1973,
at the instruction of then CIA Director Richard Helms. In
spite of persistent inquiries by both the Health Subcommittee
and the Intelligence Committee, no additional records or information were forthcoming. And no one—no single individual—could be found who remembered the details, not the
Director of the CIA, who ordered the documents destroyed,
not the official responsible for the program, nor any of his
associates..."[12]

In confirmation of my own belief that there was a vast
MKULTRA continent of which we have only been given a
glimpse is the statement of ex-CIA officer Miles Copeland,
speaking in an interview with journalist John Marks. Copeland
said, "The congressional subcommittee which went into this
sort of thing got only the barest glimpse."[13]

Dr. Sidney Gottlieb, an earlier-mentioned MKULTRA
mastermind, may have died by the same sword he lived by.
In 1999 several new court trials were in progress for victims
seeking compensation for experimentation performed upon
them by the CIA. According to persons who had talked to

Gottlieb, he suspected that current the CIA administration was going to target him as the scapegoat for the MKULTRA atrocities. There has been speculation that Gottlieb was not willing to take the fall for the Agency, and was ready to blow the whistle on what had gone in. But Gottlieb died on March 10, 1999, at a very fortuitous time for the Agency.[14]

Although the information that has been revealed about CIA mind control projects constitutes only the tip of the research, what has been revealed is a national shame that should have leveled the CIA, as John F. Kennedy had proposed doing shortly before his assassination. We know that from the beginning the CIA employed citizens in mind control experimentation and other mutilations without their consent. In these experiments lives were destroyed, minds and bodies shattered, all ostensibly in the interest of the military industrial complex's Cold War. Congress has estimated that 23,000 persons were experimented upon under the auspices of MKULTRA, but given the fact that much of the documentation for that program was destroyed, it is difficult to understand how they could have made such a precise determination. Certainly, most researchers in the field would say that the figure was a gross underestimate in horror.

It is plain that during its history the CIA has been the prime player in formulating a secret science of mind control that has only been hinted at in the controlled media. Extensive research suggests that advanced techniques of control were created far in advance of anything that the Agency has ever been willing to admit to.

The CIA and its successor agencies such as the National Security Agency must be not seen as instruments for furthering American security, but as arms of the planetary controllers for maintaining their own dominion. These agencies primarily further the elitists' own interests, including the implementation of plans of eugenics, social control, monopolistic control of resources, and other forms of the suppression of the masses worldwide.

Notes:

1. Marks, John. *The Search for the Manchurian Candidate: The CIA and Mind Control*; Bowart, Walter. *Operation Mind Control*. New York: Dell, 1977; Cannon, Martin, "Mind Control and the American Government," *Lobster* 23
2. Sutton, Antony C. *America's Secret Establishment*. Billings, Montana: Liberty House Press, 1986; Sutton, Antony C. *Wall Street and the Rise of Hitler*. Seal Beach, California: '76 Press, 1976
3. Colby, Gerard. *Thy Will Be Done*. Cited in Constantine, *Virtual Government, CIA Mind Control Operations in America*. Venice, California: Feral House, 1997; Ross, M.D., Dr. Colin, "The CIA and Military Mind Control Research: Building the Manchurian Candidate," lecture given at Ninth Annual Western Clinical Conference on Trauma and Dissociation, April 18, 1996; Krawczyk, Glenn, "Mind Control Techniques and Tactics of the New World Order," *Nexus*, December-January 1993; Bowart; Constantine; George Bush: The Unauthorized Biography; Chaitkin, Anton. *Treason in America*. New York: New Benjamin Franklin House, 1984; Pincher, Chapman. *Too Secret, Too Long*. New York: St. Martin's Press, 1984; Editors of the *Executive Intelligence Review*. *Dope, Inc*. Washington, D.C.: *EIR*, 1992; Lee and Shlain. *Acid Dreams*. Grove Press: New York, 1985; Lyttle, Thomas, "Blot Art," an interview conducted by Mark Westion. *Paranoia*, winter 1995/96; Stevens, Jay. *Storming Heaven*. New York: Harper & Row, 1987. Marks; Chaitkin, Anton. *Treason in America*; Pincher; Chaitkin, Anton, "Population Control, Nazis, and the U.N.!"; Marks
4. Brandt, Daniel, "Mind Control and the Secret State," *Prevailing Winds*, number 3
5. Stevens, Jay
6. Constantine; Cannon; Lee and Shlain. *Acid Dreams*. New York: Grove Press, 1985
7. Chaitkin, Anton, "British Psychiatry: From Eugenics to Assassination," *EIR*, October 7, 1994
8. Bowart; Lee and Shlain; *Human Rights Law Journal*, "Freedom of the Mind as an International Human Rights Issue," Vol. 3, No. 1-4; Constantine; Ross
9. Quoted in *Matrix III*, Val Valerian, ed., 1992
10. Rhodes, Tom, "U.S. 'poisoned Robeson' with mind-bending drug," *Sunday Times of London*, March 14, 1999
11. Ross; Cannon; Chaitkin, Anton, "British Psychiatry: From Eugenics to Assassination"; Constantine; "LSD, the CIA, and Your Brain: Midnight Climax," Lycaeum Drug Archives; Interview with Walter H. Bowart, July 16, 1995, conducted by Will Robinson and Marilyn Coleman
12. *Project MKULTRA, the CIA's Program of Research in Behavioral Modification*, Joint Hearing Before the Select Committee on Intelligence and the Subcommittee on Health and Scientific Research of the Committee on Human Resources, United States Senate, ninety-fifth Congress, August 3, 1977, U.S. Government Printing Office. Washington, D.C.: 1977

13. Marks
14. "Stanley Glickman LSD Overdose," *The Observer*, February 14, 1999; *MKULTRA: CIA Mind Control* by Jon Elliston, pscpdocs@aol.com:; Cockburn, Alexander and St. Clair, Jeffrey, "CIA's Sidney Gottlieb: Pusher, Assassin & Pimp," press release from *CounterPunch*

Chapter 8

Estabrooks and the Manchurian Candidate

As early as the turn of this century neurologist Morton Prince broached the subject of patients with multiple personalities or, as it is now termed by psychiatrists, Dissociative Identity Disorder. Prince believed that a person might possess several different personalities that operated at the same time, that might not be aware of each other. It took a while for men to notice that this information could be of particular use.

One man who took note of Prince's views was Rhodes Scholar, Dr. George Estabrooks, chairman of the Psychology Department at Colgate University, near Buffalo, New York. Estabrooks was well-connected with most of the major psychological figures of this century, and conducted research for all of the major branches of American military intelligence. Estabrooks was one of the first persons to realize that mind controlled intelligence agents and assassins really could be created hypnotically, Svengali aside. His experimentation in the use of hypnosis in espionage began, amazingly enough, during World War I.

In the 1920's Estabrooks engaged in research into psychic phenomena at Harvard, but he soon turned his attention back to hypnosis and its use in the overriding of the individual's will. One of Estabrooks' early and unique realizations was that if multiple personalities could be cured by hypnotism, then it followed that multiple personalities could be created in the same fashion.

In 1942, Estabrooks was appointed as an Expert Consultant to the Secretary of War, liaison with the Naval Research

Laboratory, while at the same time conducting a massive correspondence with J. Edgar Hoover. In later years Estabrooks would take on work with the CIA.[1]

According to an article penned by Estabrooks in 1971,

"One of the most fascinating but dangerous applications of hypnosis is its use in military intelligence. This is a field with which I am familiar through formulating guidelines for the techniques used by the United States in two world wars. Communication in war is always a headache. Codes can be broken. A professional spy may or may not stay bought. Your own man may have unquestionable loyalty but his judgement is always open to question. The 'hypnotic courier' on the other hand, provides a unique solution. I was involved in preparing many subjects for this work during World War II. One successful case involved an Army Service Corps Captain whom we'll call George Smith. Captain Smith had undergone months of training. He was an excellent subject but did not realize it. I had removed from him, by post-hypnotic suggestion, all recollection of ever having been hypnotized. First I had the Service Corps call the captain to Washington and tell him they needed a report on the mechanical equipment of Division X headquartered in Tokyo. Smith was ordered to leave by jet the next morning, pick up the report and return at once. These orders were given him in the waking state. Consciously, that was all he knew and it was the story he gave his wife and friends. Then I put him under deep hypnosis, and gave him— orally—a vital message to be delivered directly on his arrival in Japan to a certain colonel—let's say his name was Brown— of military intelligence. Outside of myself, Colonel Brown was the only person who could hypnotize Captain Smith. This is 'locking.' I performed it by saying to the hypnotized captain: 'Until further orders from me, only Colonel Brown and I can hypnotize you. We will use a signal phrase, 'the moon is clear.' Whenever you hear this phrase from Brown or myself you will pass instantly into deep hypnosis.' When Captain Smith re-awakened, he had no conscious memory of what happened in trance. All that he was aware of was that he must head for Tokyo to pick up a division report. On arrival there, Smith reported to Brown, who hypnotized him with the signal phrase. Under hypnosis, Smith delivered my message and received one to bring back. Awakened, he was given the division report, and returned home by jet. There I hypnotized him once more with the signal phrase, and he spieled off Brown's answer that had been dutifully tucked away in his unconscious mind. The system is virtually foolproof."[2]

Estabrooks also wrote about the creation of multiple identities for military use:

"During World War II, I worked this technique with a vulnerable Marine lieutenant I'll call Jones. Under the watchful eye of Marine Intelligence, I split his personality into Jones A and Jones B. Jones A, once a 'normal' working Marine, became entirely different. He talked communist doctrine and meant it. He was welcomed enthusiastically by communist cells, was deliberately given a dishonorable discharge by the Corps, which was in on the plot, and became a card-carrying party member. The joker was Jones B, the second personality, formerly apparent in the conscious Marine. Under hypnosis, this Jones had been carefully coached by suggestion. Jones B was the deeper personality, knew all the thoughts of Jones A, was a loyal American and was 'imprinted' to say nothing during conscious phases. All I had to do was hypnotize the whole man, get in touch with Jones B, the loyal American, and I had a pipeline straight into the Communist camp."[3]

Estabrooks went on at length about the creation of mind controlled assassins in his 1943 book *Hypnotism*. In 1945 Estabrooks, with Richard Lockridge, also penned a fictional potboiler titled *Death in the Mind*. In that book Nazis captured Allied officers and hypnotically turned them into double agents.[4]

Although the general opinion among psychologists at the time of Estabrooks' experimentation was that a person's will could not be overridden through the use of hypnosis, Estabrooks thought differently. "In fact," Estabrooks wrote, "I believe the hypnotist's power to be unlimited—or rather to be limited only by his intelligence and his scruples."[5]

In an interview with the Providence, Rhode Island *Evening Bulletin*, Estabrook talked about the creation of hypnotically controlled spies by splitting personalities. Estabrooks said that the capability "is not science fiction... This has and is being done. I have done it."

As he indicates, Estabrooks was not the only one "doing it" at the time. Morse Allen wrote that in his early days of CIA research, he attempted to "...Take an existing ego state— such as an imaginary childhood playmate—and build it into a separate personality, unknown to the first. Allen would then work with this 'new' personality and 'command it to carry out specific deeds about which the main personality would know nothing. There would be inevitable leakage between the two personalities, particularly in dreams, but if the hypnotist were clever enough, he could build in cover stories and safety valves which would prevent the subject from acting inconsistently.'"[6]

In March of 1951, 28-year-old Palle Hardrup walked into a bank in Copenhagen and shot two bank employees to death. When he was apprehended, Hardrup confessed that he had done the murders, but said that he had been hypnotized by an accomplice, Bjorn Schouw-Nielsen, to commit the crimes. Hardrup was found guilty of manslaughter and institutionalized, and his programmer, Schouw-Nielson, was also found guilty of manslaughter, but given a life term in prison.[7]

An account of the creation of mind controlled assassins was provided by Colonel William Bishop who, in 1983, made the following statement to researcher Gary Shaw:

"That was how, after the Korean War, I got involved with CIA. I have been subjected to every known type of drug. The medical doctors connected with the agency found that certain drugs work quite well in conjunction with hypnosis— hypnotic power of suggestion—with some subjects. It did with me. I speak with absolute certainty and knowledge and experience that this is not only possible, but did and is taking place today.

"I never understood why they selected me personally. There were any number of psychological or emotional factors involved in people's selection. Antisocial behavior patterns, paranoid or the rudiments of paranoia, and so on. But when they are successful with this programming—or, for lack of a better term, indoctrination—they could take John Doe and get this man to kill George and Jane Smith. He will be given all the pertinent information as to their location, daily habits, etc. Then there is a mental block put on this mission in his mind. He remembers nothing about it.

"Perhaps a month or a year later—rarely over a year, at least back in those days—the phone rings. A code word will be read to him in a voice that John Doe recognizes. That will trigger the action. John Doe will commit the assassination, return home, and remember absolutely nothing of it. It is totally a blank space.

"Now, there is a problem with this, and they never found a way that I know of to overcome it. From time to time—it happens to me now—I will see faces, names, places, gunfire, for which there is no rational explanation. I went back for deprogramming. In these sessions, they explain that this does happen from time to time, not to worry about it, just clear your mind and forget it.

"I know men who gradually lost their sight, or some of their hearing, or the use of their vocal cords. Some had chronic constipation. For entirely psychological reasons, not physical, because inadvertently these mental blocks developed. I myself became totally impotent. For obvious reasons, I don't care to go into this in any greater detail."

Within days after authorizing the release of the above information, Colonel Bishop died of heart failure, a not-uncommon fate for those who expose the Agency's dirty laundry.[8]

Judging from the information that we have, as early as World War II psychiatrists working for American Intelligence agency were able to fracture and compartment subjects' personalities, to occlude information from both the subject and from interrogators, and to insert false memories into a subject's mind. Thanks to George Estabrooks, at the mid-century mark the creation of technology of the Manchurian Candidate was complete.[9]

As many have suspected, there is evidence suggesting that George Estabrooks' Manchurian Candidate may have been employed in the field. Perhaps the most significant instance of this may have been in the assassination of President John F. Kennedy on November 22, 1963. Lee Harvey Oswald, whom evidence suggests was anything but a "lone gunman," seems to have instead been a dupe of forces that probably included the CIA, the Mafia and others, and may have programmed to kill JFK.

In a letter to the author, Kerry Thornley, Oswald's best friend at the Atsugi Japan Naval Air Base, wrote:

"In the late 1970s I was contacted by David Bucknell, who said he was in Marine Air Control Squadron Nine with Oswald and me. When he mentioned that his nickname was 'Bucky Beaver,' I recalled Bucknell—a large man with buck teeth who wore his utility cap all the way down on his head, giving it a dome shape instead of the common stretched, flat-top shape.

"Bucknell asked me if I remembered an attempt to recruit us (Bucknell, Oswald, me) to military intelligence. I did not. Then he asked if I remembered approaching he and Oswald one day and being told by Oswald that 'This is a private conversation.' That I recalled clearly. Bucknell said it happened as we were on our way to the recruitment lecture.

"Indeed, I remembered the incident occurred as all three of us were walking in the same direction toward 'Mainside' on the base and away from the radar outpost, the names Oswald, Bucknell and Thornley had been called over the P.A. system and that we were told to report to the squadron office. In the squadron office, we were ordered to report to base security over at 'Mainside' of L.T.A., the satellite of El Toro Marine Base where we were stationed.

"Bucknell said he and Oswald were running a loan sharking operation and their private conversation concerned whether or not they were now being called in for questioning about that. Oswald doubted it, because I had been called up at the same time and knew nothing about the operation.

"Bucknell says when we arrived at base security we were seated in a small auditorium or lecture room with a number of men from other outfits. Up in front, according to Bucknell, was a Marine captain and a Hispanic man in civilian clothes with a flat-top haircut. Bucknell was surprised to see that the Captain was acting as an 'errand boy' for this civilian, whom the Captain finally introduced as 'Mister B.'

"'Mister B.' said, 'We have reason to believe that Castro's new revolutionary government has been infiltrated by Soviet agents.' (This would have been in late May or early June of 1959, just after the New Year's Day Revolution, before Castro 'went Communist.' I recalled someone making that statement in a lecture I attended, but did not remember the context).

"We had all been called together, said Mr. B., because we were reputed to be admirers of Fidel Castro. As I understand it, and dimly recall it, the pitch was that Castro needed our help in getting rid of these agents. We were being asked to volunteer for a counter-espionage program!

"I'm sure I would have volunteered. To the best of my recollection, I was ostensibly turned down because I was already slated for a tour of duty in the Far East, to begin in June, and the training program was in the U.S.—But not before I signed some papers authorizing using me for intelligence purposes.

"Bucknell made detailed notes of this extraordinary event the day after it occurred, and when we met in San Francisco in the late 1970s he read me those notes.

"Volunteers were interviewed on a one-on-one basis after the recruitment lecture. Bucknell says he had a maternal grandfather named E.H. Hunt, who he listed on the recruitment form as a reference. Mister B. looked startled and said, 'Who is this E.H. Hunt?' Bucknell explained. Mister B. said, 'Oh!,' and laughed. (E. Howard Hunt was second in command under Nixon on the Bay of Pigs operation.)

""Bucknell was never contacted again in relation to this program. Neither was I.

"Bucknell says that the Marine Air Control Squadron's covert security was handled by Army Intelligence, and we now both suspect that Oswald may already have been an Army

Intelligence agent pretending to be a Marxist at the time of Mr. B.'s recruitment attempt, which may have enhanced his qualifications for Mr. B.'s program.

"At about the time all this happened, I began having vivid audio hallucinations, usually just before falling asleep."

Thornley believes that while he was in the Marines he personally was the subject of mind control experimentation, and that he was implanted at the base of his neck with a mind control device through which transmissions were directed. Kerry may have simply been paranoid, or he may have been on to something.[10]

Others in the know have suggested that Lee Harvey Oswald may have been mind controlled. Army and CIA counter intelligence agent Herman Kimsey came forward in 1975 to tell what he knew about Oswald. According to Kimsey, in an interview with journalist Hugh MacDonald, "Oswald was programmed to kill, like a medium at a seance. Then the mechanism went on the blink and Oswald became a dangerous toy without direction." Surely it was a coincidence that Kimsey died of heart failure three weeks after the interview.[11]

As documented in the Warren Report, Oswald is alleged to have lived at Cuban psychiatrist Francisco Silva's home prior to the assassination, and to have gotten a job at the hospital where Silva was employed. It is of note that Silva had collaborated in his scientific writings with brain implant scientist Robert Heath.[12]

Among the darkling creatures who populated the world of Lee Harvey Oswald was David Ferrie, believed by New Orleans District Attorney Jim Garrison to have been a key participant in the assassination conspiracy. Ferrie had been a senior pilot with Eastern Airlines, until he was fired for homosexual behavior on the job.

Ferrie was in the thick of anti-Castro activity, and associated with Mafia boss Carlos Marcello as well as members of the CIA. According to Victor Marchetti, former Executive Assistant to the Deputy Director of the CIA, he was told by a CIA agent that Ferrie had been a contract agent for the CIA in the early 60s. Ferrie allegedly became bitter with

John F. Kennedy after the failure of the Bay of Pigs invasion of Cuba, and a number of witnesses recall hearing Ferrie talking about assassinating the president.

Ferrie's earliest contact with Oswald was probably in 1954 in the Louisiana Civil Air Patrol, supposedly the same year that Oswald became wildly interested in Communism. On the day of the assassination Marcello's attorney visited Ferrie to tell him that Oswald's wallet contained Ferrie's library card.

The connections become more strange. Ferrie was a hypnotist, who allegedly used his skills in his quest for homosexual conquests. One of Ferrie's fellow travelers, Jack Martin, reportedly said that Ferrie had hypnotically programmed Oswald to kill Kennedy.

Ferrie is also alleged to have been into "black magic" and was the high priest of the Apostolic Old Catholic Church of North America, members of which were investigated by Garrison for involvement in the Kennedy hit. The Apostolic Church may have been—this is entirely speculative—a chapter of the Ordo Templi Orientis-connected Gnostic Catholic Church. Certainly it was not what would be described as your average Catholic parish. According to researcher Loren Coleman, "The church conducted services involving animal sacrifice and blood guzzling. During Lee Harvey Oswald's last weeks in New Orleans, he attended many ritualistic parties in private homes and apartments with David Ferrie." This is a curious conjunction that is seen again and again in the research: black magic, military intelligence, and mind control.

Ferrie was found dead in his apartment on February 22, 1967 while in the midst of testifying about the Kennedy assassination. There were two apparent suicide notes, but the New Orleans coroner stated that the cause of death was natural, a cerebral hemorrhage.[13]

1969 saw the publication of *Were We Controlled*, a book written by journalist Arthur Ford under the pseudonym "Lincoln Lawrence." Ford claimed to be in contact with an intelligence agency insider who gave him the details of a CIA technology dubbed RHIC-EDOM, that is, Radio Hypnotic

Intracerbral Control and Electronic Dissolution of Memory, that was used to program Oswald. According to Lincoln Lawrence, Oswald's murderer may have also been mind controlled. The evaluation of Jack Ruby's mindset by a number of doctors is suggestive. According to Dr. Walter Bromberg, a psychiatrist and clinical director at the Pinewood Psychiatric Hospital at Katonah, New York, Ruby was "preset to be a fighter, to attack." Bromberg also said, "Definitely there is a block to his thinking which is no part of his original mental endowment."

Dr. Roy Schafer, Staff Psychologist and Associate Clinical Professor of Psychiatry and Psychology at Yale University, said of Ruby that, "He appears to feel not altogether in control of his body actions, as if they occur independently of his conscious will at times."

Dr. Manfred S. Guttmacher, Chief Medical Officer of the Supreme Court of Baltimore, suggested that Ruby's brain had been damaged by undisclosed means.[14]

Perhaps the most convincing evidence that exists of the use of a Manchurian Candidate was in the assassination of John F. Kennedy's brother, Robert F. Kennedy, who was at the time of his death a strong contender in the American presidential race. Although the Kennedy case is labyrinthine in its complexity, and probably included a police/intelligence agency cover-up after the fact that makes getting at the truth difficult, I will touch on a few salient points.

Pointing to the possibility that Sirhan may have been a mind-controlled assassin, the man received a head injury while working as an exercise jockey in 1966, perhaps making him more easily hypnotizable. We do know that he received attention from a number of doctors at this time. Terry Welch, a friend from the racetrack where he worked, stated that Sirhan's personality completely changed at this time. If an operation was conducted on his head at that time, a brain implant might have been inserted without attracting attention.

Sirhan disappeared for three months during 1967, not informing his family of his whereabouts, which would have provided an excellent opportunity for mind control programming to take place. It was noted that after his return to Los Angeles, Sirhan had acquired an interest in occultism that he had never had in the past.

A search of Sirhan's room by the police in the days after the shooting turned up literature from the AMORC Rosicrucian mail order metaphysicians, and it is alleged that Sirhan had become acquainted with a member of The Process, a Scientology offshoot group that Charles Manson had also had a brush or two with. According to researcher John Judge, Sirhan had attended parties at the Roman Polanski mansion, as had Manson, and Robert F. Kennedy dined at the Polanski home the day before his murder.

A number of persons who saw Sirhan after the murder of Kennedy commented on his hypnotic-seeming demeanor. When he was questioned by the public defender who was assigned to him after the crime, Sirhan said, "I don't remember much about the shooting, sir, did I do it? Well, yes, I am told I did it. I remember being at the Ambassador [Hotel]. I am drinking Tom Collinses. I got dizzy. I went back to my car so I could go home. But I was too drunk to drive. I thought I'd better find some coffee. The next thing I remember I was being choked and a guy was twisting my knee.[15]

The "who" in Sirhan's hynosis may have been Bill Bryan, the president of the American Institute of Hypnosis, who bragged that he had worked for the CIA, and said in 1968 that Sirhan had been his client. Bryan is also known to have hypnotized Albert De Salvo, the "Boston Strangler," and references to "Di Salvo" are in Sirhan's notebook.[16]

On June 2, 1968, Sirhan was seen at the Kennedy Campaign headquarters in Los Angeles. When he was asked whether he needed some assistance, he pointed to a new volunteer who was standing nearby. The worker was Khaiber Khan, who had joined the campaign the day before. Khan, unbeknownst to the Kennedy staff, was a high-level CIA operative, who had participated in a number of major CIA actions over the years, including working as an agent in the toppling of the Iranian government in 1953.

On the day of Kennedy's shooting, Khan is reported as having provided a ride to the Ambassador Hotel for Michael

Wayne, who had earlier been seen with Sirhan. Wayne was identified by several witnesses as running out of the hotel pantry after the shooting, carrying what appeared to be a rifle.

Khaiber Khan is said to have given misleading answers when questioned about Sirhan after the death of Kennedy. He was then left alone by police investigators, perhaps because of his role in intelligence operations. One can imagine the stickiness of the L.A. police implicating the CIA in the murder of Kennedy.

It is of possible importance that the famous "girl in the polka dot dress" who ran out of the Ambassador Hotel immediately following the Kennedy shooting, exulting, "We shot him! We shot him!" was tentatively identified by two witnesses as being Khaiber Khan's daughter, Shirin Khan.[17]

Apparently the quest to create the Manchurian Candidate by intelligence agencies continues. In April of 1984 while studying at the University of Wisconsin, Dan Harr was approached by a man who identified himself as a recruiter for the CIA. Offered enlistment in a "special program," Harr turned him down. Harr believes that he was approached due to high intelligence scores, technical ability, and possibly abuse he may have experienced as a child. His maternal grandfather was chief civilian officer at the Badger Army Ammunition Ordinance plant at Baraboo, Wisconsin, and may have worked for the CIA, according to his grandmother. According to Harr, Baraboo was one location where Project Paperclip operations were conducted.

In late 1985 Harr needed money. He telephoned the CIA man, was recruited into the Agency, and during 1986 spent approximately half of his weekends at a "farm" near Fairfax, Virginia. Although the location was a working farm, it also had underground rooms for what Harr terms NOC (Non-Official Cover) training in "Pegasus" and "Orion" projects.

Harr says, "Pegasus was the operation of 'programmed responders' and Orion the operatives, the Hunters... At the NOC training I learned weapons training, extensive computer knowledge for 'hacking,' use of radios and other communication devices, and certain evasion techniques. Some of the memories are blurred because, I believe, they were later 'wiped,' and overlaid with fake trails, although I still retain the skills I was taught."

As a cover, Harr entered the Navy in January 1987 and went through electronics training. He was transferred to Mare Island near Vallejo, California, which he believes is a "special projects" submarine base with a strong CIA and NSA presence on-site. His service records from the period show a "T-secret" clearance, with additional attached code numbers.

According to Harr, he has virtually no memory of what took place at Mare Island. He believes that this was the time period in which he underwent mind control conditioning, part of it possibly conducted at Oakland Naval Hospital.

One operation Harr says he was involved with was "Bedrock-Stalemate." A former military man who had been involved in 1968 in a program of assassination of Laotian political leaders (he believes the project was called "Black Stripe") decided to become a whistleblower. Harr and two other "programmed responders" were "activated to plug the leaks."

After a knee injury, Harr recalls additional programming taking place at Oakland Naval Hospital: "I remember being strapped to the chair. My right hand was splayed out and had rubber cups on the ends of my fingers with wires running out of them. There was an IV needle in my hand. I remember hearing four drug names—Scopolamine, Sodium Pentothal, Nebutal, and Xanax. The strobes and speakers would flash and sound in sync, about one per second unless something was said to me or shown to me, which caused them to flash very fast. I think I had a metal band around my left leg, and I remember sometimes feeling shocks with the strobe lights. They would ask me questions and give directions. 'They,' I think, was a Dr. O'Connor...

"I remember some of the things I saw on the movie screen. There were many different pictures—dogs having sex, my parents with their heads cut off, a movie of a human sacrifice and some cannibalism, mixed with pictures of flowers, porno, cars, animals and such. Over and over again. Good, and bad, good and bad.

"I also remember something that felt like a coffin. It was all dark and filled with warm water. After awhile, I felt like a HEAD just floating without a body. There were also strobe lights and speakers in there as well. I remember feeling 'high' all the time. I also spent time in a small room where there was only a hole in the floor. The lights would go on and off and days would pass in hours, and hours in days. There was no sense of time."

Harr was honorably discharged after 23 months of a scheduled six-year enrollment. He returned to his hometown in Wisconsin, but was, according to his friends and family, somehow different than he had been prior to his hitch in the military. He had taken on "Right wing, Christian fanatic, Militia, Posse Commitatus" views. His belief is that these beliefs were installed to provide cover so that he could spy on right wing groups.

In April of 1995, Harr suddenly woke up in an unfamiliar restaurant in Madison, Wisconsin. A woman whom he did not know was sitting across from him. She said, "Good, you're back," stood up, and walked away. Later he found a needle mark on one arm and a puncture in his right hip. To this day, Harr labors to remember all of the details of what happened him after his recruitment by the CIA.[19]

A similar mind control project is detailed by a former member of Navy Intelligence and the CIA who was the head of a SEAL team. In "A Working Outline of a U.S. Intelligence Mind Control Program" he talks of Project Open Eyes, in which a "Clear Eyes" refers to a mind controlled subject.

"This segment is dedicated to Operation 'Open Eyes.' A preset group of our people canvass the country hospitals and immigration centers in order to find viable candidates for above named operation. We locate the target individuals, who have no close family or real good friends. They are then put under heavy stage one hypnosis, where a clear and definitive pattern of their usefulness is determined by our shrinks and field officers. If the candidate possesses a relatively high IQ he will be filed in a category file, called 'call file.'

"If the tested applicant has more than 120 IQ, he will be serviced by a trigger word or number, while under level 1 hypnosis. We then systematically do a background search and create a file for future reference. If there are no relatives to speak of, the subject will be moved to a location of our choice where further tests for vulnerability are conducted. He is then brought to level 2 hypnosis where diverse small orders and specific instructions are written into his personality.

"If subject, upon release shows that he has retained instructions and carries out small and unimportant work duties assigned under level 2 hypnosis, he will receive a recall 'Service notice' by a person we have introduced him to.

"The next step is level 3 hypnosis, where he will become an overwrite upon his own personality. He/she will be told that everything the subject does for his 'friends' is okay, even though it may very well be against all laws of the land. He will believe that he is capable of fulfilling all their (our) commands, and will be again discharged to live his normal life. (All operatives have to go to/through these 3 levels before any of us are fielded!)

"The higher the IQ of a given subject, the further the programming goes! If the IQ is high enough we will bring the subject to the Farm or one of our numerous facilities throughout the U.S. and Canada. (Dallas - 'Doctor's Hospital' is one of our main centers.

"There we will put the subject into level 4 hypnosis, where he does no longer differentiate between right and wrong. (We do this at the medical facility at the Farm—one of our contract hospitals. If he has to perform a particularly suicidal or important assignment we do our job at Stony Mountain facilities.) At level 4, diverse programs can be written/or overwritten into the brain. Any command is accepted at this level. At that level you can give the test subject a complete personality, history and make him/her believe anything the program requires for the accomplishment of any desired project. He is then given a new life in a new state and town. Driver's license, car, bank account, passport, credit cards, Birth Certificate, and all the small things—such as photos of his family (that don't really exist.) Subject and patient (one and the same) has now an agenda (that he believes is his own) and is prepared for level 5 hypnosis. At this stage, very carefully a code word or sequence of numbers or a voice imprint is etched into his brain. That is commonly known and referred to as the trigger that will activate subject to action.

"He then lives a very normal and sometimes useful life, until subject is required to perform the programs implanted/written into level 4 hypnosis at the point of activating the trigger, subject is beyond recall. That's why a level 5 person can only be approached after his/her operation. There is no actual recall in the subconscious program of any of the hypnosis. If an act of violence had been perpetrated, subject will not be able to associate with the deed. Only shrinks trained in this particular form of sub mental behavior will find any tracks leading to post level 1 or 2 mind control.

"I have personally witnessed level 1-5 programming, and was myself a subject of level 3 programming.

"Due to the fact that subject has such high IQ (preferably around 130-140) subject is very quick to learn anything fed to him/her. All major patriot groups, and normal workers and workers in big (government contract firms) corporations have at least one or more 'sleepers' attached to them.

"Project Clear Eyes is always a violent group or commune in any given community. The OKC incident was a clear cut case of Project Clear Eyes. Tom Valentine's group is the trigger mechanism for Open Eyes. Waco was an Open Eyes group that had a specific job to perform. Randy Weaver was a control subject that ended out of control. Robert Hunt is a sleeper that was put on hold. At some not too distant date you will see Bob Hunt performing his true and final role.

"Now it must be clear to you the various levels used by the Intel community to get their job done. Remember Jonestown? It was one of ours that went sour because a clear eyes was in the group. When he began firing on the runway, it all self-destructed. The man (Congressman Leo Ryan) who was killed, knew it was a government operation. Clear Eyes was accidentally—through a lone sequence—activated! There was no way to stop the killings. They were all programmed to at least level 3, the culties themselves. There were only 3 deaths attributable to cyanide, the rest died of gunfire. Now you know a little more about our line of work. I am glad I am out of it."[20]

Notes:

1. Ross, M.D., Dr. Colin, "The CIA and Military Mind Control Research: Building the Manchurian Candidate," lecture given at Ninth Annual Western Clinical Conference on Trauma and Dissociation, April 18, 1996
2. Estabrooks, G.H., "Hypnosis Comes of Age," *Science Digest*, April 1971
3. ibid.
4. Estabrooks, Dr. George, quoted in *Human Rights Law Journal*, "Freedom of the Mind as an International Human Rights Issue," Vol. 3, No. 1-4
5. Ibid.
6. Restak, Richard M. *The Brain: The Last Frontier*. New York: Warner Books, 1979
7. Lawrence, Lincoln, and Thomas, Kenn. *Mind Control, Oswald & JFK: Were We Controlled?* Kempton, Illinois: Adventures Unlimited Press, 1997
8. Russell, Dick. *The Man Who Knew Too Much*. New York: Carrol & Graf, 1992
9. Estabrooks, Dr. George, quoted in Human Rights Law Journal
10. Thornley, Kerry, correspondence with the author, August 30, 1997
11. Constantine, Alex. *Psychic Dictatorship*. Portland, Oregon: Feral House, 1995
12. Bowart, Walter, "Leading Psychiatrist Blows Whistle on Profession: Proves 50+ Years of Mind Control', *MindNet* Journal, Vol. 1, No. 94, www.visitations.com/mindnet/MN16A.HTM; Ross
13. Craig, John S., "JFK Redux: The Sinister World of David Ferrie," *Steamshovel Press*, Fall 1996; Coleman, Loren, "The Occult, MIBs, UFOs and Assassinations," *The Conspiracy Tracker*, December 1985; cited in Constantine, *Psychic Dictatorship in the U.S.A.*; Greenfield, Rev. Dr. Allen H. Greenfield, "The Secret History of Modern Witchcraft," unpublished manuscript in the author's possession
14. Lawrence
15. Kaiser, Robert Blair. *R.F.K. Must Die!* New York: Grove Press, 1970
16. Williams, Day, ed. Sirhan Sirhan is Innocent of the Assassination of Senator Robert Kennedy. "Facts About the Kennedy Assassination." Carson City, Nevada: 1998
17. ibid.
18. Terry, Maury. *The Ultimate Evil*. New York: Bantam Books, 1987; Judge, John, "Poolside with John Judge," *Prevailing Winds*, undated; Bresler, Fenton. *Who Killed John Lennon?* New York: St. Martin's Press, 1989

19. Harr, Dan, "CIA Programming," *MindNet Journal*, Vol. 1, No.47, www.visitations.com/mindnet/MN16A.htm
20. Bowart, Walter, "Operation Open Eyes: Disaffected Spook Spills SEAL Mind Control Experiences," *MindNet Journal*, Vol. 1, No. 72, www.visitations.com/mindnet/MN16A.htm

Jack Ruby exacts a nation's revenge on the assassin. BOB JACKSON

CHAPTER 9

DR. CAMERON'S CHAMBER OF HORRORS

In an effort to escape problems having to do with jurisdiction, much CIA experimentation during the MKULTRA era was conducted in Canada and in other foreign countries. Early funding of Canadian experimentation went to James Tyhurst, who in 1951 had been part of a committee providing oversight on Projects ARTICHOKE and BLUEBIRD. The Canadian Defense Research Board also provided money to Tyhurst, who did research on the effects of LSD on over 300 patients at Hollywood Hospital in Vancouver. CIA-funded research into LSD was also done in Saskatchewan, by Abram Hoffer and Humphrey Osmond.[1]

Another early CIA mind control program in Canada was 'Experimental Studies of Attitude Changes in Individuals,' with contract X-38 given to Dr. Donald O. Hebb of McGill University in 1951. Sensory deprivation and isolation in interrogation was researched, with the first subjects volunteer university students. After prolonged isolation, many of the subjects reached a point where they could no longer distinguish waking from sleep.

One of the most macabre series of experiments outside of the Inquisition was funded by the CIA and conducted by Dr. Donald Ewen Cameron, with funds also coming from the Canadian government, the Rockefeller Foundation, and the Gershickter Foundation. Cameron had studied at the Royal Mental Hospital in Glasgow, Scotland, under the tutelage of eugenicist Sir David Henderson. He later took over the psychiatric division of the Allen Memorial Institute at McGill

University in Montreal, which had been founded with Rockefeller monies. CIA Director Allen Dulles called Allen Memorial "a good source for human guinea pigs."

During the 1950s Cameron was anything but a rogue researcher; he was one of the most influential shrinks on the planet, founding the Canadian division of the World Federation of Mental Health with his friend, Tavistock's Brigadier General John Rawlings Reese. Cameron became president of many major psychiatric organizations, including the Canadian, American, and World Psychiatric Organizations.

Cameron seemingly took the Freemasonic dictum "*Ordo Ab Chao*" to heart, and set about turning patients—some of them suffering from ailments as insignificant as nervousness or mild depression—into zombies using a variety of grisly techniques. These included dosing patients with drugs including Thorazine, Nubutal, and Seconal, then giving them amphetamines to wake them up. At that point they would be blasted with electroshocks administered at voltages forty times greater than what was considered to be safe by most practitioners of the time. Patients would then be returned to their beds, tied down, and given "psychic driving" for up to thirty days, the repetition of recorded command signals with wording culled from their own psychiatric profiles. Patients were also subjected to sensory deprivation for up to 65 days, or put into comas for weeks of drugged sleep.

Cameron asked, "whether the behavior patterns of adults could be erased by a physiological process that attacked neural patterns. Could adults be made theoretically patternless? Could they be returned to a state of neurological and psychological infancy for a short period, and then could new patterns of behavior be introduced?"[2] In other words, Cameron was working at doing something not so different than the Goals 2000 approach currently being used on American schoolchildren.

Linda McDonald is one among many persons who remembers being treated by Dr. Cameron. Her experience was described by Dr. Colin Ross in a lecture given to the Ninth Annual Western Clinical Conference on Trauma and Dissociation, in April of 1996:

"She was 25 years old when she went to McGill [University] to be treated for a relatively mild post-partum depression. She turned 26 during her hospitalization from March to early September, 1963. During the course of her hospitalization, she received 102 ECT [electro-convulsive therapy] treatments, using the Paige-Russell technique, in which the button is pushed six times per treatment instead of one time. She also received about eighty days of barbiturate and neuroleptic induced sleep. During the course of her hospitalization—now, I have not only her testimony I also have the actual medical record, with all of the nursing notes documenting this and Ewen Cameron's signature in the chart—so this is not rumor or patient distortion, this is the actual record. And this is work that has been settled out of court by the CIA. She comes in a normal, somewhat depressed person... She gets regressed back to incontinent of urine, incontinent of feces, totally disoriented, unable to state her own name, year, where she is, recognize her children, recognize her husband. She gradually comes out of this. At the time of discharge she is sent home to live with her husband and children, resume normal sexual relations with her husband—she doesn't know how to drive a car, read, cook, use a toilet. Not only does she not know exactly what sex is all about, and she's not exactly sure who her husband is, she doesn't know what the concept of a husband is. She neuropsychologically pulls out of this over months, and several months down the road, she's at the point where a full time homemaker has taught her how to scramble eggs. She was a fully competent housewife and mother before this. When her children go out to play on the street, she is unable to remember thirty seconds later where they are, so she puts a map of the neighborhood up on the wall and puts pins in the map to keep track of where her kids are playing. Otherwise she goes into a panic and doesn't realize what's going on."[3]

"Mary" is another person who remembers being violated by brainwashing procedures under the hand of Dr. Cameron. She was born in Halifax, Canada, in 1947, a short time after her father left the army. Her childhood was spent in Ontario, Canada. She recalls being taken from her home on a number of occasions for mind control experimentation. These experiments, she believes, took place in upper New York state and at the Uplands Canadian Forces base near Ottawa, Canada. She says that these procedures took place in a building called "the Playhouse." Here, Mary says, in a room with walls but without a ceiling, she received an electronic mind control implant through her nostril that was fixed behind her eyeball. She also recalls being suspended in midair, with electric current flowing through her, causing her to make jerking, inadvertent body movements. "It was horrible, because my head was conscious, but they made my body do things, and I couldn't stop it. It was like being a robot."

Mary also remembers having electroshock, being subjected to sensory deprivation experiments, being drugged, and being abused sexually. She says that the experimentation ruined her life. A marriage at age twenty fell apart, and she has not been able to sustain a stable relationship since that time. In 1986 she suffered a complete nervous breakdown.

In the 1990s bits and pieces of memory involving hospitals and electroshock came to the surface and encouraged Mary to investigate what had happened to her in her childhood. She went to the local library and checked out a book about the MKULTRA experiments that included pictures of Ewen Cameron. When she saw a photo of Cameron a flood of memories of her mind control ordeal burst forth. She became hysterical and thought she was going to die.

In 1991 *Maclean's* magazine reported that the Mulroney goverment had appointed a commission composed of a single lawyer, "a defeated Conservative MP, George Cooper of Halifax...loyal to the regime that held the answer to his future..." to investigate the claims of nine victims of Dr. Cameron—nine out of the hundreds that Cameron is known to have abused. Cooper recommended that each victim be given $100,000, but not, he said, due to any government wrongdoing, but as "an expression of a collective sense of accountability for events that took place in good faith with ill effect."

Cameron retired from his chamber of horrors in 1964, and died of a heart attack while mountain climbing in 1967. Eventually the CIA also got around to cash settlements for a few of the people whose lives were destroyed by Cameron and his psychiatric henchmen.[4]

Notes:

1. Dr. Colin Ross interview, Sunday, April 6, 1997 on CKLN-FM 88 in Toronto, Canada. Interview conducted by Wayne Morris
2. Bowart, Walter. *Operation Mind Control*. New York: Dell, 1977; Lee and Shlain. *Acid Dreams*. New York: Grove Press, 1985; Constantine, Alex. *Psychic Dictatorship in the U.S.A.* Portland, Oregon: Feral House, 1995; Thomas, Gordon. *Journey Into Madness: The True Story of Secret CIA Mind Control and Medical Abuse*. New York: Bantam Books, 1989; Victorian, Armen, "United States, Canada, Britain: Partners in Mind Control Operations," *MindNet*, Vol. 1, No. 81, visitations.com/mindnet/MN16A.HTM; Chaitkin, Anton, "British Psychiatry: From Eugenics to Assassination," *EIR*, October 7, 1994
3. Ross, M.D., Dr. Colin, "The CIA and Military Mind Control Research: Building the Manchurian Candidate," lecture given at Ninth Annual Western Clinical Conference on Trauma and Dissociation, April 18, 1996
4. "Ewen Cameron and the Sleep Room," *The Fifth Estate* television show, Canadian Broadcasting Corporation, January 6, 1998; Bronskill, Jim, "Mind Games," *Ottawa Citizen*, September 13, 1997; *Maclean's*, March 13, 1991; Cockburn, Alexander and St. Clair, Jeffrey, "CIA's Sidney Gottlieb: Pusher, Assassin & Pimp," press release from *CounterPunch* at www.newsun.com/Counter.html

Chapter 10

Electronic Implants and Dr. Delgado

In 1870, two German researchers named Hitzig and Fritsch electrically stimulated the brains of dogs, demonstrating that certain portions of the brain were the centers of motor function. The American Dr. Robert Bartholow, within four years, demonstrated that the same was true of human beings. By the turn of the century in Germany Fedor Krause was able to do a systematic electrical mapping of the human brain, using conscious patients undergoing brain surgery.[1]

Another early researcher into electrical stimulation of the brain was Walter Rudolph Hess, who began research into ESB in the 1930s, jolting patients' brains with shocks administered through tiny needles that pierced their skulls.

During the decades of the 1940s and 1950s, Wilder Penfield, a neurosurgeon at McGill University, experimented with electrical brain stimulation on patients undergoing surgery. One of Penfield's discoveries was that the application of electricity on alert patients could stimulate the memory of past events.[2]

Since 1949, the Tulane University Department of Psychiatry and Neurology has done experimentation in the implantation of electrodes into patients' brains. According to one of their staff-generated reports, "By implantation of electrodes into various predetermined specific brain sites of patients capable of reporting thoughts and feelings, we have been able to make invaluable long-term observations..."[3]

Other early researchers into direct brain stimulation were Robert G. Heath, of Tulane University School of Medicine, in New Orleans, and his associate, Dr. Russell Monroe. Beginning in 1950, with funding from the CIA and the military, among other sources, they implanted as many as 125 electrodes into subjects' brains, and also experimented by injecting a wide variety of drugs directly into the brain tissue through small tubes; these drugs included LSD, psilocybin, and mescaline. One of Heath's memorable suggestions was that lobotomy should be used on subjects, not as a therapeutic measure, but for the convenience of the staff.[4]

According to Heath, "In the old days we could leave the electrodes in for only a few days; we'd stay up all night making recordings. After we refined our method, we started leaving the electrodes in up to several years so that the patients could be restimulated when symptoms recurred. Eventually, of course, we developed a pacemaker with its own internal power source to provide the patient with continuous stimulation."[5]

Heath and Monroe demonstrated that by implanting electrodes into the brains of their subjects they could switch on and off a variety of emotional and mental states, including fear, feelings of well-being, sexual sensations, as well as controlling memory and artificially inducing hallucinations. These feelings and thoughts, selectively chosen by those wielding the electric pushbutton, could in Pavlovian fashion be used for reward and punishment.[6]

One experiment performed by Heath utilized subject "B-19," a young male homosexual. Heath set about treating the man's homosexuality by inserting electrodes into his brain, including in the septum, a cerebral pleasure center. When Heath would activate the electrodes the man would experience something akin to a slow-burn orgasm. The man was shown heterosexual pornographic films while electricity was channeled through the electrodes, in an effort to rearrange his pleasure orientations, and switch his sexual interest from men to women. Eventually the man was given his own control box, which during one three-hour period he pushed 1,500 times for self stimulation. A twenty-year-old female prostitute was brought to Tulane University, and the man's brainwaves were studied while he engaged in sex with the her.[7]

By 1976 Heath had come up with the "cerebellar pacemaker," designed to electrically stimulate the brain through an array of tiny electrodes inserted at the back of the head, under the skull on the cerebellum. Although early versions of the pacemaker included a battery pack that the patient would carry in his pocket or on his belt, later versions would be implanted in the patient's abdomen.[8]

Heath was far from the only person thinking about using implants for control. In 1956, Curtiss Shafer, working as an electrical engineer for Norden-Ketay, offered the following prescription at the National Electronics Conference in Chicago. Shafer said, "The ultimate achievement of biocontrol may be man himself. The controlled subjects would never be permitted to think as individuals. A few months after birth, a surgeon would equip each child with a socket mounted under the scalp and electrodes reaching selected areas of brain tissue."

The subject's "sensory perceptions and muscular activity could be either modified or completely controlled by bioelectric signals radiating from state-controlled transmitters."[9]

Intelligence agencies have long been interested in the possibilities of direct brain electrical stimulation. A report on the CIA's MKULTRA subproject 94, issued in October 1960, said: "Initial biological work on techniques and brain locations essential to providing conditioning and control of animals has been completed... The feasibility of remote control of activities in several species of animals has been demonstrated. The present investigations are directed toward improvement of techniques."

A CIA research staff memorandum for the Deputy Director of the Agency from April 21, 1961 stated: "At present time we feel that we are close to having debugged a prototype system whereby dogs can be guided along specific courses through land areas out of sight and at some distance of the operator... In addition to its possible practical value in operations, this phenomenon is a very useful research tool in the area of the behavioral sciences. Dr. [deleted in original document] is taking appropriate action to exploit our knowledge of this area and provide adequate background for the development of future Agency applications in the general areas of influencing Human Behavior, Indirect Assessment and Interrogation Aids."

The Spaniard Dr. Jose Manuel Rodriquez Delgado, who studied medicine and taught physiology in Madrid, casts a long shadow in early CIA mind control research. Delgado is the man who perfected the stimoceiver, a tiny electronic device that is implanted into the brains of humans and animals, and is used to transmit electrical impulses directly to the brain.

Delgado came to the United States in 1950 to work at Yale University, where he was to remain for more than twenty years. He was financed by a number of agencies including the Office of Naval Intelligence, which was used to channel CIA funds. Unlike many of the researchers at the edge of behavioral control who seek anonymity, we are familiar with a good deal of Delgado's early research because he authored a book on the subject, *Physical Control of the Mind: Toward a Psychocivilised Society*, as well as several less well-known monographs.

In a 1967 medical report dated titled "Man's Intervention in Intracerebral Functions," Delgado rhapsodized about how he had:

"... Started to influence the physiological basis of the mind, and scientific investigation has established the principles that:

"We can experiment with intracerebral mechanisms responsible for the onset, development, and maintenance of specific behavioral and mental functions... The greatest challenge, however, is the possibility that we might substitute—at least in part—human intelligence for natural choices in man's design of man's highest quality: mental functions."

In the same monograph Delgado said that he had invented several types of brain implants. One type was the "radio stimulator," that provided jolts of electricity to the brain that were controlled by radio.

"Programmed stimulators" were another type of brain implant. Delgado said, "The advantage of the programmed stimulator is that it is self-contained and does not depend on a radio-link, and therefore the mobility of the subject is not limited, which is an important consideration in possible application of this unit for ambulatory therapy in humans."

Another type of stimoceiver was the "radio injector." The subjects of this type of stimoceiver are, according to Delgado, "equipped with mutilated electrodes attached to fine tunings, forming assemblies called 'chemitrodes' which are permanently implanted into the brain. Administration of chemicals is performed with a specially designed 'chemitrode pump,' which measures 40 x 18 mm. and weighs only 10 grams, and consists of two lucite compartments separated by an elastic membrane. One side is filled with synthetic spinal fluid or any other solution to be injected, and the adjoining side is filled with a solution of hydrozoan. When a current is passed through the latter compartment, gas is released and its pressure pushes the drug to be injected through the chemitrode."[10]

In an interview Delgado said that, "The brain is like an ocean through which, by relying on instrument guidance, we can navigate without visibility and reach a specific destination."[11]

What Delgado is specifically talking about when he says "instrument guidance" is locking the subject's head into a metal restraint attached to a metal arm that holds either a long hypodermic needle (for chemical stimulation) or a thin steel wire electrode that can be hooked up to dozens of other wires. Controls allow the vertical and lateral adjustment of the head until the needle or electrode is specifically targeted to a hole that has previously been drilled in the skull. The electrode is then thrust into the brain.[12]

Delgado soon came up with a new "transdermal" stimoceiver that communicates back the reactions of the subject to the electrical or chemical stimuli. Delgado reported:

"The new system described here is based on the implantation under the skin of a small instrument, without batteries, which is powered by transdermal reception of energy and is able to stimulate three different areas of the brain with remote control..."[13]

Dr. Colin Ross describes another experiment performed by Delgado:

"He...describes a technical innovation in an eleven year old boy who had brain electrodes implanted for non-therapeutic reasons. Previously you had to have wires connecting the transmitter box directly to the electrode terminals that were sticking through the skull. In this eleven-year-old boy, however, Jose Delgado had figured out how to have a remote transmitter without a direct wire connection. He describes pushing a button in this otherwise normal eleven-year-old boy's brain transmitter box and the boy starts being confused about his identity, wondering whether he is a girl and talking about wanting to marry Jose Delgado. He pushes another button, and this behavior stops."[14]

These innovations in brain implants were, in fact, a very primitive level of Delgado's research that would later be exceeded by light years. Later breakthroughs in technology were documented in "Two-Way Transdermal Communication with the Brain," published in 1975. By this time Delgado had linked his brain implants with computers. The monograph records,

"The most interesting aspect of the transdermal stimoceivers is the ability to perform simultaneous recording and stimulation of brain functions, thereby permitting the establishment of feedbacks and 'on-demand' programs of excitation with the aid of the computer. With the increasing sophistication and miniaturization of electronics, it may be possible to compress the necessary circuitry for a small computer into a chip that is implantable subcutaneously. In this way, a new self-contained instrument could be devised, capable of receiving, analyzing, and sending back information to the brain, establishing artificial links between unrelated cerebral areas, functional feedbacks, and programs of stimulation contingent on the appearance of pre-determined patterns."

The monograph further stated that:

"Two-way, transdermal exploration of the brain has the following possibilities:

"1. Long-term, depth EEG [electro-encephalogram] recording to monitor physiological, pharmacological, and psychological phenomena in unrestrained subjects;

"2. Long-term electrical stimulation of the brain to influence autonomic, somatic, and behavior responses or to provide information directly to the brain circumventing normal sensory receptors;

"3. Communication from the brain to computer and back to the brain, for the establishment of artificial intracerebral links and feedback circuits;

"4. Clinical applications to humans of 'on-demand' programs of stimulation, triggered by predetermined electrical pattern."[15]

Many popular articles on Delgado intend us to think that his primary purpose was the rehabilitation of the mentally and physically sick. This does not happen to be the case. Delgado was a blatant control freak. An example is Delgado's experimentation on changing the social orientation of animals. One staging area for this experimentation was an island in the Bermudas, where Delgado maintained a free-roving population of gibbons with electronic implants, using electrical brain boosts to build and destroy social orders among those primates as if he was knocking down a row of dominoes.[16]

Delgado returned to his native Spain in the 1970s, where he was ostensibly employed as a physiology professor at the University of Madrid. He continued his experimentation on human subjects while in Spain, although these researches have not been publicized. According to the report of a doctor who was a friend of Delgado's, one of the experiments that Delgado engaged in was the stimulation of the brains of the elderly in order to cause them to experience continuous sexual orgasms.[17]

By the 1980s, Delgado had changed directions in his work. Working at the one hundred room Ramon y Cajal hospital in Madrid, Delgado now began to emphasize changing brainwave patterns and physiology through electromagnetic broadcasting. Delgado said, "Much more research will have to be done. But with further knowledge, I am hopeful that without surgery or drugs, we will eventually be able to correct abnormal brain activity in humans."[18]

In an interview, Delgado stated that electromagnetic broadcasting for mind control had been developed to a state of effectiveness, and could be utilized at up to three kilometers.[19]

Interestingly enough, part of the thrust of Delgado's research was genetics, since he had determined that low intensity electromagnetic fields were capable of altering DNA. Delgado said, "Our understanding of genetics is very clumsy at present. But if we can produce lethal mutations with EMF fields, perhaps we will someday be able to use the technique to produce behavior changes."[20]

Summing up his philosophy, Delgado remarked, "This new knowledge is so important that I think it should radically change the philosophy of our educational system, which believes in the sanctity of individuals, thinking that an individual exists at birth. This belief is not true. And this science is going to prove the fallacy of democracy in the sense that we talk about the rights of the individual; this democratic belief is not true. Because we are forming this individual, because we are constructing his brain, we are willy nilly making the differences we either desire or dislike."[21]

Always a visionary in the Orwellian mold, Delgado said, "Looking into the future, it may be predicted that telerecording and telestimulation of the brain will be widely used."[22]

Another researcher who specialized in brain implants is Dr. Stuart Mackay, who in 1968 penned a textbook titled *Bio-Medical Telemetry*. Mackay reported, "Among the many telemetry instruments being used today are miniature radio transmitters that can be swallowed, carried externally, or surgically implanted in man or animal. They permit the simultaneous study of behaviour and physiological functioning. The scope of observations is too broad to more than hint at a few examples. The possibilities are limited only by the imagination of the investigator."[23]

In the early 1970s, in the law review *Crime and Justice*, an article by Barton L. Ingraham and Gerald W. Smith was published, titled "The Use of Electronics in the Observation and Control of Human Behavior and its Possible Use in Rehabilitation and Control." The article stated:

"In the very near future, a computer technology will make possible alternatives to imprisonment. The development of systems for telemetering information from sensors implanted in or on the body will soon make possible the observation and control of human behavior without actual physical contact. Through such telemetric devices, it will be possible to maintain twenty-four-hour-a-day surveillance over the subject and to intervene electronically or physically to influence and control selected behavior. It will thus be possible to exercise control over human behavior and from a distance without physical contact. The possible implications for criminology and corrections of such telemetric systems is tremendously significant."[24]

During the Vietnam war one of those interventions to influence behavior was done by a team of CIA psychologists at the Bien Hoa Prison outside of Saigon, where they were working as part of the infamous Phoenix Program. Suspected members of the National Liberation Front were brought into the prison, and experiments were done on them. One such experiment involved anesthetizing three prisoners and then implanting electrodes in their brains. After the prisoners were brought back to consciousness, they were placed in a room where knives had been left in the open. They were covertly observed by the psychiatrists as the electrodes were turned on, sending jolts of electricity directly to their brains. The apparent hope was that the prisoners would go berserk and attack each other with the knives, providing a juicy footnote to the CIA psychiatrists' reports. To the dismay of the CIA shrinks, this did not happen. The electrode-implanted prisoners were deemed useless. They were summarily shot; their bodies burned.[25]

In the States, doctors at the University of Mississippi in Jackson as of 1972 were implanting electrodes into the brains of black children as young as five years old, with the purpose of controlling "hyperactive" and "aggressive" behavior. A report from Dr. Peter R. Breggin states that, "Their brains were being implanted with electrodes that were heated up to melt areas of the brain that regulate emotion and intellect."[26] Although it has been a closely guarded secret, the technology of electronic brain control implants has continued to be advanced throughout this century, and continues to be applied by mind control practitioners today. One area where the technology continues to be developed is the University of Michigan Center for Neural Communication Technology. According to information on their website, "The Center was initiated to obtain resources necessary to meet the increasing demands for multichannel silicon substrate microprobes fabricated at the University of Michigan Center for Integrated Sensors and Circuits. These probes are being developed for acute and chronic recording and/or stimulation of the central nervous system."

Notes:

1. Morgan, James P., "The First Reported Case of Electrical Stimulation of the Human Brain," Journal of the History of Medicine at www3.oup.co.uk/jalsci/scope/; Zimmerman, M., "Electrical Stimulation of the Human Brain," *Human Neurobiology*, 1982
2. Project Open Mind
3. "Stereotaxic Implantation of Electrodes in the Human Brain: A Method for Long-Term Study and Treatment," Heath, John, Fontana, Department of Psychiatry and Neurology, Tulane University School of Medicine
4. Heath, Robert G. Undated interview in *Omni*; Cannon, Martin, "Mind Control and the American Government," Prevailing Winds, 1994; *Human Rights Law Journal*, "Freedom of the Mind as an International Human Rights Issue," Vol. 3, No. 1-4; Ross, M.D., Dr. Colin, "The CIA and Military Mind Control Research: Building the Manchurian Candidate," lecture given at Ninth Annual Western Clinical Conference on Trauma and Dissociation, April 18, 1996
5. Heath
6. Cannon, Martin, "Mind Control and the American Government," *Prevailing Winds*, 1994; *Human Rights Law Journal*, "Freedom of the Mind as an International Human Rights Issue"; Ross, M.D.
7. Ross
8. Heath
9. Cited in Constantine, Alex. *Psychic Dictatorship in the U.S.A.* Portland, Oregon: Feral House, 1995
10. Delgado, Dr. Jose, "Man's Intervention in Intracerebral Functions, New Haven, Connecticut: Department of Psychiatry, Yale University, School of Medicine, 1967

11. Packard, Vance. *The People Shapers*. New York: Ballentine Books, 1979
12. Packard
13. Delgado; Packard
14. Ross
15. Delgado, Lipponen, Weiss, del Pozo, Monteagudo, and McMahon, "Two-Way Transdermal Communication with the Brain," a co-operative publication of the Medical University of Madrid, Spain, and Yale University Medical School, 1975
16. Packard
17. Correspondence with the Spanish NosMan research group, April 1999
18 McAuliffe, Kathleen, "The Mind Fields," *Omni*, 1985
19. Correspondence with the Spanish NosMan group
20. McAuliffe
21. Delgado, Dr. Jose, quoted in *Human Rights Law Journal*, "Freedom of the Mind as an International Human Rights Issue," Vol. 3, No. 1-4
22. Delgado, Jose, "Radio Stimulation of the Brain in Primates and Man," New Haven, Connecticut: Department of Psychiatry, Yale University School of Medicine, 1969]
23. Mackay, Dr. Stuart, cited in Krawcyzyk, Glenn, "Mind Control Techniques and Tactics of the New World Order," *Nexus*, December-January 1993
24. Ingraham and Smith, "The Use of Electronics in the Observation and Control of Human Behavior and its Possible Use in Rehabilitation and Control," *Crime and Justice*, 1972
25. Cockburn, Alexander and St. Clair, Jeffrey, "CIA's Sidney Gottlieb: Pusher, Assassin & Pimp," press release from *CounterPunch*
26. "Recent FDA Decision Highlights Ethical Issues in Drug Research On Children," Peter R. Breggin, M.D.

CHAPTER 11

TURN ON, TUNE IN
BECOME A ROBOT

Along with CIA mind control programs, media manipulation, and Kinsey's "sexual revolution," in the 1950s and 60s America was ripe was for another ambitious operation: the restructuring of American society through the use of psychedelic drugs and mysticism.

As illogical as it may seem at first glance, the LSD drugging of the world and an accompanying injection of mystical religion fits neatly into the New World Order—and eugenics—intention for population control and a "post-technological" world. Believing that the world is overpopulated and that resources are being squandered through consumption by the masses, dystopian social visionaries epitomized by those of Tavistock and the Club of Rome have repeatedly urged that the solution is a return to a mystical primitivism—at least for the vast majority of the world's population. And that primitivism, they seem to believe, can be furthered through the use of drugs and mysticism.

Strangely, LSD may be a byproduct of German occultism. According to Captain Alfred Hubbard, the intelligence agency "Johnny Appleseed of LSD," the drug was discovered years prior to its announced discovery by Albert Hoffman, in a project mounted by members of the Rudolf Steiner's Anthroposophy—an offshoot of Blavatsky's occultist Theosophy group—to discover a "peace pill." The documented history of LSD begins much later.

The major proponent of the acid drugging of America was Aldous Huxley, the grandson of British imperialist Thomas Huxley, one of the founders of the Rhodes Round Table.

The materialist Thomas Huxley was referred to during his life as "Darwin's bulldog" for his efforts at suppressing opposition to Darwinism, and his frank advocacy of genocide for the Australian aborigine for eugenics purposes.

Aldous Huxley was a lifelong collaborator with Arnold Toynbee, who was on the council of the Round Table's Royal Institute of International Affairs, and was the head of British Intelligence's Research Division. In a 1971 dialogue with Kei Wakzizumi of Kyoto Sangyo University, Toynbee said:

"If I am right in forecasting that a world dictatorship is likely to be the way in which we shall avoid liquidating ourselves in an atomic war, and if I live to see this development, I should on the whole be optimistic, because I should not expect the dictatorship to be permanent... It is most unlikely, I fear, that it will be established by the will, or even with the acquiescence of the majority of mankind. It seems to be likely to be imposed on the majority by a ruthless, efficient, and fanatical minority, inspired by some ideology or religion. I guess that mankind will acquiesce in a harsh Leninian kind of dictatorship as a lesser evil than self-extermination or than a continuing anarchy which could end only in self-extermination. If the reluctant majority does accept this dictatorship on this ground, I think they will be making the right choice."

Huxley was tutored by Fabian Socialist and pivotal New World Order theorist H.G. Wells, author of *The Open Conspiracy* and other books detailing the intentions of the international New World Order faction. Wells was the head of British intelligence during World War I who proposed the creation of a "one-world brain"—soberingly similar in conception to that of today's Internet—that would ultimately act as "a police of the mind."

It has been reported that Huxley was a member of "the Children of the Sun," a mystical free love cult of children of the Round Table in Britain that may have shared more than just its name with the German *Sonnenkinder*, the term used to designate the eugenically bred, racially pure *Lebensborn* children of Nazi Germany.

There is more to suggest this connection than just the name of the group. Members of the British Children of the

Sun are reported to have included the fascist Sir Oswald Mosley, British intelligence agent George Orwell, and Guy Burgess. Burgess was one of the founders of the "homosexual Freemasonry" and "higher sodomy" of the Apostles at Cambridge, a founder of the pro-Nazi Anglo-German Fellowship in England, a paid agent of the Rothschild's family private intelligence network, and—his most famous role—a Soviet spy. Other members of the Apostles homosexual cabal included Soviet spies Blunt, Philby, and Maclean, who were largely responsible for the massive compromise of Western intelligence to the Soviets that began in the 1930s.

Huxley was a collaborator with Tavistock's Major John Rawlings Reese, and author of the influential *Brave New World*. Among other eugenics ideas in the book is the strict structuralization of society through test tube breeding, with the lowest members of society denied oxygen during their fetal growth to reduce intelligence.[1]

In *Brave New World Revisited*, the book's non-fictional sequel he wrote:

"The twenty-first century...will be the era of the World Controllers... The older dictators fell because they could never supply their subjects with enough bread, enough circuses, enough miracles and mysteries. Under a scientific dictatorship education will really work—with the result that most men and women will grow up to love their servitude and will never dream of revolution. There seems to be no good reason why a thoroughly scientific dictatorship should ever be overthrown. "

Huxley came to America from Britain shortly after the first published findings about LSD, in 1949. He was accompanied by his friend Dr. Humphrey Osmond who, once in America, immediately set about toiling in the MUKULTRA mindfields—including turning on his friend to acid—while Huxley was the seed crystallizing dozens of LSD and mystico-religious projects, both official and informal. Huxley was also friends with George Estabrooks, who had done early work into the creation of mind control assassins and hypnotically-installed multiple personalities, and worked with Andrija Puharich, an early researcher into the effects of electromagnetics on humans.

Certainly Huxley cannot have been unaware of the effects that the widespread distribution of LSD might bring about. He wrote,

"Now let us consider another kind of drug—still undiscovered, but probably just around the corner—a drug capable of making people happy in situations where they would normally feel miserable. Such a drug would be a blessing, but a blessing fraught with grave political dangers. By making a harmless chemical euphoric freely available, a dictator could reconcile an entire population to a state of affairs to which self respecting human beings ought not to be reconciled..."[2]

Huxley, who was also a pal of CIA mind control kingpin Louis Jolyon West, was responsible for "turning on" dozens of persons who went on to proselytize the mystical religion and acid, including Alan Watts, Ken Kesey, members of the Grateful Dead musical group, and anthropologist Gregory Bateson, who had been a "psychological planner" for the OSS. From the ranks of persons turned on directly or indirectly by Aldous Huxley, an entire generation was mentally regrooved.

Supporting the idea that Huxley may have had an agenda other than enlightening America to the Buddha-mind, an FBI memorandum from 1968 states that Grateful Dead bandleader Jerry Garcia, was used "to channel youth dissent and rebellion into more benign and non-threatening directions." It is not known whether Garcia was a witting collaborator in this channeling.[3]

Huxley's most influential acolyte was Dr. Timothy Leary, who in the 1950s coasted on eight monetary grants from the National Institute of Mental Health, a pipeline for CIA funding. Leary was first turned on to LSD by his long time friend, CIA agent Frank Barron. In an interview for *High Times* magazine in February 1978, Leary said:

"If you look back, many things that we thought were accidents turned out were not accidents. The entire LSD movement itself was sponsored originally by the CIA, to whom I give great credit. I would not be here today if it had not been for the foresight and prestige of the CIA psychologists, so give the CIA credit for being truly an intelligence agency."

Mind control researcher Walter Bowart interviewed Leary in the 1970s, and the acid guru had some interesting things to say about his association with the CIA. Asked, "Do you think CIA people were involved in your group in the sixties?" Leary responded, "Of course they were. I would say that eighty percent of my movements, eighty percent of the decisions I made were suggested to me by CIA people... I like the CIA! The game they're playing is better than the FBI. Better than the Saigon police. Better than Franco's police. Better than the Israeli police. They're a thousand times better than the KGB. So it comes down to: who are you going to work for? The Yankees or the Dodgers?" Bowart might have responded that one could simply "drop out" from the game, as Leary had counseled an entire generation.

Leary sang the praises of the CIA throughout the interview. Asked whether he had been used by the CIA, Leary said, "I've known this for ten years."

In an attempt to pin him down, Bowart asked, "You were wittingly used by the CIA?"

Leary hedged:

"Wait, when you say CIA, it's like saying 'Niggers'... I knew I was being used by the intelligence agents of this country."

Asked again whether he wittingly worked for the CIA, Leary answered forcefully, "Yes, I was a witting agent of the CIA, but I'm not a willing agent of Nixon! I did everything in my power to throw out Nixon!"

Bowart asked him, "So, you work for the Central Intelligence Agency? Is it the Deputy Director of Plans you work for? Who makes out your checks?"

"It's none of your business to know how those things work," was Leary's response. "I'll answer you no questions that have to do with business. I'll answer you any question about history or people..."[4]

After the interview, Bowart, as well as several friends of Leary who were present, agreed that "this was not the same man we'd known before he'd gone to prison. We couldn't tell if he'd changed because of the normal prison brutality, or because he was under some great pressures or had been tortured." Bowart says, "The first thought I had when seeing the altered Leary was, 'He's been the victim of one of the secret prison mind control programs.'"

There is additional confirmation that Leary himself was the guinea pig of his esteemed "intelligence agents." Bowart relates that while Leary was in Folsom Prison he was held incommunicado for a period of time, and that, according to his wife Joanna (Harcourt-Smith) Leary, when he was finally allowed to visit her, he seemed radically different: his head had been shaved, and he was bruised and pale. This information was confirmed by a former convict who told Bowart that during the period when Leary could not be located by his wife, the acid guru was given fright drugs—anectine is one drug that induces hysterical fear—and kept in solitary confinement in order to break him down. Leary returned to their cell "with his head shaved and blue lines painted on it."

According to the man, "Well, one day he comes back to the cell with lines on his head. They were actually very precise measurement lines. His head was shaved and it was marked with all these careful, precise blue lines.

"I asked him what the lines were for. He told me that they were going to give him a lobotomy. They were going to stick ice picks into his brain. He told me that it was really going to be great. They had him completely brainwashed. He said, 'This is going to be the greatest thing. All my life I've been going through this, you get up, you get down, but now,' he said, 'I'll be just as smart as I am but I won't have to feel emotions any more. Wow!'"[5]

Leary's initial intelligence handler may have been British agent Michael Hollingshead, yet another friend of Aldous Huxley. Hollingshead first provided Leary with acid, and according to reports of the period, Leary idolized him.[6]

One of Leary's major supporters was William "Billy" Mellon Hitchcock, heir to Gulf Oil, nephew to financier Andrew Mellon, and alleged to be a broker for money interests that included the Mafia and the CIA. Mellon family foundations have long been used as a conduit for CIA monies, and several members of the family have been members of American intelligence agencies. Hitchcock's father was a university roommate with David Bruce, a Chief of Technological Intelligence of the OSS. During his tenure at the Agency, CIA Director Richard Helms, the man who conceived of MKULTRA, was a close friend of the Mellons, as was Averell Harriman. Hitchcock was the largest investor in Resorts International, a consortium where a number of clandestine interests met, including British Intelligence and the networks of Mafia kingpins Tibor Rosenbaum and Meyer Lansky. Some researchers have convincingly fingered Resorts International as part the cabal that sponsored the killing of John F. Kennedy.[7]

Others involved in the acid-drugging of the world included Captain Alfred M. Hubbard of the OSS, the Treasury Department, the Federal Narcotics Bureau, and the Food and Drug Administration, and—it is alleged—the Mafia, who acted as a "Johnny Appleseed of LSD." Hubbard, who first took LSD in 1951, and guided Aldous Huxley through his second mescaline trip, distributed huge amounts of Agency acid around the world. While he was passing out LSD, Hubbard also led raids on the LSD labs of "rebel chemists" suggesting that Hubbard might have been an elitist who thought that acid was only good enough for the commisar class.

In 1968, at the height of the hippie phase, Hubbard joined the world's largest military research think tank, Stanford Research Institute, as an investigator. This was done at the behest of Tavistock-associated Willis Harmon, at that time the director of the SRI Center for the Study of Social Policy, and reported to have himself been an experimenter with LSD.

SRI was founded in 1946, reportedly by agents of the Tavistock Institute, and its first contracts were obtained from the defense establishment. SRI had already received Army money for research into "chemical incapacitants" as well as for the alleged 1958 Project Shaky, delving into using the environment as a weapon through weather wars and controlled earthquakes. SRI is linked in its database with 2,500 other organizations, including the CIA, Bell Telephone, U.S. Army intelligence, the Office of Naval Intelligence, RAND, Harvard, and MIT.

Harmon wrote to Hubbard, saying:

"Our investigations of some of the current social movements affecting education indicate that the drug usage prevalent among student members of the New Left is not entirely undesigned. Some of it appears to be present as a deliberate weapon aimed at political change. We are concerned with assessing the significance of this as it impacts on matters of long-range educational policy. In this connection it would be advantageous to have you considered in the capacity of a special investigative agent who might have access to relevant data which is not ordinarily available."

Well, who would have been promoting "drug usage...among student members of the New Left"? Surely Harmon didn't think it was the communists. This sounds more to me like a cant language proposal for carrying out "political change."

Hubbard was employed by SRI ostensibly as a security guard. In fact his actual work took place under the auspices of their Alternative Futures Program, a "corporate strategy program" that reminds one that Hubbard had his own corporate strategy of turning business and political leaders on to LSD.[8]

The LSD drugging of America was not limited to experimentation performed on adults. In the Proceedings of the 19th Annual Convention and Scientific Program of the Society of Biological Psychiatry, that took place in Los Angeles, May 13, 1964, it is reported:

"In the children's unit of Creedmore State Hospital with a resident population of 450 patients, ages 4 to 15, we have investigated the responses of some of these children to lysergic acid and related drugs in the psychiatric, psychological and biochemical areas. Two groups of boys receiving daily LSD, UML (which is a methylated derivative of LSD) or psilocybin...at first the medication was given weekly but was eventually given daily for periods of up to several months. Dosages remain constant throughout, LSD 150 mcg, psilocybin 20 mg. daily or UML 12 mg. daily, all given in two divided doses. The average duration of treatment was 2 to 3 months."[9]

It is not necessary to comment at length on the magnitude of the LSD drugging program and its mystical retooling of the American psyche in the 1960s. The varied results of that operation—the destruction of much of political activism in America; the birth of the quiche-breathed lockstepping Yuppies; the alienated and politically impotent Punks and Gen X; and the drug gang fetishism of both black and white "gangsta" culture—are testimony to the effectiveness of this far-reaching pacification program.

Notes:
1. *EIR*, volume 14, number 23; Lockhart, Robin Bruce. *Reilly: The First Man*. London: Penguin Books, 1987; Pincher, Chapman. *Too Secret, Too Long*. New York: St. Martin's Press, 1984; Lively and Abrams. *The Pink Swastika: Homosexuality in the Nazi Party*. Keiser, Oregon: Founders Publishing Corporation, 1995; White, Carol. *The New Dark Ages Conspiracy*. New York: New Benjamin Franklin House, 1980; Editors of *EIR*. *Dope, Inc.* Washington, D.C.: *EIR*, 1992; Desmond, Adrian. *Huxley: The Devil's Disciple*. London: Michael Joseph, 1994; Costello, John. *Mask of Treachery: Spies, Lies, & Betrayal*. New York: Warner Books, 1988
2. Huxley, Aldous, "The Doors of Perception," *Collected Essays*. New York: Harper and Brothers, 1958
3. *Dope, Inc.*; Lee and Shlain. *Acid Dreams*. New York: Grove Press, 1985; White, Carol. *The New Dark Ages Conspiracy*. New York: New Benjamin Franklin House, 1984; Ross, M.D., Dr. Colin, "The CIA and Military Mind Control Research: Building the Manchurian Candidate," lecture given at Ninth Annual Western Clinical Conference on Trauma and Dissociation, April 18, 1996
4. Bowart, Walter, "Timothy Leary and the CIA or The Spy Who Came In From the (Ergot) Mold"
5. ibid.
6. Constantine, Alex. *Virtual Government. CIA Mind Control Operations in America*. Venice, California: Feral House, 1997; Bowart, Walter. Unpublished manuscript, cited in Constantine; Bowart, "Timothy Leary and the CIA or The Spy Who Came In From the (Ergot) Mold"
7. Lee and Shlain; *Dope, Inc.*; Interview with Walter H. Bowart, July 16, 1995, conducted by Will Robinson and Marilyn Coleman
8. Constantine; Coleman, John. *Conspirators' Hierarchy: The Story of the Committee of 300*. Carson City, Nevada: America West Publishers, 1992

9.   Recent Advances in Biological Psychiatry, the Proceedings of the 19th
     Annual Convention and Scientific Program of the Society of Biological
     Psychiatry, Los Angeles, volume 7, May 13, 1964. "Autonomic Ner-
     vous System Responses in Hospitalized Children Treated with LSD
     and UML"

Dr. Jolly West.

CHAPTER 12

JOLLY WEST
AND THE VIOLENCE CENTER

A ir Force Major Louis Jolyon "Jolly" West signed up early on as a co-conspirator in the CIA's MKULTRA, although most of his activities in the program are shadowed. In the most famous event of his career, while he was chairman of the Department of Psychiatry at the University of Oklahoma, West injected an elephant named Tusko with a huge dosage of LSD in an experiment supposedly designed to provide insight about animal behavior. Not surprisingly, Tusko collapsed into a stupor and, while trying to bring the elephant back to consciousness with a variety of drugs, West succeeded in killing the animal.

West lived in Haight-Ashbury in the summer of 1967 and was supposedly involved in a project of studying the hippie in his native habitat. This was at the time that CIA chemists were allegedly collaborating in setting up laboratories for the production of LSD in the Bay Area, and one can only speculate just what West was up to.[1]

West was in charge of the Department of Psychiatry at UCLA, and director there of the Neuro-Psychiatric Institute until his death in 1999. In 1973, during Ronald Reagan's governorship in California, West proposed the creation of what he dubbed a Center for the Study and Reduction of Violence, that would have been located in an abandoned Nike missile base in California. In a letter to Dr. J.M. Stubblebine, the Director of Health in the California Office of Health Planning, West said:

"Comparative studies could be carried out there, in an isolated but convenient location, of experimental or model programs for the alteration of undesirable behavior." West said that there were certain factors that militated toward violent behavior, including "sex (male), age (youthful), ethnicity (black), and urbanicity."

In a secret memo he discussed projects that the center might employ in more detail. He said, "... Now by implanting tiny electrodes deep within the brain [it] is even possible to record bioelectrical changes in the brain of freely moving subjects through the use of remote monitoring techniques. They are not yet feasible for large scale screening that might permit detection of a violent episode. A major task at the center should be to devise such a test..."

Other techniques that West planned on using on violent offenders at the Center included castration by chemicals, drugs for mood manipulation, and brain surgery. The Center would collaborate with the California state police and share a database that would keep track of "pre-delinquent" children in order to treat them before they became delinquents, a foreshadowing of programs currently in operation in Clinton's Goals 2000.[2]

One critic of West was Dr. Isidore Ziferstein, associate clinical professor of psychiatry at the UCLA Neuropsychiatric Institute. "We have a new situation on our hands," Ziferstein said. "Because of the intensifying economic decline it is inevitable that more and more jobless will go beyond the limits of the law to satisfy their needs. There are probably upwards of 30 percent of our population who are permanently impoverished... And once these 30 percent become convinced that the democratic process is not working for them, they become desperate and may resort to violent means. There is a rising radicalism in their midst and there is an uppitiness among the blacks and Chicano prisoners which prison officials find intolerable. To subdue them, the authorities are using new methods. They're employing the psychiatric armamentarium and a new technological tool set—what has come to be known as psycho-technology. Under the guise of therapeutic behavior modification they're applying anything from [the terror drug] Anectine and other aversive drugs to psychosurgery."

Despite Reagan's support, the idea for the Violence Center was tabled, although he retained the concept of the Center in his active file until his election to President.

After the demise of the Violence Center, West seems to have moved into the role of a "fixer" for the CIA, always on the spot for high profile psychiatric intervention, character assassination, or an off-the-cuff interview when the Agency sought damage control. West examined Jack Ruby after the killing of Lee Harvey Oswald, and determined that Ruby was in a "paranoid state manifested by delusions, visual and auditory hallucinations, and suicidal impulses." This diagnosis was probably influenced by Ruby's insistence that a conspiracy had been responsible for the murder of John F. Kennedy, and that Ruby was being troublesome by virtually begging the authorities, including Chief Justice Earl Warren of the Warren Report, to listen to his take on who had done the deed.

In correspondence that journalist Lincoln Lawrence had access to, Ruby wrote:

"...to start my story off, they found some very clever means and ways to trick me... I was used to silence Oswald. I walked into a trap the moment I walked down that ramp Sunday morning."

Ruby also wrote, "The reason I have gone through all, the explanation is, that knowing of my complete innocence and their framing me as they have, there certainly was a tremendous motive for it. The old war lords are going to come back. S.A. [South America] is full of these Nazis! They will know that it is only one kind of people that would do such a thing...that would have to be the Nazis and that is who is in power."

If the idea of Nazi involvement in the assassination seems far-fetched, then a perusal of the Torbitt Document would be in order.[3]

Ruby finished his letter by say, "The rest depends upon you. You can be of some help some way. Be careful...they are after my blood. See if my prediction will be correct."

In the end, no one listened to what Ruby had to say, except for journalist Dorothy Kilgallen, who was found "suicided" shortly after her interview with him. Ruby himself was to die soon after from a cancer that he believed had been injected into him.[4]

At the end of his life West was associated with the Cult Awareness Network, founded by deprogrammer Ted Patrick, who had been an aide to Ronald Reagan at the time that the Violence Center was proposed.[5]

Notes:

1. Interview with Walter H. Bowart, July 16, 1995, conducted by Will Robinson and Marilyn Coleman
2. Neill, Patricia, "Mass Testing for 'Delinquency' Gene', *Parascope* at www.parascope.com/main.htm; Krawczyk, Glenn, "The New Inquisition: Cult Awareness or the Cult of Intelligence?," *Nexus*, October/November 1994
3. Torbitt, William. *Nomenclature of an Assassination Cabal*, republished by Torbitt and Thomas/ *NASA, Nazis, and JFK*. Kempton, Illinois: Adventures Unlimited Press, 1996
4. Lawrence, Lincoln, and Thomas, Kenn. *Mind Control, Oswald & JFK: Were We Controlled?* Kempton, Illinois: Adventures Unlimited Press, 1997
5. Krawczyk

Chapter 13

Occult Connections

It is difficult to overestimate the role of religion and occultism in the history of world control. This is one means by which zealots are molded who are unable to evaluate effectively, and who thus can be turned to the purposes of their controllers. In many religious or occult groups the zombieism of the mind controlled is the entry fee, and the "disposal" problem for getting rid of the victims of mind control is not so formidable since cult members have often become disaffected with their former friends and family.

A quick scan through cultic history in recent years reveals significant, branching connections, a few of which I will cover in this book.

A prime instance of CIA involvement in a cult in recent years is the case of Jim Jones' Peoples' Temple, although nary a word of these dark underpinnings has slipped into mainstream accounts of the group. Evangelist Jim Jones started out as a member of Bertrand Russell's Fellowship of Reconciliation, which sponsored him at Butler College in Indianapolis. The Fellowship is reported to have financed his first trip to Brazil, in 1961. Jones at the time told the Brazilians that he was in the employ of Naval Intelligence, and both his food and lodging during his stay were provided by the U.S. embassy.

While in Brazil, Jones took regular trips to Belo Horizonte, the location of CIA headquarters in the region, and returned to the United States with an unexplained $10,000 cash windfall. Apparently Jones was doing more than missionary work. According to one account, Jones had been part of a CIA effort attempting a government overthrow in South America, and distributed leaflets and stirred up revolutionary sentiments during his stay.[1]

It is alleged that one of Jones' earliest source of financing for his work was Rabbi Maurice Davis, who provided him a church in Indianapolis. Davis was on the board of the American Family Foundation, the founding group for the Cult Awareness Network, and worked as a chaplain at the National Institute for Mental Health's infamous Lexington Addiction Research Center, where MKULTRA research had been done.[2]

Jones moved his growing fellowship to Ukiah, California, where reports from the disaffected from his group said that behavior modification experiments were performed on the congregation. According to People's Temple researcher Michael Meiers:

"Early Temple experiments in sensory deprivation are not well documented, but it is known that Jones imparted his expertise to Donald DeFreeze, who utilized the technique to brainwash Patricia Hearst."[3]

Also, according to Meiers, "Tom Grubbs, a psychologist with the University of California, was in charge of 'the box.' Grubbs, who was also principal of the Jonestown school, personally constructed Jones' sensory deprivation chamber."

In Ukiah, Jones became chairman of the county grand jury, and worked with many wealthy collaborators, including persons connected to military and intelligence agencies. The Jones group also infiltrated and took over the Mendocino State Hospital as part of a government pilot project to evaluate the feasibility of deinstitionalizing mental patients. After a reduction in state funding for psychiatric institutions, most of the patients at Mendocino were released into the custody of the Peoples' Temple.[4]

In 1971, the People's Temple relocated to San Francisco, where Jones and many of his followers are said to have smoothly integrated as part of the Jerry Brown political machine. Jones became the head of the San Francisco Housing Commission, and used the city welfare department to recruit members for the People's Temple.

Among the most important of Jones' supporters were the Layton family, whose head, Dr. Lawrence Laird Layton, had relocated to America from Germany after World War II. Layton had worked on the Manhattan Project, and was Chief of Chemical and Ecological Warfare Research at Dugway Proving Grounds in Utah, where Army LSD research was carried out. Layton's wife Eva had worked for the CIA at Berkeley University. According to Dr. Colin Ross, "...her job at the library was to keep track of all the left-wing literature taken out of the library and the names of the people who took those books out and report that to the CIA."

Another home for Jones' flock was set up in Guyana at the former site of the Shalom Project, allegedly a CIA training camp for guerrillas to be used in operations in Angola between 1973 and 1975. Jones received assistance from the U.S. embassy in Georgetown, Guyana, which was also the headquarters for the CIA in the area. It has been alleged that all of the members of the embassy in Georgetown were agents of the CIA.

At Jonestown, children were kept in line with electric cattle prods. When Congressman Leo Ryan attempted to investigate Jonestown, members of the U.S. embassy attempted to prevent him. This was finally left up to Jones' followers.[5]

The Jonestown deaths were the ultimate in "assisted suicides." According to the officiating pathologist in Guyana 80-90% of the victims had fresh needle marks on their bodies. Other victims had been shot or strangled. Orders were sent to U.S. military officials by an aide to national security advisor Zbigniew Brzezinski to remove "all politically sensitive papers and forms of identification from the bodies."

Jim Jones may have survived the destruction of the People's Temple compound. The body identified as being Jim Jones was so decomposed as to be unidentifiable, although it is reported that the corpse did not have Jones' distinctive chest tattoos.

Examining the evidence, the conclusion is simple, inevitable: Jonestown was a project of U.S. intelligence agencies and the psychiatric establishment, and the mass murders or suicides there probably took place to cover that fact up. American media is in collusion in keeping the information from the public.[6]

—The Esalen Institute, located at Big Sur, is a New Age-style group with a myriad of interesting connections. One of the founders of the group was Aldous Huxley, the primary advocate for the LSD dosing of the world. The first seminar on Human Potential at Esalen was led by Willis Harmon of Stanford Research Institute, who was anything but a hippie. Charles Manson and members of his group played a concert at Esalen three days before the Helter Skelter murders.

Physicist Jack Sarfatti reports on "weird stories" that he heard at the Esalen Institute in Big Sur that the occultist philosophy Arica had been founded in Chile by fugitive Nazis who were occult adepts. Sarfatti says, "Many of the regulars at Esalen, including some of our group like Dr. John Lilly and Claudio Naranjo had been in the first Arica training in Chile." Sarfatti also lists Soviet officials who were at Esalen in the late '70s and early '80s: "Valentin M. Berezhkov, Yuri A. Zamoshkin, Andrey A. Kokoshin, Henrikas Jushkevitshus, Vladimir M. Kuznetsov, Victor M. Pogostin, Vlail Pl Kaznacheyev, Joseph Goldin. This list is not complete."

One of the people said to have been involved in the Russian presence at Esalen is the Rockefeller-funded John Mack, formerly on the board of advisors of Werner Erhard's est. Mack has lately achieved prominence as a UFO abduction researcher. Donna Bassett, who infiltrated Mack's group, says that he has been funded by an "ex-CIA" source.[7]

—The Unification Church of Reverend Sun Myung Moon, has since its beginning maintained close connections to the South Korean Central Intelligence Agency. At least four of Moon's early acolytes were army officers closely connected to the founding director of the KCIA. One of Moon's most influential aides, Bo Hi Pak, liased with the CIA for the KCIA, and is said to have made many trips to the National Security Agency at Fort Meade, Maryland.

Moon's church is enormously rich and influential, with at least 600 front groups by last count. Among the group's notable acquisitions has been the *Washington Times* newspaper, which Moon admits has cost him more than a billion dollars, and the University of Bridgeport in Connecticut, that has hired as a trustee Jack E. Thomas, former assistant chief of staff for U.S. Air Force Intelligence.[8]

—On March 23 through 25, 1997, 39 members of a UFO/apocalyptic cult group called Heaven's Gate killed themselves with phenobarbitol and vodka in the Rancho Santa Fe suburb of San Diego. As with many apparent cults, when a thread is pulled, it often leads to the shadowy denizens of American spookdom. In the case of Heaven's Gate, one of these connections is via the Internet. The web server for the Heaven's Gate website is a small company, Spacestar, staffed by one man in Eden Prairie, Minnesota. Fracturing coincidence, another group that uses the services of Spacestar is the Scientific Applications International Corps, or SAIC ('CIAs' spelled backward. Doubly coincidental is that SAIC is located in La Jolla, California, near Rancho Santa Fe.

SAIC is the parent company to a group called Network Solutions, which in turn owns a company called InterNIC. That group is in charge of all the website addresses on the Internet. The board of directors of SAIC includes NSA Director Bobby Ray Inman, as well as retired U.S. Army General W.A. Downing. Other alum of SAIC include William Casey, former head of the CIA [until], former CIA director John Deutch, former Defense Secretary Melvin Laird, Donald Kerr, former director of Los Alamos National Laboratory, and William Perry, the head of the Department of Defense. SAIC has been involved in remote viewing experimentation with American intelligence agencies, for which medical oversight, according to researcher Jim Schnabel, was provided by Louis Jolyon West.

San Diego must be a hotbed of strange research at the edges of American spy biz, since it is also the location for Naval Electronics System Command, who have been reported to have been another one of the funding sources for Hal Puthoff's early remote viewing experiments at Stanford Research Institute.

Another interesting connection to Heaven's Gate is alleged by researcher John Judge. Judge has said that the murdered CIA and British Intelligence operative Ian Spiro, who lived within a few blocks of the Heaven's Gate group, was also a member of the group.

What would be the purpose of putting together and manipulating a group like Heaven's Gate? Like People's Temple, such a group might provide a model for larger societal manipulation, for the fine-tuning of larger scale "New Age" religious manipulation, and perhaps a testing ground for drug or electronic manipulation.[9]

—Intelligence agencies seem to have infiltrated, interfaced, and created some satanic groups, with the resurgence of groups of this type beginning in 1966, with the birth of the Church of Satan, founded by Anton LaVey. LaVey studied criminology at the San Francisco City College, and worked in the crime lab of the SFPD. According to journalist Linda Blood, "He maintained a cordial relationship with the SFPD..." An associate of LaVey's has also told me that he has personal knowledge that the Satanist also functioned as an informant for Interpol.

Prior to the Church of Satan, LaVey ran a group called the "Magic Circle," whose members were a surprisingly un-satanic bunch that according to LaVey biographer Burton Wolfe included an anthropologist who would hold professorships at Yale, Columbia, and Berkeley, and chair the New School for Social Research; a billionaire and accused pederast; a feminist who would go on to direct the National Women's Political Caucus; and a number of San Francisco Police Department employees. The most interesting member of the group is said by Wolfe to have been the heir to the Vickers munitions empire.

Although I do not know specifically which member of the Vickers family was involved with LaVey, the family background is telling. Sir Peter Vickers Hall is a Fabian Socialist, member of NATO, and alleged to be a senior member of British MI6. His father-in-law Sir Peter Vickers worked on the Stanford Research Institute "Changing Images of Man" project, a definitely Tavistock-influenced endeavor. To quote Vickers Hall reeling off his own one world propaganda:

"I am perfectly happy working with the Heritage Foundation and groups like that. True Fabians look to the New Right to push through some of their more radical ideas. For more than a decade the British population has been subject to a constant propaganda barrage of how it was on the industrial skids. All of this is true, but the net effect of the propaganda was to demoralize the population.

"This will happen in the United States as the economy worsens. This [demoralizing] is necessary to make people accept difficult choices. If there is no planning for the future or if constituencies block progress there will be social chaos on a scale which is currently hard to imagine. The outlook for urban America is bleak. There is a possibility of doing something with the inner cities, but basically the cities will shrink and the manufacturing base will decline. This will produce social convulsions."[10]

Michael Aquino was a prominent member of the Church of Satan who went on to form his own group, the Temple of Set. Aquino, at the time of his entrance into LaVey's group, was an Army specialist in intelligence and psychological warfare. In 1973 he became the executive officer of the 306th Psychological Operations Battalion at Fort MacArthur in California. Several other members of the military and military intelligence are alleged to have been involved in the Temple of Set, including a member of the Naval Reserve; a captain in Psyops; an intelligence officer; and a reserve Army major.[11]

Aquino and others were alleged to have been involved in child molestation at the Child Development Center at the Army's Presido in San Francisco, one in a string of abuse investigations of military daycare centers that have taken place in the past by the Army. Investigations of child abuse have taken place at West Point, Fort Dix, Fort Leavenworth, and Fort Jackson. Other daycare centers investigated for allegations of abuse include a Navy day care center in Philadelphia where a man was sentenced to three years in prison for child abuse, two Air Force daycare centers, and a Department of Defense elementary school in Panama.[12]

Reporter Linda Goldston describes what she found when she conducted an on-site investigation at the Presidio:

"Inside a concrete bunker behind the military intelligence building at the Presidio, the words 'Prince of Darkness' are painted boldly in red on one wall. Used decades ago to house artillery guns, the reinforced concrete batteries appear to have been converted to something like ritual chambers.

"Emblazoned next to the 'Prince of Darkness' is the word 'Die,' and what looks like a list of names, painted in red, that have been crossed out with heavy black paint. One wall is covered with the numerals 666, a sign of the devil, and occult drawings. A clearing in the center of the concrete floor, where the ground is exposed, is filled with refuse and partly burned logs. On the front wall beneath the window that faces the Military Intelligence Building is a huge pentagram inside a circle. In the rear, where sunlight gives way to darkness, white and black candle drippings sit atop a dome shaped recession in the wall, apparently a crude altar. Incense sticks lie half burned to the side.

"At another battery farther up Lincoln Boulevard, a large drawing of Satan, with red eyes and horns appears on an outside concrete wall. Doors to the battery are secured shut...no entry is possible here."

Notes:
1. Judge, John, "The Black Hole of Guyana," *Secret and Suppressed*, Jim Keith, Ed. Portland, Oregon: Feral House, 1993; Krawczyk, Glenn, "The New Inquisition: Cult Awareness or the Cult of Intelligence?," Part 2, *Nexus*, December 1994/January 1995; Ross, M.D., Dr. Colin, "The CIA and Military Mind Control Research: Building the Manchurian Candidate," lecture given at Ninth Annual Western Clinical Conference on Trauma and Dissociation, April 18, 1996
2. White, Carol. *The New Dark Ages Conspiracy*. New York: New Benjamin Franklin House, 1980
3. Meiers, Michael. Cited in Constantine, Alex. *Virtual Government*. Venice, California: Feral House, 1997
4. Ross; Constantine; Krawczyk
5. Judge; Krawczyk; Constantine; Ross; White
6. Judge; Krawczyk; Constantine

7. *Doc Hambone*, John Mack listing at wwww.io.com/%7Ehambone;
    Sarfatti, Jack, "Sarfatti's Illuminati: In the Thick of It!," *MindNet
    Journal*, Vol. 2, No. 2A, www.visitations.com/mindnet/
    MN16A.HTM; Editors of *EIR*. *Dope, Inc.* Washington, D.C.: *EIR*,
    1992; listing for Esalen at Doc Hambone
8. Brandt, Daniel, "Cults, Anti-Cultists, and the Cult of Intelligence,"
    NameBase NewsLine, number 5, April/June
9. *Sightings*, "Heaven's Gate!" by J.P. Essene, at www.whatshotin.com;
    Constantine; Schnabel, Jim. *Remote Viewers: The Secret History of
    America's Psychic Spies*. New York: Dell, 1997; Knight, Robert,
    "Heaven's Gate to Higher (Income) Sources," at the Earthwatch website
10. Coleman, John. *Conspirators' Hierarchy: The Story of the Committee
    of 300*. Carson City, Nevada: America West Publishers, 1992; Blood,
    Linda. *The New Satanists*. New York: Warner Books, 1994
11. "Re: Former ToS Member on Satanic Crime," posted at alt.mindcontrol
    news group
12. Blood, Linda. *The New Satanists*. New York: Warner Books, 1994;
    Goldston, Linda, "Army of the Night," San Jose Mercury News, July
    24, 1988

CHAPTER 14

CONSOLIDATING CONTROL

During the Nixon administration, psychiatric and police organizations merged their efforts on many fronts. Richard Nixon and members of his staff met with agents of the Justice Department's Law Enforcement Assistance Administration, and Dr. Bertram Brown, director of the National Institute of Mental Health. LEAA was also involved in plans for the creation of a national police force, and urban warfare preparation that went by the names Operation Cable Splicer and Operation Garden Plot.

Incredibly, the LEAA began the financing of 350 National Institute of Mental Health psychiatric projects, with LEAA directly monitoring the NIMH doctors. These projects included screening children for psychological problems, experiments in behavior modification and psychosurgery, drugging programs in prisons including the use of nausea and terror-inducing drugs, and shock treatment programs.

By the 1960s, due in part to an increasing uproar from the public for accountability by the government, some officials had begun to scrutinize, at least at a superficial level, the excesses of intelligence and other official agencies in experimentation and mind manipulation of the public. Concerns of U.S. intelligence agencies about this scrutiny were expressed in a 1962 "Inspector General's Report on Inspection of MKULTRA." The report said:

"(a) Research in the manipulation of human behavior is considered by many authorities in medicine and related fields to be professionally unethical, therefore the reputation of professional participants in the...program are on occasion in jeopardy.

"(b) Some [of these] activities raise questions of legality implicit in the original charter [of the CIA].

"(c) A final phase [of certain projects] places the rights and interests of U.S. citizens in jeopardy.

"(d) Public disclosure of some aspects could induce serious adverse reaction in the U.S. public opinion, as well as stimulate offensive and defensive action in this field on the part of foreign intelligence services."

In the U.S. government publication "Individual Rights and the Federal Role in Behavior Modification," a study prepared by the staff of the Subcommittee on Constitutional Rights of the Committee of the Judiciary in 1974, it was revealed that "A number of departments and agencies, including the Department of Justice, the Department of Labor, the Veterans Administration, the Department of Defense, and the National Science Foundation, fund, participate in, or otherwise sanction research involving various aspects of behavior modification in the absence of effective review structures, guidelines or standards for participation."

One of the results of Senate scrutiny of these programs was that the head of the LEAA was interrogated. He announced that the LEAA would discontinue funding for psychosurgery and that funding for other behavior modification programs would be discontinued by the organization.

Nothing of the sort happened, with LEAA funding for behavior control continuing. At the Atmore State Prison in Alabama at least 50 psychosurgical operations took place. According to Dr. Swan of Fisk University, these were lobotomies performed on black political activists.[1]

In 1977, a Senate hearing into Central Intelligence Agency drug experimentation was launched, which had the effect of driving CIA programs underground, according to ex-CIA agent Victor Marchetti. To secure the survival of their projects, networks, and funding the mind controllers had to a great degree abandon scientific and military laboratories and seek deeper cover.

A probable by-product of the scrutiny that Congress was applying to behavior control is that researchers in mind control began to work unofficially, or hid their activities through a variety of other ruses; by performing their experimentation on the voiceless incarcerated of the prison and psychiatric systems, or in the inner city; by manipulating or starting cults and using them as a cover for their projects; by hiding their work within the tentacles of criminal enterprises; or by undocumented mind control projects performed on an unsuspecting populace.

Now, for the sake of secrecy, there would be no official paper trail. The great majority of documentation relating to MKULTRA and its related projects was destroyed, and never again would the mind controllers make the mistake of documenting their evil. Mind control operations were hidden in undocumented 'black' projects and intelligence agency 'cutouts' of all types, providing cover and deniability for the perpetrators. Government and heads of intelligence agencies looked the other way at violations of human rights, or sometimes they continued to gaze with unconcealed delight.

Notes:
1.   Martin, Harry V., and Caul, David, "Mind Control," *Napa Sentinel*, 1991 2. Constantine, Alex, "The False Memory Hoax: CIA Connections to Mind Control Cults," *Paranoia*, Winter 95/96

CHAPTER 15

GUERRILLA MINDWAR

The Symbionese Liberation Army, the revolutionary group that kidnapped heiress Patty Hearst in 1974, like Jonestown, was created at the fringes of U.S. intelligence. The group's leader, Donald DeFreeze, known as "Cinque," was employed as a paid informant by the Los Angeles Police Department's Public Disorder Unit from 1967-69, then directed the Black Cultural Association at the prison deceptively titled the Vacaville Medical Facility, which researcher Alex Constantine has alleged to be "a covert mind control unit with funding from the CIA channeled through SRI." Behavior modification was performed on DeFreeze at Vacaville—where documentation suggests electronic brain implanting and lobotomies, among other techniques, have been employed.

The Black Cultural Association was run by Colston Westbrook, a black CIA expert in psychological warfare who had participated in the Operation Phoenix assassination and mind control program in Vietnam. Westbrook's controller is alleged to have been the CIA's William Herrmann, the man who originated the idea of the violence center that Louis Jolyon West would champion during Reagan's governorship of California.[1]

Veteran conspiracy watcher Mae Brussell asked, "Why was CIA agent Colston Westbrook educated in psychological warfare and the indoctrination of assassination and terrorist cadres, chosen to select and train the group that became the SLA? Joseph Remiro and Nancy Ling Perry, important to the SLA for military tactics and cover story rhetoric, were dependent upon drugs. Both were political conservatives with a 'kill-a-Commie-for-Christ' background. Their transition into 'radicals' could have been assisted by the same chemical and psychological controls our intelligence agencies are using and experimenting with daily.

"Bill and Emily Harris, and Angela Atwood, worked together as a 'mod squad' narc team back home in Indiana, for the Indiana State Police. What brought them all scurrying to the Bay Area in the summer of 1972? Russell Little and Robyn Steiner, college chums from the University of Florida, drove out together from Florida to Oakland in the summer of '72. Though neither had shown any previous interest in blacks or prisoners, both immediately began working with Colston Westbrook and Donald DeFreeze at Vacaville Medical Facility. Camilla Hall and Patricia Soltwk were at least authentic residents of the Berkeley community. What controls were used to draw them into the SLA and ultimately to their deaths in Los Angeles?"

According to Brussell, "In March, 1974, a prisoner in Soledad was offered a chance to 'escape' by three prison officials if he would 'join the SLA army.'"[2]

Heiress Hearst, abducted by the SLA, was subjected to sophisticated mind control programming that turned her into a "changeling," as defined by CIA brainbanger Louis Jolyon West, who commented on her case:

"Prolonged environmental stress or life situations profoundly different from the usual, can disrupt the normally integrative functions of personality. Individuals subjected to such forces may adapt through dissociation by generating an altered persona, or pseudo-identity."[3]

According to West, "[Patricia Hearst], violently abducted by members of the Symbionese Liberation Army in February of 1974, [was] brutalized, raped, tortured and forced to participate in illegal acts beginning with the bank robbery for which she was later (in our view wrongly) convicted. The traumatic kidnapping and subsequent two months of torture produced in her a state of emotional regression and fearful compliance with the demands and expectations of her captors.

"This was quickly followed by the coerced transformation of Patty into [her alter ego] Tania and subsequently (less well known to the public) into [alter ego] Pearl, after additional trauma over a period of many months. Tania was merely a role coerced on pain of death; it was Pearl who later represented the pseudo-identity which was found on psychiatric examination by one of us (West) shortly after Heart's arrest by the FBI. Chronic symptoms of PTSD [Post Traumatic Stress Disorder] were also prominent in this case."[4]

According to Dr. Colin Ross, Jim Jones and the People's Temple were closely connected to the SLA:

"Jim Jones was a good PR guy. When Patty Hearst was kidnapped he offered William Randolph Hearst a program to set up a collection/donation of money to pay the ransom to the SLA. And the SLA was demanding something like $170 million from Hearst for the release of Patty Hearst. Jim Jones offered to set up this fund, but Hearst said no. The next outcome was that the SLA also wanted food donated to poor people that they said they were representing in a revolution. So a committee was set up to do food distribution, financed by William Randolph Hearst. According to this book, the way that food distribution ws done was Jim Jones got control of the mechanisms and he brought people down from the People's Temple down to be the homeless and poor people who received the food and the same food was distributed around the network six times, constantly being picked up by new People's Temple people, and taken back to the distribution point. So actually only one-sixth as much food was purchased as it appeared, and the rest was skimmed by the People's Temple."[5]

One person who survived the Jonestown deaths relates that Hearst's boyfriend Steven Weed had been to the People's Temple compound in Ukiah, and was seen talking to Jim Jones three months prior to the kidnapping of Hearst.[6]

Another example of government funding of "counterculture" political groups involved in terrorism: According to an Associated Press report from January 10, 1976, "The FBI created and funded a...group called the Secret Army Organization (S.A.O)...in the early 1970s the 'San Diego Union' reports."

The S.A.O., a division of the Weather Underground, was involved in urban guerilla warfare including murder, kidnappings, bombings, and arson and was, according to AP, a "centrally designed and externally financed infrastructure designed for terror and sabotage... These acts were sanctioned by the nation's most powerful and highly respected Law Enforcement Agency: the FBI."

The San Diego Union reports that the S.A.O. was guided and funded by Howard Berry Godfrey, who 'paid the expenses of the secret army, recruited new members, supplied the explosives, and picked out targets.' Godfrey was a paid FBI informer who had helped to found the SAO on the orders of the FBI.

Notes:
1. Ross, M.D., Dr. Colin, "The CIA and Military Mind Control Research: Building the Manchurian Candidate," lecture given at Ninth Annual Western Clinical Conference on Trauma and Dissociation, April 18, 1996; Brussell, Mae, "Why Was Patty Hearst Kidnapped?" *Paranoid Women Collect Their Thoughts*. Joan D'Arc, ed. Providence, Rhode Island: Paranoia Publishing, 1996; Constantine, Alex. *Virtual Government, CIA Mind Control Operations in America*. Venice, California: Feral House, 1997
2. Brussell
3. West, Louis Jolyon, "Pseudo-Identity and the Treatment of Personality Change in Victims of Captivity and Cults," in *Dissociation: Clinical and Theoretical Perspectives*, Lynn, S.J. and Rhue, J.W., eds. Guilford Press, 1994
4. West
5. Ross
6. ibid.

Chapter 16

The Greening of America: Monarch

One of the problems of researching covert control is obvious: we are attempting to delve into programs that are secret, and meant to remain so. For this reason there is often no paper trail to follow, and the researcher must pick his way through thickets of conflicting information and first person accounts that sometimes lack substantiation and challenge our current belief systems. It is often a difficult task to sort out fact from fiction, reality from delusion or disinformation.

After CIA mind control programs were severed as official projects in the 1960s and 1970s, the paper trail becomes sporadic. The Freedom of Information Act, which has provided at least a partial view of what took place during the MKULTRA era, now fails us entirely. One is forced to access primarily first person accounts, some of them contradictory, some of them plainly delusory. Determining the truth becomes difficult, and it is evident that there are many areas of our knowledge of mind control programs that will take years to understand, to clarify.

An area of research that still demands corroboration and definition is what has come to be known as Project MONARCH. On June 25, 1992, psychologist Dr. Corydon Hammond gave a talk to an audience of psychology professionals at the Fourth Annual Eastern Regional Conference on Abuse and Multiple Personality in Alexandria, Virginia. The title of the lecture was "Hypnosis in MPD: Ritual

Abuse," and it was one of the first public presentations which seems to expose a vast *terra incognita* in the area of mind control research.

Dr. Hammond began his presentation by commenting on the prevalence of multiple personality disorder cases who had apparently suffered ritual abuse at the hand of mind controllers, and his own efforts to understand what was going on by interviewing other psychologists and psychiatrists who were encountering the same type of cases around the country. Carefully, "without leading or contaminating," as Hammond says, he cross-checked with other mental health care professionals, comparing cases until he felt that he had had a good sense of what was going on.

Hammond stated that in as many as two-thirds of the ritual abuse cases that existed, the victims had been subjected to a highly developed and uniform technology of mind control, suggesting that there is a large network of practitioners of this kind practicing. This observation goes along with my own belief that the CIA, beginning in the 1940s, labored long in creating a secret science of mind control, the details of which are only now coming to light. What we know of MKULTRA is the tip of the iceberg.

Often, according to Hammond, these will be "bloodline people," that is persons programmed by their parents who are involved in cultic practice such as Satanism, or in intelligence agency programs.

Hammond said, "When you start to find the same highly esoteric information in different states and different countries, from Florida to California, you start to get an idea that there's something going on that is very large, very well coordinated, with a great deal of communication and systematicness to what's happening. So I have gone from someone kind of neutral and not knowing what to think about it all to someone who clearly believes ritual abuse is real and that the people who say it isn't are either naive like people who didn't want to believe the Holocaust or—they're dirty."

According to Hammond, "What they basically do is they will get a child and they will start this, in basic forms it appears, by about two-and-a-half after the child's already been made dissociative. They'll make him dissociative not only through abuse, like sexual abuse, but also things like putting a mousetrap on their fingers and teaching the parents, 'You do not go in until the child stops crying. Only then do you go in and remove it.' They start in rudimentary forms at about two and a half and kick into high gear, it appears, around six or six and a half, continue through adolescence with periodic reinforcements in adulthood.

Basically in the programming the child will be put typically on a gurney. They will have an IV in one hand or arm. They'll be strapped down, typically naked. There'll be wires attached to their head to monitor electroencephalograph patterns. They will see a pulsing light, most often described as red, occasionally white or blue. They'll be given, most commonly, I believe, Demerol... Then they will describe a pain on one ear, their right ear generally, where it appears a needle has been placed, and they will hear weird, disorienting sounds in that ear while they see photic stimulation to drive the brain into a brainwave pattern with a pulsing light at a certain frequency... Then, after a suitable period when they're in a certain brainwave state, they will begin programming, programming oriented to self-destruction and debasement of the person."

Hammond says that many of the cases dramatizing MPD phenomena have connections to the CIA and military installations. He describes one patient who went to a "cult school," where mind control sessions would take place several times a week. "She would go into a room, get all hooked up... When she was in a proper altered state, now they were no longer having to monitor it with electroencephalographs, they also had already had placed on her electrodes, one in the vagina, for example, four on the head. Sometimes they'll be on other parts of the body. They will then begin and they would say to her, 'You are angry with someone in the group.' She'd say, 'No, I'm not' and they would violently shock her. They would say the same thing until she complied and didn't make any negative response. They would continue. 'And because you are angry with someone in the group,' or 'When you are angry with someone in the group, you will hurt yourself. Do you understand?' She said, 'No' and they shocked her. They repeated again, 'Do you understand?' 'Well, yes, but I don't want to.' Shock her again until they get compliance. Then they keep adding to it. 'And you will hurt yourself by cutting yourself. Do you understand?' Maybe she'd say 'yes,' but they might say, 'We don't believe you' and shock her anyway. 'Go back and go over it again.' They would continue in this sort of fashion."

She said typically it seemed as though they'd go about thirty minutes, take a break for a smoke or something, come back. They may review what they'd done and stopped or they might review what they'd done and go on to new material. She said the sessions might go half an hour, they might go three hours. She estimated three times a week. Programming under the influence of drugs in a certain brainwave state and with these noises in one ear and them speaking in the other ear, usually the left ear, associated with right hemisphere non-dominant brain functioning, and with them talking, therefore, and requiring intense concentration, intense focusing. Because often they'll have to memorize and say certain things back, word-perfect, to avoid punishment, shock, and other kinds of things that are occurring... There will be very standardized types of hypnotic things done at times. There'll be sensory deprivation which we know increases suggestibility in anyone. Total sensory deprivation suggestibility has significantly increased from the research."

Hammond has come to believe that there are several levels of programming within the patients with whom he has worked, that can be accessed by letters of the Greek alphabet. Although Hammond does not mention it, these designations may have been roughly derived from the classifications in the classic eugenics tract *Brave New World*, by Aldous Huxley. Some of these letter designations follow:

—The first level, ALPHA, is generalized mind control, the base level of programming of the subject, and characterized by augmented memory and the splitting of the mind into left and right brain divisions.

—BETA is apparently programming of sexuality and the destruction of moral inhibitions.

—GAMMA is a level providing mind control system protection involving deception and misdirection.

—DELTA is the assassin programming level, and includes killers trained to perform ritual sacrifice.

—THETA is termed the "psychic killer" level. According to Hammond, "You know, I had never in my life heard those two terms paired together. I'd never heard the words 'psychic killers' put together, but when you have people in different states, including therapists inquiring and asking, 'What is Theta?' and patients say to them, 'psychic killers' it tends to make one a believer that certain things are very systematic and very widespread. This comes from their belief in psychic sorts of abilities and powers, including their ability to psychically communicate with 'mother' [and] including their ability to psychically cause somebody to develop a brain aneurysm and die.

—OMEGA is the level of programming dictating self destruction, and is intended to cause the subject to commit suicide when they are interrogated or begin therapy.

Hammond believes that this type of program was originally created by the CIA, and in particular by Dr. L. Wilson Greene, whose original name Hammond reports was Greenbaum. Among the code names used for the programming is Green Tree and Ultra-Green.

Hammond describes a self-destruction programming: "This was called the 'Green Bomb.' B-O-M-B. Lots of interesting internal consistencies like that play on words with Dr. Greenbaum, his original name. Now in this case it was done to her at age nine for the first time, only hers was different. Hers was a suggestion for amnesia. 'If you ever remember anything about Ultra-Green and the Green Tree you will go crazy. You will become a vegetable and be locked up forever.' Then finally the suggestions added, 'And it will be easier to just kill yourself than have that happen to you, if you ever remember it.'

"At age twelve then, three years later, they used what sounds like a [Sodium] Amytol interview to try to breach the amnesia and find out if they could. They couldn't. So then they strapped her down again, gave her something to kind of paralyze her body, gave her LSD...and reinforced all the suggestions. Did a similar thing at the age of sixteen."

One area where mind control programming takes place, according to Hammond, is in southern Utah. "Remember the Process Church?" Hammond asked in his presentation. "Roman Polanski's wife Sharon Tate was killed by the Manson Family who were associated with the Process Church? A lot of prominent people in Hollywood were associated and then they went underground, the books say, in about '78 and vanished. Well, they're alive and well in southern Utah. We have a thick file in the Utah Department of Public Safety documenting that they moved to southern Utah, north of Monument Valley, bought a movie ranch in the desert, renovated it, expanded it, built a bunch of buildings there, carefully monitored so that very few people go out of there and no one can get in, and changed their name. A key word in their name is 'Foundation.' 'The Foundation.'"

Hammond's allegations about ritual abuse in Utah are supported by a document I received in 1991. This was a copy of a memo authored by a General Authority of the Mormon Church, Second Counselor in the Presiding Bishopric, Glenn L. Pace, directed to the "Strengthening Church Members Committee." Suffice it to say that I am not a Mormon—I am not a member of any organized religious group—but that members of the church sent it to me.

According to the memo, which has "Do Not Reproduce" emblazoned across its masthead, Mr. Pace has met with sixty victims of ritual abuse in Utah. Pace writes, "That number could be twice or three times as many if I did not discipline myself to only one meeting per week... Of the sixty victims with whom I have met, fifty-three are female and seven are male. Eight are children. The abuse occurred in the following places: Utah (37), Idaho (3), California (4), Mexico (2), and other places (14). Fifty-three victims are currently living in the State of Utah. All sixty individuals are members of the [Mormon] Church. Forty-five victims allege witnessing and/or participating in human sacrifice. The majority were abused by relatives, often their parents. All have developed psychological problems and most have been diagnosed as having multiple personality disorder or some other form of dissociative disorder."

Pace reports, "I don't pretend to know how prevalent the problem is. All I know is that I have met with 60 victims. Assuming that each one comes from a coven of 13, we are talking about the involvement of 800 or so right here on the Wasatch Front [in Utah]. Obviously, I have only seen those coming forth to get help. They are in their twenties and thirties for the most part. I can only assume that it is expanding geometrically and am horrified the numbers represented by the generation who are now children and teenagers."

Pace goes on to detail the mindset of these cultic victims with information more reminiscent of the type of intelligence agency mind manipulation that Hammond speaks of than straight Satanism:

"The memories seem to come in layers. For example, the first memory might be of incest; then they remember robes and candles; next they realize that their father or mother or both were present when they were being abused. Another layer will be the memory of seeing other people hurt and even killed. Then they remember having seen babies killed. Another layer is realizing that they participated in the sacrifices. One of the most painful memories may be that they even sacrificed their own baby. With each layer of memory comes another set of problems with which they must deal."[1]

Is the Pace memo an accurate representation of what is going on? Is Hammond correct in his view about a vast mind control underground? The main problem with Hammond's testimony is the difficulty in substantiating his statements. We do know, however, that the reports of many persons who believe that they have been victims of mind control coincide with the information that Hammond has brought forward.

Notes:
1. Pace, Bishop Glenn L., "Ritualistic Child Abuse," memo to the Strengthening Church Members Committee of the Mormon Church, July 19, 1990

Chapter 17

Claudia Mullen

In March 1995 Claudia Mullen spoke before a U.S. presidential advisory committee investigating government radiation experiments after World War II. Mullen stated to the commission:

"Between the years 1957 and 1984, I became a pawn in the government's game. Its ultimate goal was mind control and to create the perfect spy, all through the use of chemicals, radiation, drugs, hypnosis, electric shock, isolation in tubs of water, sleep deprivation, brainwashing, verbal, physical, emotional and sexual abuse. I was exploited unwittingly for nearly three decades of my life and the only explanations given to me were 'that the end justifies the means' and 'I was serving my country in their bold effort to fight communism.' I can only summarize my circumstances by saying they took an already abused seven-year-old child and compounded my suffering beyond belief. The saddest part is, I know for a fact I was not alone. There were countless other children in my same situation and there was no one to help us until now. I have already submitted as much information as possible including conversations overheard at the agencies responsible. I am able to report all of this to you in such detail because of my photographic memory and the arrogance of the people involved. They were certain they would always control my mind. Although the process of recalling these atrocities is not an easy one, nor is it without some danger to myself and my family, I feel the risk is worth taking."

Mullen fingered Dr. Sidney Gottlieb and members of the TSD, or "Technical Science Division of the CIA" as being the primary co-conspirators in her abuse.

"In 1958 they told me I was to be tested by some important doctors from the Society, or the Human Ecology Society and I was instructed to cooperate. I was told not to look at anyone's faces, and to try hard to ignore any names because this was a very secret project. I was told all these things to help me forget. Naturally, as most children do, I did the opposite and remembered as much as I could." According to Mullen, "I was told by Sid Gottlieb that I was 'ripe for the big A' meaning [Project] ARTICHOKE."

Mullen continued: "The next year I was sent to a lodge in Maryland...to learn how to sexually please men." Mullen said that this was an attempt by high-ranking members of the CIA to fill "...as many high government agency officials and heads of academic institutions and foundations as possible so that later when the funding for mind control and radiation started to dwindle, projects would continue. I was used to entrap many unwitting men including themselves, all with the use of a hidden camera. I was only nine years old when the sexual humiliation began. I overheard conversations about part of the Agency called ORD which I found out was Office of Research and Development." One occasion Mullen heard a high-ranking CIA mind control doctor state "that 'in order to keep more funding coming from different sources for radiation and mind control projects' he suggested stepping up the amounts of stressors used and also the blackmail portions of the experiments. He said, 'it needed to be done faster then to get rid of the subjects or they were asking for us to come back later and haunt them with our remembrances.'

Mullen said that, "I would love nothing more than to say that I dreamed this all up and need to just forget it. But that would be a tragic mistake. It would also be a lie. All these atrocities did occur to me and to countless other children, and all under the guise of defending our country. It is because of the cumulative effects of exposure to radiation, chemicals, drugs, pain, subsequent mental and physical distress that I have been robbed of the ability to work and even to bear children of my own. It is blatantly obvious that none of this was needed, nor would ever have been allowed to take place at all, and the only means we have to seek out the awful truth and bring it to light is by opening whatever files remain on all the projects, and through another Presidential Commission on Mind Control.

"I believe that every citizen of this nation has the right to know what is fact, and what is fiction. It is our greatest protection against this ever happening again. In conclusion, I can offer you no more than what I have given you today—the truth."[2]

Mullen recalls that one of her government tormenters had a Scottish accent and called her "lassie." "I almost fell off my chair," Mullen's therapist Valerie Wolf recalled, when she saw a film of CIA mind controller Dr. Donald Ewan Cameron addressing a female patient and calling her "lassie."[3]

Later, in a radio interview, Claudia Mullen further described the extent of her mind control ordeal, which she says continued from 1957 to 1983:

"I was tested at Tulane and at several other places outside of New Orleans, and then once they decided I could become part of the projects—and they had a series of projects, the Umbrella project, and the Bluebird which became Artichoke and then came MKULTRA and each one on down the line. Each one had a different purpose. I was taken on train trips, planes—small planes to different military bases. I was taken to places out in the woods—I guess Tulane was the worst where I would receive intensive electric shock, isolation for days, sleep deprivation where they would attach electrodes to me and if I started to fall asleep, they would shock me—enough to wake me up. You couldn't sleep for days. The messages would start: 'Your mother doesn't love you, she left you here, your mother doesn't want you, you are too much trouble for her, you are a very evil child, you want to hurt people, you want to entice men.'

"My adoptive father was very ill and he died when I was very young, so I was taught to take to older men and encouraged to become friendly with older men and eventually, when

I was old enough, I was sent out into what they called the operational field and I would be photographed with government and agency officials (CIA), doctors who were consulted, heads of universities and private foundations—all under the chance that if the government funds started dwindling they wanted to be able to blackmail or coerce the men into making sure the projects continued. That was the ultimate goal. The projects had to continue at all costs. They had to train a certain amount of young females to go around and I was sent to a camp in Maryland for three weeks when I was nine years old, and that was my first training on how to sexually please men.

"I went through a training course, like a seminar. There were children of all ages, even younger than myself. Teenagers, young adult girls were there. We were all assigned someone there, and at the end of three weeks we were taught. They decided it was a success. It was a CIA project. It was called Imaginative Research. They had to give a name to it that they could release and document because they couldn't really put down what it really was. It came under the heading MKULTRA, project 74, and I was subject #3. I remember we were given a number. We were allowed to choose a name and after the three weeks I was sent home. For the next few years they worked on making sure I was amnesia controlled, making sure the amnesia barriers were in place so that if something should ever happen to me and the memories should ever start coming back, the pain would come first. I would seek help from the doctors who I was taught were the only people who could help me, the 'good doctors.' I was taught that doctors were the answer to everything. I had no reason to disbelieve that because every time I was sent home, I was told you are a good girl, you are cured, you are going to be just fine, you are going to grow up and have lots of kids. I didn't even realize that they had taken that away from me. I didn't know I couldn't even bear children."[4]

According to Mullen some of her initial programming was done at a camp for boys and girls, run by an official at Tulane University Medical Center. She says that her programming continued until she graduated from high school in 1968, and that by that time she had been programmed with nearly one hundred different personalities.

Most of this material was unknown to her until October, 1992, when she was attacked and raped in her home.

"It took two and one-half years to go to trial," Mullen states, "and during the time I was in therapy, that's when the memories started coming back... I would never recommend going back to any place where abuse happened by yourself, because you immediately go into a flashback... We went to some places around New Orleans that I had been to. One was a camp, an arsenal, that's now a police training facility and they allowed us to go in and look around... I went back to Tulane University... I showed her the room—I said, 'It's room 301' and I described what the hall would look like, what was on the wall, and sure enough a lot of it was the same. ...It was exactly the way I described it."

Mullen says that she was experimented on at Edgewood Arsenal, and is able to verify her account through the memories of some people who were there at the time:

"It did turn out that one of the people that was verifying the information that I sent interviewed different people. A couple of times they interviewed people that I actually remembered from my childhood that remembered me, only they remembered me as 'Crystal Stone' which was my name back then. That's what they called me for the experiments..."

Mullen says that Dr. Sidney Gottlieb was involved in her programming "From eight years to sixteen years—about eight years. He told me he raised goats..."

Of Ewen Cameron: "They called a lot of them in as 'consultants.' ...Next thing I knew I would be called back to Tulane and here was 'Camera Man' [her nickname for him], Cameron. He came in around 1960 when I was about 9 or 10. He was there a lot at first, testing how much electricity was too much, they didn't want to fry my brain or anything because they needed me to seem fairly intelligent because I had to associate with people..."

Her memories of Dr. Greene are extensive: "Next to Heath, I guess he had the most authority or whatever you wanted to call it. He was a German doctor. Liam was his first name, but he hated being called anything but Dr. Greene. He was head of Edgewood Arsenal, that's where his office was...in Fort Dietrich, Maryland but he came to Tulane quite a bit and worked with Dr. Heath on the projects. He told me, when I was about fourteen or fifteen, he told one of my shadows [or multiple personalities] the story...how he got involved. He said he was Jewish, and he was in a concentration camp when the war ended and the Nazis had killed his sister and put him in a concentration camp. He had met the Angel of Death [Mengele] there, and that was his hero and he used to love to watch him do experiments on twins and everything. Dr. Greene said he was put in the camp when he was fifteen...but when the war ended, the United States paid to bring him back to the U.S. and put him through medical school and now they paid him to do these experiments."

Mullen recalls, "They had no reason to think they had to hide anything from me, so they would have conversations about the projects, about so-and-so, what he's working on, where he is, where he is from, they would call each other by name. They would have suitcases with their nametags on them, briefcases. I met with Richard Helms who was Deputy Director of the CIA for a long time. I met with him lots of times. I mean I got to know them all on a first-name basis. They would say, 'call me Uncle.' Of course, every now and then they would expect 'a favor' but then you would be assured they were not being filmed. Somehow they managed to film almost everything... Until you got sent out into the field as, you know, an operative—to target these officials and get them on film. The idea being they wouldn't want a child who had been abused over a long period of time. They would want a child who was innocent and pure, and this was your first time. You were taught other ways to please men—anal intercourse, oral sex, everything else...

"Under the Umbrella Folder, the first one was Artichoke which could produce amnesia and also to develop polygraph techniques. There was MKDELTA, MKNAOMI which was germ warfare. They were laughing about how they would drop canisters of toxins— they had no idea what effect it was going to have—they would just wait five or ten years and see what the effects on this neighborhood was—a poor neighborhood. I was told about using retarded children in East New Orleans and exposing them to large doses of massive radiation and they saw no reason to use them because they were already retarded, they just wanted to see what anomalies would develop over the years."

On October 23, 1997, Claudia Mullen was shot. For months she was hooked up to a respirator, and is still undergoing a series of surgeries at this writing in May, 1999. She believes that she knows who the assailant was, but is unable to discuss the person's identity pending litigation.[5]

Notes:
1. "Mind Control Survivors' Testimony at the Human Radiation Experiments Hearings," CKLN-FM radio, July 1, 1997
2. ibid.
3. Bronskill, Jim, "Mind Games," Ottawa Citizen, September 13, 1997
4. Mullen, Claudia, Interview conducted by Will Snodgrass for CKLN-FM radio, July 15, 1997, Toronto, Canada; "Mind Control Survivors' Testimony at the Human Radiation Experiments Hearings"
5. Mullen, Claudia, correspondence with the author, March 5, 1999, and May 20, 1999

CHAPTER 18

BRICE TAYLOR

Other believed survivors of government mind control programs have come forward to tell their stories. One such person is the pseudonymous Brice Taylor. Born in 1951, Taylor speaks without hesitation about being the victim of CIA mind control programming, although in an interview with the author she confides that she fears that one day all of the information that she has stored in her mind will suddenly come pouring forth and overwhelm her.[1]

Taylor recalls that after a 1985 auto accident in which her head was smashed through a windshield she began recovering memory, experiencing flashbacks of her programming and mind controlled missions. Beginning in 1988, Taylor sought deprogramming from a therapist. Her therapy continued every day for six years, and she spent, according to her estimate, a total of $300,000 on recovery.

In an attempt to escape mind control, Taylor left her husband and children, whom she believes are still victims of programming. At present, the mind programming of her twenty-year-old daughter is breaking down, Taylor relates to me, so that the woman is currently in a near-catatonic state: drooling and in diapers.[2]

According to Taylor, from infancy her personality was progressively shattered by her father. She believes that he was also a victim of programming, and used CIA dissociative techniques on her in order to transform her into a mind controlled slave. Taylor believes that from childhood she was sold as a prostitute, and used in pornography. She states that at the Baptist Sunday school she attended as a child, the minister and secretary of the church practiced witchcraft.[3]

In a short memoir of her experiences, Taylor reported, "I started menstruating. This heralded abuse in rituals involving getting raped and impregnated, sometimes twice a year. When the fetuses were two to three months old, they were aborted at rituals and ingested to fulfill the beliefs of the group that it made those participating more powerful. These were devastating, deeply traumatizing and painful experiences that were repressed along with the other traumas."

Brice Taylor believes that throughout childhood she was abused and programmed at military bases including Edwards AFB, Twenty-Nine Palms, and Point Magu Naval Base.[4] Among the techniques she says were employed on her were sensory deprivation chambers, "spin chambers," and light and sound entertainment technologies. She says that she was programmed at a number of other locations including Barking Sands missile base in Hawaii and the UCLA Neuropsychiatric Institute, where drugs, light and sound, and sophisticated computerized methods were used on her under the supervision of Louis Jolyon West.[5]

Taylor reports that her "owner" was a popular Hollywood entertainer whom she names. He was "much more than an entertainer. Entertainment was actually just a clever hobby of his. I witnessed his participation as a strategically placed, influential, and integrated part of an underworld group that secretly sought to control the world. He maintained direct ties to the White House."[6]

She recalls that for her sixteenth birthday, her husband-to-be surprised her with a visit by train to the San Diego zoo. According to Taylor, once on the train she was delivered to a private car where the entertainer, a well-known politician, and two other men awaited her. "I had sex with each of them as the others watched."[7]

Starlite was the name that the entertainer gave her. "Starlite was one of my alter personalities. She was to become his 'starlet'..." The entertainer "took me to several of Hugh Hefner's penthouse parties in Los Angeles. There were windows all around and at night you could see all the twinkling lights of the city." According to Taylor she was prostituted to members of "the Rat Pack" of Hollywood celebrities.[8]

As an adult, Taylor says that she had fully taken on the characteristics of a multiple personality "presidential model" mind-slave, used as a courier, and sexual toy for government leaders and other world figures. She says that she was also used as a "human tape recorder," to store the text of secret documents by the use of her photographic memory. This was done so that these high level players could communicate without records or physical connections within their cabal, a group whose total intention is to bring about a fascist New World Order.

Taylor alleges that she was programmed to sexually service politicians:

"I was used extensively on and around 1968 by top politicians...guaranteed by the Central Intelligence Agency that my training in Project Monarch...insured the highest level of security. The level of mind control I possessed guaranteed that I could be used with these leaders who were involved at the highest levels of 'national security,' without my own awareness."[9]

Taylor says she went to Alcatraz and other locations, and saw mind control programming being done at those sites. Taylor indicates that she was also prostituted to several presidents.[10]

"[W]hat many of the CIA may or may not have been aware of was that a powerful group of men, whom I will call The Council, secretly ran the government. The Council was also able to access me and had programmed me to subversively influence top government officials in ways that benefited them. The CIA's latest technology was being used against our own government...

"The Council studied people's psychological profiles and knew exactly what their likes and dislikes were, their sexual preferences, what perfumes they liked, and any other information that could be used to influence individuals in ways of which they were never even aware. The Council would pre-program me with instructions (all based on careful research of the targeted person) of what to wear, how to act, what type of sexual stance to take...specific words or phrases to say, and the best time to deliver them. The Council always worked up a complete strategy and never sent me to a person unprepared."[11]

Taylor has penned an autobiography titled *Starshine,* written in fictionalized format, she says, in order to protect her from reprisal, and as of May, 1999 has finished a more complete statement of her experiences called *Thanks for the Memories: The Truth Has Set Me Free.*[12]

Perhaps the most persuasive validation of Taylor's recollections comes from mind control researcher Walter Bowart, who recalls seeing Taylor at a charity event in Palm Springs in the company of the entertainer who say alleges controlled her. He says that she was "just another of the many 'hostess' types that you find working the parties in the Coachella Valley." Other physical proof consists of what she characterizes as numerous stun gun marks over her body.

What is the truth about what happened to Brice Taylor? Admittedly, her story is incredible, outrageous, and bears little resemblance to what is commonly thought of as reality. Because of the outlandish details of her story, linking mind control programming to various prominent entertainers and politicians, one is tempted to reject her story out of hand. The difficulty is that, when speaking with her, one does not detect lying.

Notes:
1. Taylor, Brice, telephone interview with Jim Keith, December 19, 1998
2. Bowart, W.H. Operation Mind Control. Fort Bragg, California: Flatland, 1994; interview with Don Trainor, September, 1998; "Special Report: Mind Control Goes Public", Chicago Health Television, 1998; Taylor, Brice, lecture for the Global Sciences Conference, Daytona, Beach, Florida, 1998
3. Bowart; "Special Report: Mind Control Goes Public"
4. ibid.
5. Taylor, Brice. "Naming The Names," videotape presentation, 1998
6. Bowart
7. ibid
8. ibid
9. Bowart; Taylor, Brice. "Naming The Names"

10. Taylor, Brice. "Naming The Names"; Taylor, Brice, telephone interview with the author, December 19, 1998
11. Bowart
12. Taylor, Brice, with Patrick Stone. Starshine. Carbondale, Illinois: Brice Taylor Foundation, 1995; Taylor, Brice, lecture for the Global Sciences Conference

CHAPTER 19

KATHERINE SULLIVAN

Katherine Sullivan speaks plainly, without hesitation, with a hint of a Southern accent, offering a wealth of detail to flesh out an incredible story. As she speaks one cannot help but wonder if what she says is a particularly twisted brand of science fiction. But the ease with which the woman answers questions put to her, and her sense of sincerity is compelling. Finally, one fears that she is telling the truth.

Sullivan says that she realized that something was terribly wrong when it became apparent that she did not have many childhood memories. Born in 1955, it was only in 1990, while in treatment for codependency with her daughter, that she began to have memories of sexual abuse and torture by her father, as well as experiences of cultic ritual abuse.

Later, in a hospital in Dallas, Texas, Sullivan uncovered what she believes was another whole layer of programming. She began to remember being imprinted with CIA "assassin programming," which she believes was inadvertently activated during the course of her therapy, causing her to attempt to kill hospital nurses and staff. Sullivan says that memories of being programmed to become an assassin came back to her before she knew anything about the subject of intelligence agency mind control, and that her initial reaction was denial. Eventually, however, she says that she could deny her memories no longer. She finally had to admit to herself that she had been utilized in government mind control operations for twenty years.

During the years that followed, Sullivan remembered many more details of her programming. She came to believe that she had been victimized from the time she was six or seven years old by members of the CIA, NSA, and other groups and individuals.

According to Sullivan, her principal programmer was her father, an electrical, mechanical and chemical engineer who worked for AT&T. She says that he was employed in overseas work for the CIA, and had also worked as an interpreter in the infamous Operation Paperclip transferal of Nazis to the U.S. He was also, according to Sullivan, the head of a satanic coven in Reading, Pennsylvania. She believes that her father had been programmed as a child, and that her mother was "definitely a multiple," in other words a person who had been programmed to have multiple personalities.

Sullivan has said that, "Two older male relatives from my childhood were also involved with dad in criminal, 'black' activities that included ritual murders and orgies attended by invited 'guests,' kiddy pornography, filmed bestiality, black marketing of dismembered parts 'pickled' in glass jars of formaldehyde; and more. Around my age eight, Dad began to force me to sit by myself on an altar each week, usually late on Friday nights. I would watch in horror and great grief as he and his criminal associates would murder and mutilate quite a few humans...from babies on up to adults! They would usually accuse the adult victims of having been 'traitors,' which also conditioned me to believe that 'to talk is to die.' I was forced to ingest small, raw pieces of the murder victims' bodies, and was usually forced to eat excrement, drink urine, and drink human blood...often laced with powdered opium. On several occasions I was also forced to ingest human brain matter."[1]

According to Sullivan, her father was a confidant of CIA superspook James Jesus Angleton, who also programmed her. Early on, she recalls, she was offered as a piece of human chattel to the White House, usually referred to by her programmers as "1600 Pennsylvania Avenue," but which was also called the Hub, and Emerald City. The President, she says, was referred to as Oz or God, and she was conditioned to return to the White House like a "homing pigeon."

Another of her programmers was a mysterious Dr. Black (aka Dr. Schwartz), a tall man with curly black hair who spoke German fluently, and whose primary interest in research seemed to be the study of aspects of aggression. She calls Dr. Black a major figure in her childhood, and remembers that his office was a black train car. Whether it actually traveled on railway tracks, she does not remember.

Sullivan claims that one of her mind controllers was Henry Kissinger, of whom she says, "I still love Henry Kissinger, even though I should be absolutely furious at him, I haven't found that anger yet." She states that Kissinger was one of the few controllers who did not rape her, and was "a very lonely man, an absolute genius," and in a "lot of pain and fog somewhere." Oddly, she still has a degree of respect for him because he was "honest about being a bastard."

Sullivan believes that the Luciferians see the lower classes as cattle, and are determined to phase out what they consider to be inferior races. They are determined to create a one world order where Luciferianism can be openly practiced, and where such activities as pedophilia and bestiality will be legalized.

Sullivan believes that the Bilderbergers are at the top of the heap in terms of international control, the "top of the top," she says, and remarks that the members of the group associate mainly with each other, thus fostering a cultish mentality in their ranks.

Other groups that Sullivan was involved with, or was aware of included:

—The Austrian Order of the Reich, "actively working, under supervision of Ford Foundation, Rockefeller Foundation and Rothschilds, to create a new world government"

—The Black Brotherhood, "direct ties to the Vatican, American Military Intelligence, CIA, etc."

—Order of the Golden Dragon, "Asian ties. Americans. Small, politically powerful group. Elite."

—Black Star Rising, "consider themselves to be the antithesis of the Order of the Golden Dawn"

—NOWD (Nazi Order for World Domination), "One of the think-tank groups actively planing world takeover (neo-Nazi government) to be accomplished by the year 2000"
—The PLAN "Public (or) Political Liberation for All Nations, belief systems & plans based on Orwellian society presented in 1984"
—The Organization, "New, more streamlined, large, radical terroristic neo-Nazi organization based in Alabama & Mississippi"
—Knights of the Golden Armor, "an elite subgroup of the Black Brotherhood."
—The Code, "organization comprised of top worldwide new age & occultic channelers"
—Society of the Inner Light, "metaphysical, mystical group. One of five main Illuminati families";
—Western Mysteries, "occultic organization, also one of the five main Illuminati families"
—BNO, "(Brave New Ones/Order) - group of the newer generation of politically active Illuminati members. Newer, more radical beliefs and plans to create a worldwide Orwellian society"
—Wolffen, "neo-Nazi, secret underground organization. Hitler, their idol... Based in West Germany, at least partly... Militaristic, use semi-automatic weapons. Practice paramilitary takeover of various countries. War games"
—Thornless Rose, "More local Satanist, criminal cult practicing in the Southwest"
—The Brotherhood of the Hand, "last known to be headquartered in Louisiana. Local criminal occultic group"
—AOR, or in Italy AORI, standing for Austrian Order of the Reich. The purpose of the company was to bring world leaders to facilities where they were taught to increase theta brain wave activity. Once there, they would be recruited to a Nazi, one world orientation.[2]

One approach to the creation of the New World Order, Sullivan says, is by the promotion of Gaia worship. Sullivan says that she was told that Benjamin Creme's reclusive messiah Maitreya will be the main public figure used in the transition to the New World Order, and that other leading Christian evangelists would be the means to convert the world to Luciferianism.

She states that many Luciferians are involved in the Golden Dawn occultic organization, which has many members in in Washington, D.C.

Sullivan believes that she participated in ritual sacrifices performed by her father since the time she was four years old. She indicates that another child of her father by a later marriage was also sexually abused by him. She believes that he traumatized her, as well as many other children, in order to split off parts of their personalities into many "alters" for mind control programming.

Sullivan also states that "screen memories and scrambles," injecting false details into her memory, were used to cover up what had been done to her, and operations that she had been forced to engage in. Drugs, hypnosis, and electric stun guns, as well as the use of virtual reality systems were used to program her, as well as to make it nearly impossible for her to access her own mental programming.

The list of covert intelligence operations that Sullivan believes she engaged in is long: smuggling of drugs and children, being a courier of information, programming of children, disposing of bodies, participating in porn movies, torture and interrogation, sex with political dignitaries, the seduction of female politicians and wives of politicians.

When employed as a bodyguard she was called "Plain Jane" and dressed in a brown jacket and skirt. She believes her usefulness as a bodyguard was because she was not an identifiable employee of any agency. She also was utilized for assassinations, and remembers putting a poisonous substance in the lemonade of a cult of young people, perhaps in a foreign country. Another assassination technique was scratching people through their clothes with a pin that stuck out of her purse. The pin was coated with a fast-acting poison.

Sullivan: "By my eighteenth birthday, my assassin/ops training was complete. I was introduced to other members of what I was told was "Illuminati.' I was then made to join a 'religious' mind-controlled 'cult' During the three-and-a-half year stint, my previous programming was overlaid by the religious God/submission/spiritual realm programming. My basic personality was further split into two almost completely separated parts. Because I had also been extensively, sexually abused by one female relative in particular during my childhood, a number of split-off parts of my personality had been further conditioned to 'sexually service' females. This was another business 'bonus' for my father and other owners. I was occasionally assigned to 'service' wives of politicians, both locally and otherwise. To the best of my recollection, most (if not all) of them were members of a secret pagan organization. Although a number of lesser gods and goddesses were mentioned in their rituals, the main 'god' was known to me as 'Ra.'³

"Some of the women would get together around high noon in privately owned greenhouses or rooms with overhead windows to practice divination and to do Greco-Roman type rituals. They would dress in distinctive garments, and would drink a clear, gelled liquid containing what seemed to be tiny yellow flecks that seemed to 'sparkle' when a clear glass container of the liquid was held up to direct sunlight. The women called the odd, clear liquid the 'elixer of life.' Approximately two years ago, while skimming through Texe Marrs' book of the New Age cults and religions for verification concerning these memories, I discovered the true ingredient of the 'elixer of life'—human semen!

"I believe that many people would be deeply shocked to learn how many politicians and other leaders in our society are practicing pagans—going to church on Sundays, and then gathering together to do secretive pagan rituals. (Often in female gatherings, I was forced to do female/female sex with participants). It is no surprise to me that Hillary Clinton placed a sun ornament atop the White House Christmas tree, several years ago!"

Sullivan has identified a large number of participants in Washington, D.C., some of them prominent politicians or the wives of same, but has asked me not to divulge their identities. She has also provided a transcript of a long occultic ceremony she remembers that was practiced at these meetings.

One of the facilities where she believes she was conditioned was called The School or The Fortress, where she received some type of surgery on her head. There were other children there, with units designated A, B, and C, and the "Romper Room." There she recalls children being indoctrinated into government ops conditioning, part of which involved disemboweling teddy bears.

Another facility, she recalls, was in Reading Pennsylvania, where there was a building with large theatrical stages. She remembers being there at the age of eight, and remembers being forced to kill men who were dressed like "street bums." "I still don't want to actually believe that I killed these men at my age," she says, suggesting that the event may have been staged; a mock murder meant to traumatize her. This and another location where Sullivan believes she was programmed have been tentatively identified in the Reading area.

Another programming location was Coffeesville, Maryland. She was taken from public school to a facility consisting of several trailers and pavilions. There she was given "chameleon" training and shown how to behave around dignitaries.

According to Sullivan she was programmed by NASA personnel at various locations including Huntsville, Alabama; Houston, Texas; Cape Canaveral, Florida; and Goddard Air Force Base, outside of Washington, D.C. At Goddard, she says that the programmers dressed in Star Trek uniforms in order to confuse and discredit the memories of those they programmed—as a "scramble" for their memory. She believes that at Goddard she was hooked up to a helmet that was linked to a computer system, apparently some kind of virtual reality system, since when she closed her eyes images would "flash in front of [her] face."

Sullivan describes alleged NASA conditioning called "Father Time" training, which involved real or imaginary dimensional travel. Sullivan says that NASA specialized in "time folding" and "going back in time at least in our minds." The children involved in these program read Madeleine L'Engle's juvenile science fiction books, including *A Wrinkle in Time,* about dimensional travelling children. Sullivan believes that NASA is trying to find ways to explore alternate dimensions, and that this kind of programming, "Really messed up my head."

By 1991—interestingly, before Dr. Hammond's voicing of his own discoveries about mind control, as confirmed by dated drawings that she has sent the author —Sullivan had come to the conclusion that there were five principal mind control programming systems, closely paralleling the systems that Hammond later described.

"Another form of verification that is important to me," she states, "is that I was remembering and diagramming my programming (Alpha, Beta, Delta, Theta and Omicron) back in the summer of 1991, years before anyone else came forward and exposed that stuff. When I received independent verifications that the programs exist, and that they are used the way I had remembered, I was very depressed and upset... I had wanted this stuff to be fantasy!"[4]

—Alpha, she says, is the most basic programming.

—Beta, also referred to as "Barbie" (she believes this type of programming was invented by the Nazi Klaus Barbie) is sexual programming.

—Delta is military programming, involving loyalty and submission.

—Theta programming is also called "psychic killers," and involves the programming of mental energy in telepathic killing and to influence events. She also performed remote viewing, which may have been a subset of this kind of programming.

—Omicron, she says, was special programming for mind control programs run by the Mafia.

She has detailed a number of programming techniques that she believes are used, including electroshock to the head and spine, a "neck choker" to shock her throat, and the injection of a drug related to the South American drug curare, that would paralyze her so that she could not move but could still think and feel.

According to Sullivan, one technique that her father specialized in was "shell programming," which she alleges took place at or near Georgia Technical University. There children were programmed into split personalities by being placed in large *papier mache* shells where gallons of bugs were poured on them. Sometimes the children went catatonic which, Sullivan indicates, was not an acceptable outcome. When used as codes, the numerals three, two, and one all had to do with CIA activities. The numeral zero specified an "inactive" case or agent. "Naomi" was a code used to specify biochemical projects, while "Birdcage" indicated a location where biochemical weapons were kept.

Sullivan recalls that mind control subjects were frequently programmed through music, including chords, sequences of notes, and lyrics. Music by the Beatles was used more than any other type, but also Pink Floyd ("used in NASA time programming") and The Who, especially portions of the rock opera "Tommy." Movies were also used as programming devices, with the most common being "the Wizard of Oz" and Disney's "Alice in Wonderland".

Some of the designations for projects that she remembers participating in, or was aware of were: Seabase (or C-Base), Goldilocks, Massacre, Sandstone, Royal India, Dot Purple or Deep Purple, Larkspur, Chronic Headache, Marigold, Z-Bomb, Top Hat, Messiah, Overlord, Fire and Ice, Delta Blue, Deep Blue, Blowfish. Code Failsafe was a system for creating amnesia in mind control victims. One computer system was referred to as Brandon. "Goldstar Operations Systems" and Mongoose were supposedly a brainchild of George Bush; "The Link," is apparently a liason operation between NSA and NASA; Centipede is an information compartmentalization system in the CIA and National Security Agency. A mind control program that created an entire fantasy world in a person's mind was called "Heaven's Gate." Mensa, not connected to the organization of the same title, was a program for using genius IQ mind control victims in think tanks. *Pax Romana* and The Plan were Aryan-related code names. Project Armageddon had to do with war games and preparation for World War III, with "the Keys of Solomon" providing code information for the Armageddon scenario.

According to Sullivan, the CIA and the KGB have been working together for many years—with cross-training taking place in Russia—while at the same time being in competition. KGB codes included Dark Chocolate, Sasha, Mink, and Ermine. In CIA numerical code, negative one, negative two, and negative three referred to the KGB.

Sullivan remembers that there was a location near Dallas where a full-sized UFO equipped with an hydraulic lift had been transported to or constructed in a large room. Her understanding is that government UFOs were based on World War II German technology, and that there are several UFO bases that are currently in operation, including one in the Himalayas, and another at an underwater base near Hawaii.

Inside the UFO were "people that looked like aliens," and this UFO prop was used to make people think that they had been abducted by extraterrestrials. Based upon the bragging of her father and other information, Sullivan believes that these "aliens" were first created in German labs during World War II experiments on embryos. She calls these pseudo-aliens "The Children," and says that they are programmed so that they believe that they are extraterrestrials.

Sullivan claims to have met several of The Children, including one young boy who spoke English and what was referred to as "Trilateral" language, containing lots of clicks and symbolic gestures. She also says that she met several breeders of these mutated humans, and that one distinguishing characteristic is that some wear a "bird's nest" haircut, shaved part way around the top of their head.

Sullivan believes that the purpose of faking UFOs and aliens is to prepare the people of the world to believe in aliens. She explains that she has heard discussions about the possibility of a faked UFO invasion that would psychologically decimate the populace so that they would gladly submit to total control.

According to Sullivan she heard other possible plans for initiating the New World Order, including using Christian evangelists to push belief in the "tribulation" or "last days" of the Earth. Sullivan says that she was led to believe that AIDS was created specifically to key into belief in the biblical Revelations. Another possibility that was talked about was the assassination of a president, providing the opportunity for FEMA to take over the country and to institute totalitarian control.[5]

—Evaluating Sullivan's statements, her description of some aspects of the New World Order sound too reminiscent of the stock-and-trade of conspiracy literature. This suggests contamination of her story by reading the work of others; in fact, Sullivan at one point mentioned that she had read something by radio evangelist and conspiracy author Texe Marrs. It does not, however, disprove that she is a victim of mind control.

In terms of physical evidence, Sullivan has said in correspondence with the author, "I have little round white stun gun marks all over my forearms and on other parts of my arms and legs. There might be some on other parts of my body, too, but I can't see them. (an investigator/police officer in Atlanta verified, without my saying what I knew they were, that they are stun gun marks). I have a discoloration on the left side of my head/eyelashes/eyebrow from where Dad used to make a blank gun go off... I don't have much physical evidence, because every ten years or so, my then-current handler would make me literally throw or give away everything I owned, right down to my bed sheets and all my jewelry, and start from scratch again. I guess that was their way of making sure I wasn't holding onto any evidence."[6]

Another form of verification offered by Sullivan to the author is a lengthy series of lecture notes that her father used for what was apparently a philosophical self-help class that he taught. What these notes show is a wide-ranging familiarity with psychological and philosophical teachings, with several interesting emphases. He mentions the use of "chemotherapy, surgery and shock therapy" in psychiatry, the work of Dr. Jose Delgado, as well as "ancient sacrifices of children." He also references "Russia's mental reconditioning" and "T.V. flash techniques & editing." Obviously her father was not completely unaware of mind control techniques.

Sullivan has also provided a photocopy of a letter from a district attorney in Georgia—I respect her desire for me to not to be more specific than that—that confirms that her father was arrested for sexually molesting her half-brother. In the letter, the D.A. states, "I feel we would have been successful at trial because the evidence against him was overwhelming and also because he had made some admissions to the charge."[7]

Before he could go to trial, her father committed suicide.

Notes:
1. Sullivan, Katherine, "Like Father, Like Daughter" at Mind Control Forum at www.mk.net/ ~ mcf/resrc-hm.htm, CAHRA; CKLN interview at Mind Control Forum
2. "Questionnaire for Survivors Abused Over the Age of Eighteen", February 21, 1993, copy furnished to the author by Katherine Sullivan
3. Sullivan, Katherine, "Like Father, Like Daughter"
4. Katherine Sullivan, correspondence with the author, March 23, 1999
5. CKLN
6. Sullivan, Katherine, correspondence with the author, March 23, 1999
7. Letter from a district attorney in Georgia, name withheld at request, dated January 30, 1990, to Katherine Sullivan's mother

CHAPTER 20

EVALUATING MONARCH

The problem with evaluating the account of many believed victims of mind control is the problem with psychological therapy itself. It is ultimately a subjective process in which the patient is influenced by the therapist, and the therapist by the patient. It is a private process where two persons collaborate to hopefully heal the patient and bring forth the truth about what happened to them. Sometimes that goal is not accomplished.

In some cases the accounts of believed victims may have been influenced by the tales of others. They may be referencing things that they have read or heard from others. Thus, not to make light of such things, an incident of childhood sexual abuse might be turned into an abusive encounter with a prominent politician. A childhood nightmare of cloaked Satan-worshippers might be remembered as fact. Daddy's clients in the insurance trade might fit all the earmarks of members of the Illuminati.

Even Dr. Colin Ross, a well-known researcher on multiple personality disorder and mind control admits this difficulty in evaluating these cases:

"You cannot tell just by listening to a patient's story…you can't tell that it is true. Also you can't tell that it is false. In other words you can't tell without some sort of outside proof. That is proof that it really happened, or proof that it didn't happen. What I have learned especially in the last five years, there is really no limit to how detailed, how compelling, how full of feeling…how detailed a bunch of memories can be and actually be totally real, or never have happened. I have worked with people who have had really elaborate memories of all kinds of things with tremendous amounts of detail and then we have been able to prove it never happened. You can't tell."[1]

While there is no question that many people have been the victims of mind control and ritual abuse—in my opinion far more than have ever been acknowledged—there are also many people who proclaim themselves mind control victims whose accounts I do not find entirely credible. Like copy cat criminals, there seem be copy cat victims who source their current problems to the stories of others, who may or may not be actual victims themselves.

An example of possible delusion and contamination in the memory of an alleged mind control victim is the story of Pat Burgess, who in the mid-1980s experienced post partum delivery trauma after the birth of her second son. Prior to that time Burgess seems to have lived a normal life, and to have had no psychological problems. Complaining of depression, Burgess consulted hypnotherapist Ann Marie Bauman, who over the course of many visits came to believe that she had discovered at least thirty personalities within the recesses of Burgess' psyche. Feeling that a therapist more experienced in Multiple Personality Disorder was called for, Bauman referred Burgess to Dr. Bennet Braun, who ran a clinic at the well-known Rush Presbyterian St. Luke's Medical Center in Chicago. In March of 1986 Burgess checked into Braun's clinic.

During the course of her therapy Braun prescribed large doses of psychoactive drugs for Burgess, including Halcion, which is known to in some cases induce hallucinations. Braun came to believe that he had eventually summoned forth three hundred hidden personalities in Burgess, and that the woman had been a leader in a worldwide satanic cult that had engaged in numerous murders, cannibalism, rape, and other crimes. Braun, it is reported, had long believed in a huge satanic cult engaging in mind control and ritual abuse, and at one point, according to Burgess, told her that the Pope was the head of the cult and had sexually abused her son. Burgess called the FBI to investigate, but having heard her stories, they chose not to pursue the matter.

Both of Burgess' sons, aged three and five, were checked into the hospital for evaluation, and put on a course of drugs and therapy, spending three years in the locked child psychiatry department of the hospital.

After twenty-seven months in the hospital Burgess went home. She has concluded that her beliefs that she was a member of a satanic cult and engaged in murder were the product of the mind altering drugs that she was prescribed, and the paranoid world view of Dr. Braun and the MPD unit at Rush Presbyterian. Burgess sued Dr. Braun and the hospital, who settled out of court for 10.6 million dollars. Braun's clinic was closed, but he is still practicing psychiatry at Rush. What has only been recently revealed is that Braun had not been a licensed psychiatrist to begin with, but only obtained his license some time after Burgess had gone into therapy with him. The state of Illinois has brought formal charges against Dr. Braun to revoke his license.[2]

As another example of possible delusion in tales of mind control, I noted in my *Mind Control, World Control* that the book *The Illuminati Formula Used to Create an Undetectable Total Mind Controlled Slave* by Fritz Springmeier and Cisco Wheeler contains much that does not seem credible to me. Their narrative seems to be a conglomeration of horror tales oft-told in the fundamentalist Christian underground without much regard for evidence, credibility, or even possibility. Since my first write-up, I have obtained a lengthy taped interview with Cisco Wheeler that has in many ways confirmed my opinion of her story.

Wheeler, who frames her story within a strong Christian religious belief structure, believes that she came from a multi-generational satanic family, and that her father was a 33rd degree Mason, a mind control programmer for the U.S. government, as well as being a grand master of the Illuminati secret society. She believes that he was involved with the shipment of drugs from Vietnam during the Vietnamese War; he was one of the guys who picked up the kilos of heroin sewn into corpses sent home for burial. "The purpose of that,"

Wheeler says, "was to destroy the structure within the family unit. The drug culture was the real purpose behind the Vietnam War."

"Structure within the family unit" and the purpose of the Vietnam War aside, Wheeler reports that in the late 1940s the Illuminati set upon a plan to infiltrate churches "because they understood the power of God within the structure of the church, and they had to find a way to infiltrate the church to break down that spiritual strength within the church, the power of the holy spirit that works within the church." Her father, she says, was used to further this purpose, and married a woman who was not Illuminati or involved in ritual magick, but who did have a Christian background so that he could obtain entrance into fundamentalist circles.

Wheeler believes, like many others, that she was adversely conditioned by trauma while still in the womb, and that, "By the time I was 18 months, because my father was a programmer, he could control my liver, my kidneys, my heart rate, my pulse, my respiration." Later, she says, she was sexually groomed to service the top politicos of this country. This programming, according to Wheeler, took place at China Lake Naval Base, Alcatraz Prison, the Presidio, and Scotty's Castle in California, and at the state mental hospital and Dorenbecker Masonic hospital in Oregon. Wheeler estimates that there were a total of ten million children who were programmed in MKULTRA.

"I was part of the Illuminati function within the British Royal Family during elite meetings," she reports. The first American president that sexually abused her, she recalls, was Eisenhower. She also believes that she endured mind control procedures under the hand of the infamous Dr. Greene, who she identifies as actually being the Nazi Dr. Josef Mengele working under an alias. Her father, she says, was Mengele's number two man.

As to the books that she and Springmeier have self-published, Wheeler says, "If we had a publishing company distributing them, the Illuminati would buy them all up and have the right to them, and we would lose our books."

Perhaps providing insight into how Wheeler came to believe that she was the victim of mind control abuse is the
information that her therapy took place in the context of a
group of four woman, all of whom believed that they had
been programmed at about the same time by the same programmers. She says, "In our healing process the first thing
we had to acknowledge within ourselves, and we each had to
do this separately, is to acknowledge that we are MPD [Mul-
tiple Personality Disorder], that we are DID [Dissociative
Identity Disorder], and that we were generational families of
Satanism."

Again, like many other recovered memories of mind
control and ritual abuse and being dawdled on President
Eisenhower's lap, Cisco Wheeler's version of history is long
on Christian sermonizing about the End Times and, so far as
I can tell, devoid of proof. It is obvious that Cisco Wheeler
believes what she is saying—I do not doubt her sincerity—but
her recollections are so scanty and so generalized in detail
that they do not comprise anything approximating proof, or
even a possibly credible account. This, of course, may not be
vital for widespread acceptance of her story in an era where
seemingly half of the population believes that extraterrestrial
aliens collaborate with the American government in underground bases, but it is vital to me. Horror of horrors to some
researchers, in order to accept reports of this nature as being
true, one absolutely must rely on proof.

It is obvious to me that Cisco Wheeler has had problems
in her life, and those problems may even have stemmed from
mind control programming. I do not rule that out as a possibility. But the simple fact is that she has not proven that she is
a subject of mind or control, or that the CIA or the Illuminati
are responsible.[3]

To repeat, I do not say that all people who believe that
they have been mind controlled, or who believe they have
been victims of ritual abuse are deluded. Far from it, as evi-
denced by the time I have spent writing this book. I believe
that many of these persons are actual victims, and that there
is an underworld of mind control and ritual abuse that has
been only partially exposed at this time. It is simply cases

such as these must be evaluated carefully and individually. To uncritically accept every account, even the most outrageous and obviously paranoid, as many so-called researchers do, discredits real mind control abuse that does take place. It is also important to realize that the contamination of stories of actual as well as believed victims, may be a way of discrediting the truth. By injecting outlandish details into these stories, by linking intelligence agency mind control with extraterrestrial aliens and such, a pallor of doubt is cast upon real cases of abuse. This is the activity of "scrambling" that Katherine Sullivan and others talk about. It is also true that traumatic abuse and conditioning confuses and disorients the victim, causing cross-referencing of mental information, and potentially adding to the nightmarish quality of many reports of this sort.

Finally, there are many reports of mind control conditioning that I find credible, and many witnesses whose testimony holds up under scrutiny.

Notes:
1. Dr. Colin Ross interview, aired on Sunday, April 6, 1997 on CKLN-FM 88 in Toronto, Canada. Interview conducted by Wayne Morris
2. *Dateline*, NBC television, October 28, 1998
3. Wheeler, Cisco, interview conducted by Wayne Morris for CKLN-FM radio, Toronto, Canada, October 5, 1998

CHAPTER 21

CONCEALING
MIND CONTROL ABUSE

One strategy for concealing actual mind control is to
erect pseudo-scholarly fronts to disprove that such
misdeeds exist. One such group is the False Memory
Syndrome Foundation, a group of psychiatrists whose mission is to prove that cult abuse and mind control are figments
of the imagination. While it is no doubt true that some cases
of mind control and ritual abuse are imagined and that false
accusations do take place, there is a solid body of evidence
showing that such abuse does exist. For starters, documentation on the CIA's MKULTRA program is not in question.
But the Foundation is intent on proving that this is not the
case.

Of the False Memory Syndrome Foundation, mind control researcher Walter Bowart has said, "This is a Central
Intelligence Agency action. It is an action aimed at the psychological and psychiatric mental health community. To discredit you, to keep you in fear and terror."

The membership of the Foundation is telling. Many of
the psychiatrists in the group's advisory board are linked to
CIA mind control operations or to the military. These persons are often called upon in court cases to discredit testimony of cult sexual abuse and mind control.[1]

One of the original members of the group, Martin T.
Orne, a researcher at one time funded through MKULTRA
and the gamut of military agencies, is employed at the University of Pennsylvania's Experimental Psychiatry Laboratory. Orne was friends with George Estabrooks, the early

researcher on the creation of hypnotic Manchurian Candidates, and bragged to researcher John Marks that he was routinely briefed on advances in CIA mind control research.

Some of Orne's early researches, including studies of post-hypnotic amnesia, were financed by the Human Ecology Fund, a conduit for CIA monies at Cornell University. HEF financed numerous major mind control experiments worldwide, including those of the infamous Ewen Cameron at the Montreal Allen Memorial Institute.[2]

Orne was called in to examine Patty Hearst after the Agency-created Symbionese Liberation Army was immolated by the LAPD. Also evaluating Hearst were Robert Jay Lifton, a founder of the CIA-contracted Human Ecology Fund, and infamous MKULTRA shrink Louis Jolyon West.

Another person testifying at the trail of Patty Hearst was retired Berkeley Ph.D. Dr. Margaret Singer, also on the advisory board of the False Memory Syndrome Foundation. Singer had studied American prisoners of the Korean War at the Walter Reed Army Institute of Research in Maryland during the 1950s.

FMSF founder Ralph Underwager, director of the Institute of Psychological Therapies in Minnesota and the publisher of a magazine titled *Issues in Child Abuse Allegations*, is another member of the group who may have an axe to grind. It is reported that Underwager said in an interview in an Amsterdam journal that it was "God's Will" that adults have sex with children. Underwager later filed an affidavit in France for members of the Children of God cult, whose tenets at least at one time promoted sex with children. Underwager testified that they were not guilty of child abuse.[3]

The story of Peter and Pamela Freyd, who are executive directors of the Foundation, may also be significant. The Freyds have been accused of sexual abuse by their daughter Jennifer, who is a professor of psychology at the University of Oregon. Pamela Freyd called in her own psychiatrist, Dr. Harold Lief, an original board member of the FMSF. His determination was that Jennifer had not been abused. Lief himself was a major in the Army medical corps, was on the University of Pennsylvania faculty during the time that the university was conducting federal-funded experiments in behavior modification, and assisted Dr. Orne in studies on hypnotic programming.[4]

Another strategy for discrediting victims of mind control abuse and therapists who are investigating this subject are criminal charges. In 1998 the federal government initiated criminal charges against Texas psychologist Dr. Judith Peterson, charging that she had intentionally implanted false memories into her clients in order to extend their period of therapy. Dr. Peterson was also charged with mail fraud for mailing those clients bills through the mail. At the time of this writing, the government had only interviewed disgruntled patients and their attorneys, neglecting to interview Dr. Peterson or clients whose experience with her has been positive. Earlier, the same alleged victims of fraud complained to the Texas Department of Mental Health and Mental Retardation, and the Texas Department of Health. After investigations by those bodies, Dr. Peterson was found to be innocent of the charges.[5]

Notes:
1. Constantine, Alex, "The False Memory Hoax: CIA Connections to Mind Control Cults," *Paranoia*, Winter 95/96
2. Constantine; Ross, M.D., Dr. Colin, "The CIA and Military Mind Control Research: Building the Manchurian Candidate," lecture given at Ninth Annual Western Clinical Conference on Trauma and Dissociation, April 18, 1996
3. Constantine
4. Constantine; Blood, Linda. *The New Satanists*. New York: Warner Books, 1994
5. Morris, Wayne, preface to an interview with Professor Alan Scheflin on CKLN-FM radio, Toronto, Canada, June 22, 1998

Chapter 22

Electronic Mind Control

A giant leap forward in the technical capability for mind control came with the discovery that electromagnetic energy could be used to influence, disable, or kill humans at a distance. The famous scientist Nikola Tesla was one of the first persons to delve into the effects of electromagnetics on the human organism, with E.L. Chaffee and R.U. Light following in 1934 with the monograph "A Method For the Remote Control of Electrical Stimulation of the Nervous System."

In the same year Soviet scientist Leonid L. Vasiliev wrote "Critical Evaluation of the Hypogenic Method" about the discoveries of Dr. I.F. Tomashevsky and his research into remote influencing of the brain through radio waves. Vasiliev wrote: "As a control of the subject's condition when she was outside the laboratory in another set of experiments, a radio set-up was used... Not many experiments of this sort were carried out, but the results obtained indicate that the method of using radio signals substantially enhances the experimental possibilities."

Later in the paper Vasiliev wrote: "Tomashevsky [I.F. Tomashevsky, famed Russian physiologist] carried out the first experiment with this subject at a distance of one or two rooms and under conditions where the participant would not know or suspect that she would be experimented with. In other cases, the sender was not in the same house and someone else observed the subject's behavior. Subsequent experiments at considerable distances were successful...one such experiment was carried out in a part at a distance... Mental suggestion to go to sleep was complied with within a minute."[1]

Another researcher into the potential of electromagnetics in the 1930s was Professor E. Cazzamalli. Cazzamalli bombarded subjects with VHF radio waves and "told an astounded world that his subjects would hallucinate when under the influence of his *"oscillatori telegrafica."*[2]

Andrija Puharich was another early researcher into the effects of electromagnetics who delved into the effects of radio waves on animals, working at Northwestern University in the late 1940s. Puharich founded a laboratory he called the Round Table Foundation of Electrobiology in what he modestly termed "a barn in the woods" outside of Camden, Maine, in 1948. It was hardly a barn, sized one hundred by fifty feet, with a basement and upper story. It had been used by the Navy, reportedly for storage, during World War II.

Among Puharich's associates at the Round Table were Warren S. McCulloch, one of the founders of cybernetics theory, who had worked at Bellevue Hospital in New York. McCulloch was an early advocate of electronic brain implants, and chaired conferences sponsored by the Josiah Macy, Jr. Foundation, a channel for CIA mind control funding. Another associate of Puharich's was John Hays Hammond, said to have been Nikola Tesla's only student. Hays was also interested in the use of electromagnetics to influence the human mind.

After the demise of Puharich's Round Table he spent time with social engineer Aldous Huxley in Tecate, Mexico, again studying the effects of electronics on the human organism. Puharich was also employed at the Army's Chemical and Biological Warfare Center at Fort Detrick, Maryland, researching the effects of LSD for the CIA in 1954. He delved into the effects of digatoid drugs at the Permanente Research Foundation, with funding from the Sandoz Chemical Works.[3]

Among Puharich's accomplishments was the design of what is described as a radio tooth implant, the technical specs of which were sold to the CIA. At a conference on electromagnetism in September of 1987, Puharich described this invention: "We were able to develop a hearing device that fit under the cap of a tooth and we could hear very clearly from a small little relay and receiver and transmitter and unfortunately it was promptly classified by an agency of our government. But we did solve the problem in terms of hardware."

The radio tooth implant may still be in use. According to the *Chemical and Engineering News* for February 5, 1996, in a story titled "Hong Kong professor sues U.S. for mind control":[4]

"The *South China Morning Post* reported on January 25 that an assistant professor at the University of Science & Technology, Hong Kong, has filed a $100 million suit against the U.S. government for implanting mind-control devices in his teeth. Huang Si-ming charges that the devices were implanted during root canal work in 1991 while he was studying at the University of Iowa, according to *Morning Post* reported Patricia Young. Another student at Iowa University, who like Huang, was born in China, had gone on a shooting spree, and the Feds, Huang says, put the devices in his teeth to find out if he was involved.

"The Hong Kong professor says he suffered an Alzheimer's disease-like memory loss that hampered his teaching. It stopped, he says, only when he sought legal aid to mount his lawsuit. Besides the U.S., the suit names the University of Science & Technology on the grounds that it was involved in continuing the mind-control work. It also seeks punitive damages of $1 million from the defendants for 'low ethical standards.'

"Huang claims that one of the devices in his teeth can read his thoughts and talk to his mind when he's asleep. A second device, he believes, transmits pictures of what he sees to a receiver for recording. The mind controller, he says, can drive him to 'bad' behavior. He gives two examples, one of which cannot be mentioned in a family magazine."

Huang is not alone in his complaints about having mind control devices implanted in his teeth. David B. recounts his story:

"X-rays revealed a metal object on the left side of my skull under the jaw in the soft tissue of my neck. In May 1996, I finally had it removed, I asked many doctors about the possibility of it falling there during an extraction—they

said, 'possible, but remote.' Most of them thought it punc-
tured my neck from the outside. I sent X-rays to Dr. Sims,
and he arranged removal. The strange thing that came out of
this was the discovery of the small object in my shoulder.
Dr. Leer called after receiving my X-rays and asked if I had
ever broken my shoulder, if I had ever been in an explosion.
I replied no. He said the reason was that the X-ray clearly
showed a screw in my left shoulder. He said it looked like an
operation for a broken shoulder. I have never broken a bone
to my knowledge, and called my mother to ask. She said I'd
had no operations as a child. This part is a complete mystery.

"During the first six months of torture (extreme at that
time), I went to a dentist and reported pain under my new
dental bridge, installed a few months before the assault. He
removed it and I was still in contact. So I wrote off my teeth
and concentrated on my throat, wrongly. In my X-rays and
CAT scan, one tooth is very bright and in one frame of the
CAT scan it shows rays of white emanating from it. People I
asked said it was probably an interference effect with the
metal."[5]

An insight into the state of early Soviet research into
electromagnetics is provided by an account of a meeting held
on May 22, 1963, in the office of Professor Zinoviev at the
Ministry of Higher and Secondary Specialized Education in
the Soviet Union. In a meeting of sixteen scientists, a Professor Artemov mentioned what he called a "mental work machine." Artemov said that in the near future an electromagnetic broadcasting unit the size of a transistor radio would be
used to stimulate creativity and mental energy. Artemov said
that the first models of the machine that had been constructed
were desk-top size, but that now the units were portable and
were in use.[6]

The Soviets also worked on less benign applications of
electromagnetics. About 1960, as microwave scientist Milton
Zaret recalls it, he was approached by the CIA. Zaret had
worked on an Air Force project evaluating potential eye damage to radar and microwave technicians, but the CIA was
interested in more arcane matters. They asked about the effect of microwaves on human behavior, and the possibility of

using microwaves for brainwashing. Later, in 1965, they finally disclosed to Zaret why they were interested: the U.S. Embassy in Moscow was being bombarded with microwaves by the Soviets—with radiation that they dubbed the "Moscow Signal."

Zaret was briefed on Project Pandora, a government program in progress that was aimed at finding out why the Soviets were irradiating the embassy, and perhaps turning that research to the CIA's own purposes. In one Project Pandora experiment chimpanzees were irradiated with microwave bursts. The head of the program determined that "the potential for exerting a degree of control on human behavior by low level microwave radiation seems to exist and he urged that the effects of microwaves be studied for possible weapons applications."

Zaret conducted his own tests and determined that "Whatever other reasons the Russians may have had, they believed the beam would modify the behavior of the personnel."[7]

Zaret's recommendations were simple. The American government should demand that the Soviets stop irradiating its employees. Persons stationed at the embassy should also be briefed on what was going on, which they had not been, and be given the option of transferring to other areas of the world. Zaret was assured that his suggestions would be followed, but they were in only one particular. President Lyndon B. Johnson issued a demand to the Soviets that the irradiation end. They ignored him.

Embassy personnel were never told that they were being subjected to electromagnetic irradiation, nor that tests showed many of them were afflicted with terrible medical problems. Ambassador Walter J. Stoessel had problems with bleeding from the eyes, and was diagnosed with a blood disease similar to leukemia. The two previous ambassadors had both died of cancer. State Department tests also found what they described as a "slightly higher" white blood cell count in one-third of the employees tested, but in fact their lymphocyte count was forty percent higher than normal. Several children of embassy employees were found to have blood disorders.

They would only learn of the source of their illnesses in 1972, when newspaper columnist Jack Anderson would blow the whistle on the "Moscow Signal" in his newspaper column. A possible by-product of Project Pandora is that in 1961 Dr. Alan Frey reported that microwaves are sometimes audible to humans, although the discovery was dismissed by many scientists as being a case of outside noise. Frey's experiment was later described in detail by James C. Lin, in his *Microwave Auditory Effects and Applications*:[8]

"Frey...found that human subjects exposed to 1310 MHz and 2982 MHz microwaves at average power densities of 0.4 to 2 mW/cm2 perceived auditory sensations described as buzzing or knocking sounds... The peak power densities were on the order of 200 to 300 mW/cm2 and the pulse repetition frequencies varied from 200 to 400 Hz... Frey referred to this auditory phenomenon as the RF (radio frequency) sound. The sensation occurred instantaneously at average incident power densities well below that necessary for known biological damage and appeared to originate from within or near the back of the head."[10]

There were important ramifications to Frey's discovery. In his paper, "Human Auditory System Response to Modulated Electromagnetic Energy," Frey explained "...how voices can be beamed directly into an individual's head." Among other areas of research, Frey also delved into the induction of heart seizures by beamed electromagnetics.[11]

Other Pandora personnel included Operation Paperclip Nazis like Dr. Deitrich Beischer, who irradiated 7,000 Navy crewmen with dangerous levels of radiation at the Naval Aerospace Research Laboratory in Pensacola, Florida. Beischer simply disappeared in 1977, with records of his employment—and his existence—expunged.

Spanish researchers maintain that brain implant specialist Dr. Jose Delgado was also involved in Pandora.[9]

In 1972 the Department of the Army released a report titled "Controlled Offensive Behavior—U.S.S.R.," documenting five hundred Russian studies of the use of "Super-high frequency electromagnetic oscillations." "SHF may be used as a technique for altering human behavior," the report stated.

"Lethal and non-lethal effects have been shown to exist. In certain non-lethal exposures, definite behavioral changes have occurred."[12]

In the same year the U.S. Army Mobility Equipment Research and Development Center released a study titled "Analysis of Microwaves for Barrier Warfare." The report discussed the use of truck-portable microwave broadcasting systems that would be used to irradiate and immobilize people, and suggested that with the current state of armament there was no way of protecting against the use of such a system.[13]

At about the same, electronics engineer Tom Jaski was conducting experimentation using a low-power oscillator broadcasting at 300-600 MHz to irradiate subjects. In repeated trials, subjects were able to detect the electromagnetic sweeps and, "at these 'individual' frequencies, the same subjects announced having experienced pulsing sensations in the brain, ringing in the ears and an odd desire to bite the experimenters."[14]

As research in mind control progressed, the potential of directly and precisely influencing the human brain with microwaves became apparent. Technologies whereby emotions, messages and subliminal commands could be beamed directly to the brain of unwitting subjects were researched by both the American and Soviet governments. Among many other projects, the Department of Defense funded work of J.F. Schapitz, who in 1974 proposed the use of radio broadcasting in conjunction with hypnotic control:

"In this investigation," Schapitz wrote, "it will be shown that the spoken word of the hypnotist may be conveyed by modulate electromagnetic energy directly into the subconscious parts of the human brain—i.e., without employing any technical devices for receiving or transcoding the messages and without the person exposed to such influence having a chance to control the information input consciously...

"The second experiment was to be the implanting of hypnotic suggestions for simple acts, like leaving the lab to buy some particular item, which were to be triggered by a suggested time, spoken word, or sight. Subjects were to be interviewed later. It may be expected that they rationalize their behavior and consider it to be undertaken out of their own free will."

The results of Schapitz' experimentation have never been released to the public.[15]

In 1978 Dr. Andrew Michrowski wrote that, "Potentially, almost anything could be inserted into the target brain mind systems, and such insertions would be processed by the biosystems as internally-generated data/effects. Words, phrases, images, sensations, and emotions could be directly inserted and experienced in the biological targets as internal states, codes, emotions, thoughts and ideas."[16]

On April 20, 1976, an "Apparatus and Method for Remotely Monitoring and Altering Brain Waves" was patented. Its inventor was Robert G. Malech, of New York. According to the patent abstract, it is an "Apparatus for and method of sensing brain waves at a position remote from a subject whereby electromagnetic signals of different frequencies are simultaneously transmitted to the brain of the subject." Although somewhat technical in its jargon, the "Summary of the Invention" in the patent bears wading through for the interested researcher:

"The present invention relates to apparatus and a method for monitoring brain waves wherein all components of the apparatus employed are remote from the test subject. More specifically, high frequency transmitters are operated to radiate electromagnetic energy of different frequencies through antennas which are capable of scanning the entire brain of the test subject or any desired region thereof. The signals of different frequencies penetrate the skull of the subject and impinge upon the brain where they mix to yield an interference wave modulated by radiation from the brain's natural electrical activity. The modulated interference wave is retransmitted by the brain and received by an antenna at a remote station where it is demodulated, and processed to provide a profile of the subject's brain waves. In addition to passively monitoring his brain waves, the subject's neurological processes may be affected by transmitting to his brain, through a transmitter compensating signals. The latter signals can be derived from the received and processed brain waves."[17]

In the years 1980 to 1983 the Marine Corps sponsored research into electromagnetic weaponry, with the project run by Eldon Byrd, a specialist in medical bioengineering. The lion's share of the research was conducted at the Armed Forces Radiobiology Research Institute in Bethesda, Maryland, with research done on small animals and even Byrd himself. Byrd's focus was an attempt to see if electromagnetic waves could be used to influence or entrain the brain activity of living organisms.

Using electromagnetic broadcasting, Byrd says, "We could put animals into a stupor by hitting them with these frequencies. We got chick brains—in vitro—to dump 80 percent of the natural opioids in their brains. The effects were nonlethal and reversible. You could disable a person temporarily,' Byrd suggests that, "It [would have been] like a stun gun."

Byrd's program was scheduled for four years, but was closed down after two. Byrd believes that it wasn't because the research was unsuccessful: "The work was really outstanding. We would have had a weapon in one year."

Byrd believes that the work was not discontinued, but was instead simply taken out of his hands and turned into a black project. That statement is hardly outlandish, and numerous other researcher in electromagnetics tell a similar tale of having their work taken away from them at the precise point when they began to get successful results.

As conservative a publication as the International Review of the Red Cross in 1990 acknowledged the ascendancy of "beam weapons" in the field of warfare. The authors of an article titled "The Development of New Antipersonnel Weapons" stated:

"The effects induced in human beings by electromagnetic waves have been known, albeit imperfectly, for a long time and have been the subject of continuous research. Depending on the frequency used, the emission mode, the energy radiated, and the shape and duration of the pulses used, electromagnetic radiation directed against the human body may produce heat and cause serious burns or even changes in the molecular structure of the tissues they reach.

"Research work in this field has been carried out in almost all industrialized countries, and especially by the great powers, with a view to using these phenomena for anti-materiel or anti-personnel purposes. Tests have demonstrated that powerful microwave pulses could be used as a weapon in order to put the adversary *hors de combat* or even kill him. It is possible today to generate a very powerful microwave pulse (e.g. between 150 and 3,000 megahertz), with an energy level of several hundreds of megawatts. Using specially adapted antenna systems, these generators could in principle transmit over hundreds of meters sufficient energy to cook a meal. However, it is important to mention that the lethal or incapacitating effects which can be expected from weapon systems using this technology can be produced with much lower energy levels. Using the principle of magnetic field concentration, which permits the control of the geometry on the target, by means of antenna systems especially designed for the purpose, the radiated energy can be concentrated on very small surfaces of the human body, for example the base of the brain where relatively low energy can produce lethal effects."

In 1991, the ITV News Bureau reported on the first known use of electronic subliminals on the battlefield and the "true reason for the seemingly illogical and apparently suicidal attack by Iraqi troops on the deserted city of Al-Khafji…12 miles south of Kuwaiti border…" According to ITV the Iraqis had launched a successful attack meant to destroy an FM radio station that had been installed in Al-Khafji by the U.S. Defense Department's PsyOps branch. Although the station outwardly appeared to be broadcasting "Tokyo Rose" style propaganda, deserting Iraqi soldiers claimed that the real purpose of the station was to broadcast "the new, high tech, type of subliminal messages referred to as ultra-high-frequency 'silent sounds' or 'silent subliminals.'"

According to ITV, "Although completely silent to the human ear, the negative voice messages placed on the tapes alongside the audible programming by psyops psychologists were clearly perceived by the subconscious minds of the Iraqi soldiers and the silent messages completely demoralized them and instilled a perpetual feeling of fear and hopelessness in their minds."[18]

In 1993 a "Method of Inducing Mental, Emotional and Physical States of Consciousness, Including Specific Mental Activity, in Human Beings" was patented by its inventor, Robert A. Monroe. The now-deceased Monroe was an early practitioner of what is termed "remote viewing," or out of body travel, and is the founder of the Monroe Institute in Charlottesville, Virginia. He is reported to have had close connections to the CIA.[19]

The abstract of Monroe's patent says that specific states of consciousness can be induced "through generation of stereo audio signals having specific wave shapes" and that "In accordance with the invention, human brain waves, in the form of EEGs, are superimposed upon specific stereo audio signals, known as carrier frequencies which are within the range of human hearing."

Monroe followed up his initial invention with a "Method of and Apparatus for Inducing Desired States of Consciousness," apparently a new and improved form of his first offering.[20]

The U.S. Air Force Review of Biotechnology in 1982 warned that: "Radiofrequency radiation (RFR) fields may pose powerful and revolutionary anti-personnel military threats...RFR experiments and the increasing understanding of the brain as an electrically-mediated organ suggests the serious probability that impressed electromagnetic fields can be disruptive to purposeful behavior and may be capable of directing and or interrogating such behaviour. Further, the passage of approximately 100 milliamperes through the myocardium [of the brain] can lead to cardiac standstill and death, again pointing to speed-of-light weapons effect. A rapidly scanning RFR system could provide an effective stun or kill capability over a large area."

The article continued:

"There is little doubt that crowd control devices using Radio Frequency Radiation do exist. The development of such devices would complement sonic and infra-red weapons, which are well known, and were advertised in the British Defense Equipment Catalogue until 1983. These included the Valkyrie, an infra-red device causing night blindness and the Squawk Box or Sound Curdler, developed by the U.S. for use in Vietnam. The Squawk Box was designed to induce feelings of giddiness and nausea in the victim, and is highly directional, so that as individuals are hit by the invisible effect, distress and confusion is spread amongst a crowd... In 1984 the Ministry of Defense ordered that all advertisements and references to 'frequency weapons,' but cut from the Defense Catalogue."[21]

By 1993 the National Institute of Justice, an office of the Justice Department, was recommending in its "NIJ Inititative on Less-Than-Lethal Weapons," that state and local police departments in America utilize psychotronic, electromagnetic and other mind control weapons against American citizens involved in "domestic disturbances"—a description so broad as to include family arguments. The report said, "Short-term research will be completed to adopt military technologies to use by domestic law enforcement...including laser, microwave, and electromagnetic" weapons. The *Washington Post* reported: "The Pentagon and the Justice Department have agreed to share state-of-the-art military technology with civilian law enforcement agencies, including exotic 'non-lethal' weapons."

This new approach to law enforcement was showcased in a three-day secret conference on non-lethal weaponry at the Applied Physics Laboratory at Johns Hopkins University in Maryland. The conference head was Col. John B. Alexander, Program Manager for Non-Lethal (psychotronic) Defense, Los Alamos National Laboratory. Attending the meeting was Attorney General Janet Reno, military weapons specialists, and representatives from state and local police departments. A wide variety of subjects were covered at the conference, including "radio frequency weapons, high powered microwave technology, acoustic technology, voice synthesis, and application of extreme frequency electromagnetic fields to non-lethal weapons."

The U.S. Air Force has installed high-power microwave generators on air-launched cruise missiles. The stated purpose for the beam generators is to wage computer warfare, frying delicate computer components, but these generators would also theoretically be able to fry the delicate mental components of human beings.[22]

Has electromagnetic weaponry ever moved beyond the experimental stage and been used on citizens? Has it ever been utilized in experiments upon an unsuspecting population, the way that drugs and other forms of behavior modification were used in MKULTRA? Literally thousands of persons worldwide believe that they have. They claim that electronic assault weapons have been used on them, either for experimentation, or possibly for harassment. The sheer number of these accounts, the parallels to what has been verified in terms of government testing, and the credibility of many of the persons making these claims strongly suggest covert use of these weapons on civilians.

One man who believes that he has been irradiated with electronic beam weapons is Martin C. Mack. In an open letter Mr. Mack describes his experience:

"I'm a former truck driver, now retired. My troubles with what I am about to recount began in the fall of 1987 when I rented a room in Seattle, Washington. The renter...next to me had visitors who tried to avoid being seen by me. Comments were made about me describing my actions, as if coming from his room. Somehow, they were able to make me hear and also pick up on the process of my hearing—hear what I heard. As if my head, strange as this sounds, was a sort of antenna, and I picked things up—not subliminally but audibly.

"They knew when I was coming and going and commented on such. While I was at the hotel; talk was heard about what I was doing. They could account for much of what I did in my room and in that building. They must have some way of watching me, I thought.

"Statements to throw me off as to what they were doing were heard, such as: 'This stinger will reach 35 feet' and 'There is a two-way mirror in the lobby.' 'Let us test him' was heard.

"This was before I moved out, and afterward: 'He has a microphone in his throat.' I do not have a material one there, of course. It was implied that they could pick up on what I voiced. All this seemed like an impossibility. Due to what has transpired over the years, I know these things as fact— regardless of what others might think.

"One night my spine was made very warm. That region is thermal sensitive and part of the central nervous system. The reflex arc which passes through the spine was triggered and gave my body a jerk.

"They could heat sting my back shoulder blades. The bone coverings of those are pain sensitive. They decided to drive me out of there and did before the month was up.

"There is a way that a person can be made selectively receptive to a modulated radio frequency carrier and that was resolved while I was there. Before leaving, I inquired as to how long the two previous tenants stayed in that room. 'A month or two,' the manager said. I was not hurt so very badly after they drove me out.

"Concerning the behavior and mind control: There is not much of a point in stimulating a person unless you can get a visual or audible response from the subject. They do get an audible one from me, a curse for one thing.

"How I think it is done: An unmodulated radio frequency carrier is sent out from one location—preferably lower in frequency. It passes into the spine and head regions of the subject. The carrier is modulated by the electromagnetic nature of the hearing process—speech and inner speech of the victim. The fields of the processes piggy back onto the carrier. It thought that the unwanted fields are filtered out on arrival at the point of reception. If what is received by the offenders displeased them—then a hurtful stimuli is sent out on a carrier to cause pain to the subject—hence behavior and mind control. There is much more to it than that.

"All sorts of responses can be brought about in the body and head—by modulation of a radio frequency carrier with various frequencies of sound and energy—hearing and cranial pain, ear pain, and others—yes, heart pain, torture and death. They are able to resolve motion or the absence thereof. A very loud snap sound can be caused at the rear of the head. The sound modulation can be spiked and cause hurtful jolts of pain. Eye stinging and eye pains have been caused. The heat pain sting torture is believed to be caused by vibrating the molecules in nerve endings of the thermal receptors. While in the process of thinking about what they are doing or reading, some people use inner speech or subvocalization. The trachea, i.e. wind pipe is piezoelectric and should act as a transducer.

"Subvocalization has been recorded directly off the throat by researchers. The indications have long been good, that they can take off the electromagnetic field associated with inner speech. They have commented on that of which I inwardly voiced—many times. The shoulder muscles can be made stiff and sore—those of the neck also. The heart muscle can be made sore. I am monitored round the clock. Sleep deprivation is caused each night. The offenders needed a scapegoat to field test their equipment on and with me they got lots of practice..."[23]

Regina Cullen, a resident of the UK, also reports that she has been the victim of electronic assault. She feels that she was targeted for such harassment because of a complaint that she made against local police in 1984. After numerous examples of more overt forms of harassment, including having her bicycle tires slashed, her car broken into, and being physically assaulted twice, she says, "A new element of harassment appeared: my home was rendered uninhabitable by 'frequency assault.' What I now know to be microwaves and/or infrasound were used to turn the room into a torture chamber."

Cullen reports that she was harassed with an "irregularly pulsed 'humming' sound, impossible to tell which direction it came from, seeming louder when one was lying down... It reverberated most in the area just behind the ear, the mastoid bone area which is filled with air pockets, and caused my eyes to ache and my forehead to feel fuzzy and interfered with."

The woman was forced to change residences repeatedly during the ensuing years. She says, "Sometime, in outrage at being forced out of my home, I would return in the middle of the night to find complete peace and quiet, but ten or twenty minutes later the frequency assault would begin again."

At one location, she says, "I believe the source of the assault was the flat above, unless microtechnology is hidden in one's own flat, for this took place on the 11th floor. There were no houses of comparable height nearby, and the flat above was inhabited by the building's caretaker... On the day this happened there had been a man pretending to be asleep in a red car parked half onto the sidewalk in front of the building's entrance. I was instantly afraid of him, but warned myself not to be paranoid. Two weeks later, as I was running suddenly for a bus and looking over my shoulder, I caught him ducking behind a van to avoid being seen following me."

Cullen says that, "Earlier, back at the bedsit [a single occupancy room], intuition had given me another clue to look out of my spyhole just as the hooligan was being handed a strange box with orange hemispherical plastic knobs on each corner by a trench-coated detective type, who did not speak and took care not to creak the hallway doors... [Not] long after that I saw him carrying in full view a small Christmas tree-shaped aerial, and he seemed upset that I had seen it."

On one occasion, as Cullen sat in her garden, "Something shot through my head with a strange 'fzzzzzzzzsssst' sound as it happened, seeming to come from behind the fence. I was terrified and could no longer sleep there anymore. A year or so later, sitting in front of the window with the curtains open, the same thing happened again and the TV instantly turned to snow. The alignment that time of the invisible beam was such that it came from above and on the other side of the garden, from the very area where in '86 had appeared a momentary pencil-like beam of white light which was aimed at my bathroom window."

Cullen describes two types of electronic assault:

"Symptoms of Type 1 include a bizarre feeling that the right and left halves of the brain are separating, with a cap in between, as if parts of the head and face are rearranged spatially, as in a Cubist painting. There is an impression of slight puffiness in the face, a flattening of the nose, and 'definement' of features." Type 2 symptoms include the feeling that "I could hardly breath and felt like I was in an oven. Each breath is like trying to inhale searing desert air, along with the usual headache and severe lassitude, sore tired eyes, fatigue, hot burning skin, old scars throbbing, and an overwhelming sense of oppression, evil and helplessness."[24]

Further substantiating these claims of electronic assault are the reports of believed victims of mind control harassment who have observed suspect equipment in areas adjacent to where they live. A number of reports of this kind have been compiled by the Association of National Security Alumni in their Electronic Surveillance Project, intending to document and expose mind control abuses in the United States.

One individual documented by the Electronic Surveillance Project talked to her next door neighbor who claimed that he was a military intelligence officer employed by a space technology firm, and that he was on a year-long temporary duty in the individual's apartment building. It was later determined that the individual was not employed in the military. When the pretended military intelligence officer moved out of the apartment building, the contact went into his apartment and found a microwave oven size device, and that an "excavation" had been made in the wall facing her apartment.

Another believed victim of mind control harassment looked through the window of her neighbor's apartment to see a one by five foot gray box. A black-framed lens projected from the box, facing in the direction of her apartment. According to the witness, the box was being operated in some fashion by a man in a three-piece suit, who was startled when he realized that he was being observed.[25]

Notes:
1. Wall, Judy, "Synthetic Telepathy," *Paranoid Women Collect Their Thoughts*, Joan D'Arc, ed. Providence, Rhode Island: Paranoia Publishing, 1996; Vasiliev, Leonid L., cited in Lawrence, Lincoln, and Thomas, Kenn. *Mind Control, Oswald & JFK: Were We Controlled?* Kempton, Illinois: Adventures Unlimited Press, 1997
2. Cannon, Martin, "Mind Control and the American Government," *Prevailing Winds*, 1994
3. Milner, Terry, "Ratting out Puharich," at *Doc Hambone*, www.io.com/%7Ehambone
4. Welsh, Cheryl. *Mind Control is No Longer Science Fiction*, Volume 2. Davis, California: Citizens Against Human Rights Abuses, 1997
5. Constantine, Alex. *Virtual Government*. Venice, California: Feral House, 1997
6. Lawrence
7. Cited in Constantine, Alex. *Psychic Dictatorship in the U.S.A.* Portland, Oregon: Feral House, 1995
8. Kaufer, Scott, "The Air Pollution You Can't See," *New Times,* March 6, 1976
9. Wall; Constantine, Alex. *Psychic Dictatorship in the U.S.A.*; Correspondence by the NosMan group
10. Lin, James C. *Microwave Auditory Effects and Applications.* Springfield, Illinois: Charles C. Thomas, 1978
11. Cannon; Lin; Wall
12. Constantine, Alex. *Virtual Government*
13. Wall
14. Cannon
15. Robert O. Becker. *The Body Electric.* New York: William Morrow, 1985; Welsh
16. Welsh
17. U.S. Patent 3,951,134, "Apparatus and Method for Remotely Monitoring and Altering Brain Waves," April 20, 1976
18. "High Tech Psychological Warfare Arrives in the Middle East," ITV News Bureau, Ltd. 1991
19. Porter, Tom, "Government Research into ESP & Mind Control," *MindNet Journal*, Vol. 1, No. 46, www.visitations.com/mindnet/MN16A.HTM
20. U.S. Patent 5,356,368, "Method of and Apparatus for Inducing Desired States of Consciousness," October 18, 1994; U.S. Patent number 5,213,562, "A Method of Inducing Mental, Emotional and Physical States of Consciousness, Including Specific Mental Activity, in Human Beings," May 25, 1993
21. Kennard, Peter, "Field of Nightmares," *The Weekend Guardian*, February 2-3, 1991
22. Baker, C.B., "New World Order & ELF Psychotronic Tyranny," *Youth Action Newsletter*, Dec. 1994; *Microwave News*, March/April 1998; *Aviation Week*, January 19, 1998
23. "Re: Assault by Remote Technology methods," statement by Martin C. Mack, undated

24. Cullen, Regina, "The Traveling Torture Chamber: Microwave Harassment, Gangsterism and Freemasonry." *Paranoid Women Collect Their Thoughts*. Joan D'Arc, Ed. Providence, Rhode Island: Paranoia Publishing, 1996
25. Microwave Harassment and Mind-Control Experimentation, published by the Association of National Security Alumni, Electronic Surveillance Project

CHAPTER 23

MIND PRISON

From the earliest days of such research, a ready source of human fodder for experimentation has been found in prisons. This has not exactly been kept secret. In 1962, James V. Bennett, at the time the director of the U.S. Bureau of Prisons, encouraged psychiatrists and social scientists to use the "tremendous opportunity" that 24,000 incarcerated and helpless prison inmates offered for experimentation. He said, "We here in Washington are anxious to have you undertake some of these things...perhaps on your own—undertake a little experiment on what you can do with the Muslims, what you can do with...sociopath individuals."[1]

In 1971 the Director of Corrections for California proposed the broad implementation of neurosurgery for violent inmates of prisons. That does not mean that this sort of surgery had not been done earlier. As an example, in 1968 three inmates at Vacaville Medical Facility had a portion of their brains' amygdalas mutilated, reportedly in an attempt to quell their violent urges.[2]

In 1974 a prisoner at the Arizona State Prison wrote in the *New York Times* about a program of electroshock at the prison that was aimed at discouraging the activities of "jailhouse lawyers" and political radicals. The term the prisoners used for the program, he said, was "Edison's medicine."[3]

In October, 1988, David Fratus, a 38-year-old prisoner at the Utah State Prison serving a one-to-fifteen year sentence for second degree burglary penned an open letter describing his experiences, protesting that he was being subjected to mind control torture. He indicated that eleven months prior he had had an altercation with another prisoner that, he believed, was the reason that a program of systematic mind control torture had been instituted against him.

Fratus' account is detailed and believable. According to his letter, "Day after day they tampered with my food, smashing and removing items from my tray, and threatened to poison me with carcinogens and diseases. My mail received similar treatment. I was constantly verbally badgered as well as physically assaulted, and was told my parents would be murdered should I fail to maintain silence."

Fratus believes that these harassment's were used to drive him over the edge into losing his temper, thus providing justification for placing him in solitary confinement and for more intense harassment.

"Once isolated," Fratus relates, "some extremely peculiar things began to occur. I became disoriented to the extent that my cell and surrounding area would take on a surrealistic appearance as though I were under the influence of a hallucinogenic drug, and I was plagued by severe headaches and insomnia for weeks at a time... I began to receive, or hear, high frequency tones in my ears. Like the test pattern on a TV set. The volume or intensity of these frequencies is adjustable and some are so high and piercing that they've literally had me climbing the walls. When I plug my ears with cotton or fingertips, the tones are still inside and become amplified. It's as if they had become electrified echo chambers with the sounds coming from the inside out."

When Fratus complained, he says that he was thrown into a "strip cell" without clothes, mattress, toilet paper, or drinking water.

After five months of harassment, Fratus says that the torture escalated to the point that he admits that what happened would sound crazy to anyone not familiar with current capabilities of mind control technology. "I began to hear voices in my ears," Fratus reports. "Voices that change pitch and timbre in contrast from being a cartoonish high and squeaky, descending through the octaves, including everything from sinister Darth Vaderish to basically normal characteristics. The reception of these voices into my inner ears is as vivid as though I were listening to a set of stereo headphones, and they are able to mix, match, and blend them in conjunction with the frequency tones creating a raucous cacophony of audio discord that disheartens the soul."

Fratus believes that eventually advanced technology was brought to bear upon him, to the extent that a computer mind scanning machine was used on him capable of monitoring—"picking apart," he describes it—his thoughts as well as physical functions. Fratus said, "With the apparent ease of manipulating a keyboard they can, with the flick of the switch, strip me of all energy and motivation to where I'm forced to lie on my bunk and stare at the wall like a zombie. I've been left in this state for weeks at a time—literally chained to my bed without the actual use of physical restraints, having not the energy to walk back and forth in my cell even a few times."

Fratus describes a list of devastating effects used to debilitate his body and his psyche, and admits that it would be hard for people to believe that prison officials would torment their captives in this manner. Corroborating his tale, he says, is a conversation with a paralegal advisor who told him that he had received similar complaints from other prisoners at the facility, and when Fratus launched a legal suit against medical personnel at the facility, several inmates came forward to substantiate his claims, strikingly describing similar symptoms to those described by Fratus.

Forty-six year old Robert LaSalle, also an inmate at Utah State Prison, who had been housed in a cell adjacent to Fratus, described with complete coherence and in great detail his own torment at what he believed was an electronic mind control technology. In an affidavit dated 11 July, 1991, LaSalle stated:

"That for approximately five years now I have been subjected to some type of device or technology that causes me to receive voice transmissions into my inner ears just as if I have little radio speakers in my head...

"That the voices I am hearing respond to my thoughts and punish me with electrical current cooking sensations when I do not cooperate or respond the way they want me to...

"That I have experienced periods of torment where I felt as if my body were made of metal and a giant magnet was pulling me to the floor so that I could not hardly get up from bed and move around...

"That I often hear different tones of high and low frequency signals in my ears—like the test pattern on a T.V. set."

LaSalle describes a variety of other effects, including itching and vibrating in the inner ear, electronic tones changing from high to low, and electronic assault that is so intense that he is completely incapacitated. He speaks at length about voices in his head, primarily female, that are sometimes interrupted by male authority figure voices. These voices tell him that he will be punished until he becomes cooperative, and that he is being punished for his past crimes. One telling factor, LaSalle states, is that the voices sometimes use the names of prison or medical staff or inmates that he seldom comes in contact with, and thus would be unlikely to think about.

In another affidavit, Utah State Prison inmate Frank Moxley, also imprisoned in a cell adjacent to Fratus, stated that he has also "been subjected to the influence of some type of device or technology that causes me to receive voice transmissions into my head, just as if I had little radio speakers in my inner ears." Moxley also reported "That there are many inmates here in Utah Maximum Security having this mental communications system used on them, but that due to the methods employed in so doing, not many inmates are willing to speak of it."

Robert Varner, also at Utah State Prison, stated, in an affidavit dated 10 June, 1991, that he had also endured apparent electronic assault and was aware of at least six other inmates who had similarly complained of these activities. Varner said, "That the sounds I experience in my inner ears consist of frequency like ringing noises from which I can sometimes, but not always distinguish voices... That when the voices are distinguishable, I sometimes hear things concerning my past history" and that "these voices sometimes respond to my thoughts."

Varner also reports "high and low ringing sounds in my ears" and "pressure sensations in my ears."

Another inmate of Utah State Prison, James F. Gardner, testified about his own mind control harassment in an affidavit dated 10 June, 1991. Gardner describes a variety of symptoms corresponding to electronic bombardment, including "the effects of a device or technology that caused me to hear voices—in my inner ears—that gave me behavior instructions." Gardner experienced "torturous headaches and intense pressure chamber sensations in my inner ears, to the end that I was driven to explosively aggressive behavior... That the mental voice communication process I am describing definitely involved thought comprehension because the voices were able to respond to what I was thinking, and on one occasion the voices advised me that certain inmates— with whom I had had an altercation—would be waiting to jump me with weapons (on A-block): the voices told me exactly who the inmates were and where they would be hiding, and all information was correct—there is no way I could have hallucinated such a situation."

The experience of David Fratus and other inmates at Utah State Prison is hardly solitary. Many other inmates have attempted legal action against the prison system, complaining that they have been subjected to electronic torture, some of it corresponding strikingly to the testimony of the men at Utah State Prison. These legal actions have uniformly been struck down by the courts as being frivolous. And yet, given our knowledge of advances in electronic mind control by the CIA and other agencies, and the similarity of statements between these inmates, these complaints seem very credible. They strongly suggest that electronic mind control technology is currently being used at prisons throughout America.[4]

America is not the only country where mind control techniques and experimentation have been employed on prisoners. In August of 1971 an experiment began in England using torture and sensory deprivation on Irish political prisoners. Many prisoners suffered permanent psychological debilitation and some died during the course of the experimentation, while some attempted suicide in order to escape the torture.

After the protestations of a number of civil rights group, including Amnesty International, a number of prisoners who had endured the torture were released without charges.[5]

Further confirmation of the use of electronic torture device comes from *Electromagnetics News*, detailing information originally published in the *London Observer*, for Jan 13th, 1990. According to the article, "An electronic torture chamber, using a white noise generator designed to pulse sound at 11 Hz—apparently ultimately capable of destroying the human body—has been installed by a British company, Electronic Intelligence, inside the headquarters of the Special Branch of Dubai. Called 'The House of Fun,' the torture chamber also houses a strobe light, also set at 11 Hz and synchronized with the white noise generator, the combined effect of which is to reduce anyone inside the cell to a 'screaming, helpless suppliant within moments.'

"According to the *Observer*, the equipment was referred to as 'Prisoner Disorientation Equipment' within Electronic Intelligence, run by three former London policemen, while the bulk of the 1 million pound contract involved the installation of bugging equipment and concealed video cameras in the rooms and cells of the Special Branch HQ."[6]

Notes:
1. Mitford, Jessica. *Kind & Usual Punishment*
2. Packard, Vance. *The People Shapers*. New York: Bantam Books, 1977
3. DiSpoldo, Nick, "Arizona's Clockwork Orange Bill," *New York Times*, June 20, 1974
4. Russell-Manning, Elizabeth. *Mind Control in U.S. Prison System*. San Francisco: Self-published, 1996
5. Victorian, Armen, "United States, Canada, Britain: Partners in Mind Control Operations," *MindNet*, Vol. 1, No. 81, visitations.com/mindnet/MN16A.HTM
6. "Electronic torture chamber of Dubai's Special Branch," *Electromagnetics News*, undated clipping

CHAPTER 24

BEAM WARFARE

B y the mid-1970s full-scale electromagnetic warfare was in progress between the United States and the Soviet Union, although full details of that war would not leak out until years later. On October 30, 1976, the *New York Times* published a report revealing that a broadband shortwave radio signal was being broadcast from the Soviet Union that disrupted radio and other electronic communications worldwide. The radio signal, varying in frequency between about 3.26 and 17.54 megahertz, was initiated on July 4, 1976, the date of the U.S. bicentennial, and continued to be broadcast in the years to follow. The signal came from a high power transmitter located near Kiev in the Ukraine. Due to pulse modulation the radio signal produced a unique woodpecker-like chatter on radio receivers, hence its informal name, the "Russian Woodpecker."

According to electromagnetics expert Robert Beck,

"The signal is so strong it drowns out anything else on its wavelength. It first appeared on the UN International Telecommunications channels, including the emergency frequencies for aircraft on transoceanic flights. Now the woodpecker leaves 'holes'; it skips the crucial frequencies as it moves up and down the spectrum. The signal is maintained at enormous expense from a current total of seven nations, the seven most powerful radio transmitters in the world."

Since the first broadcasts of the Russian Woodpecker, at least thirty similar transmission centers have been set up by the Russians, sending signals in the same dangerous frequency range.

Shortly after the Russian Woodpecker began broadcasting, complaints were heard from numerous locations in the United States and Canada, but mostly centered in Oregon, of people experiencing headaches, anxiety, lack of body coordination, and other symptoms.[1]

Dr. Andrija Puharich, who had been researching electromagnetics at the fringes of spookdom since the early 1950s, commented on the Soviet signal in 1983:

"When the Soviets went on the air in July 4, 1976 with their 100 megawatt transmissions of extremely low frequency waves (ELF), the intelligence community of the U.S. was caught unaware of this new technology. The Soviet's ELF pulses covered the frequency range of the human brain. No one knew what the purpose of this new technology was. I had a hypothesis that this was a new mind control weapon that could entrain a human being's EEG. Bob Beck and I designed an experiment that conclusively proved that the Soviet Transmissions could indeed entrain the human brain, and thereby induce behavioral modification. I reported this finding to the intelligence community in the U.S. and my paper was promptly classified. A CIA commission of inquiry reported to President Carter that there was no substance to our findings. Today, five years later, all of our findings have been confirmed by various agencies of the U.S. government. However, they went one step beyond our findings, and proved that a certain ELF frequency (Classified) will cause cancer. I have repeated these experiments and found this to be true... A single ELF frequency can produce cancer."[2]

Elsewhere Puharich said:

"The U.S. Air Force identified five different frequencies in this compound harmonic the Russians were sending through the earth and the atmosphere. The intention was to affect a change of consciousness in mankind. The extremely low frequency waves will penetrate anything and everything, the specially shielded Faraday cage, the ocean. Nothing stops or weakens these signals."

Referring to himself in third person, he said,

"Dr. Puharich and Robert Beck designed receiving equipment which could measure these waves and their effect on the human brain. Their experiments proved that a signal of 6 Hertz easily penetrated the copper walls of a Faraday cage. So could a rate of 6.6—of the rates being used by the Russians. This caused depression.

"7.83 Hertz could make a person feel good. This is the so-called Schumann Resonance, the earth's pulse rate.

"10.80 Hertz could cause riotous behavior. As far as he could determine, the Soviets never sent out a signal in the 8 Hertz range that would be beneficial to people.

"When Dr. Puharich presented this information to certain U.S. military leaders they would not believe him! He then made up a secret report and had it hand delivered to President Carter, to the head of the French Intelligence Service, to Prime Minister Trudeau of Canada, and to certain dignitaries of other Western nations.

"Heavy action was then taken by our government to shut him up. His home in Ossining, New York, containing the results of much of his research work, was burned to the ground. He fled for his life to Mexico. From there he continued to monitor the Russian ELF wave signals and the higher harmonics in the Megahertz range (5.340 MHz).

"Through his Washington contacts a group meeting was arranged with the CIA. A showdown ensued, an agreement reached, since then no trouble with the CIA—except for the publication of his books! The government program is now called the ELF (for Extreme Low Frequency) and the Navy set up a research program on it, two years late!

"Puharich's secret report was expanded into a book, under contract to Dell publishing company, but publication has been blocked for the past four years; meanwhile the Russian attack goes on, unknown to the general public.

"Whole populations can be controlled by ELF waves. Intensive research on such 'behavior modification' is now being conducted by the United States government, to find out just what such waves do to people. This electromagnetic research is similar to the secret drug experiments conducted on the unsuspecting populace in the 1950s. Dr. Puharich did identify one ELF wave as a cancer-causing agent in mice....

"These waves cannot be jammed. The lower frequency Hertz waves are as long as 300,000 miles. The government has built huge transmitters in South Africa, Australia and other places to beam ELF waves back at Russia. There is no shield that will stop these signals."[3]

At a conference on Electromagnetism in September of 1987, Puharich said:

"...In 1981, the U.S. government went into full scale ELF warfare and set up all their big transmitters down under in Australia and Africa so on and now they're in business and everything's classified and you can't say a goddamned thing about it, a tough situation. And you can't get any real information out of any government agency. And I know all of them, that they do the work. I know the people who head the projects, etc. When they're in trouble, they usually come and ask me. And they classify what I tell them. Insanity."[4]

Although the United States government did not officially acknowledge that the country was under electromagnetic assault from a foreign power, they apparently did respond in kind, beyond what Puharich documented. Stefan Rednip, a journalist living in England, reported that he had gotten access to secret documents about an American electromagnetics program called Operation Pique, that involved firing electromagnetic signals off the ionosphere, to ricochet down on Eastern Europe, with a particular focus being Eastern European nuclear installations. [Beck]

What is apparently the most recent and largest escalation in the beam war is the construction of the HAARP project in the Alaskan wilderness.

HAARP is the world's largest electromagnetic broadcasting station, composed of 180 high frequency broadcast antennae, with power estimated at 72,000 times more than the next most powerful radio transmitter. The project is the creation of the U.S. Air Force Phillips Lab, the Naval Research Laboratory, and the Office of Naval Research. Although announced as a facility for ionospheric research, HAARP seems to have a number of other potential uses, including weather control and electromagnetic sweeps that can be used for mind control of large populations.

Of odd note, is the observation of a civilian who was monitoring the output of the HAARP transmissions at precisely the times that the recent mass murder in Littleton, Colorado took place. According to Kent Steadman, "A peak in HAARP transmission occurred between 10:40 PDT and 1:20 PDT. The shootings began between 11:00 and 11:30 PDT.[5]

Notes:
1. Welsh, Cheryl. *Mind Control is No Longer Science Fiction*, Volume 2. Davis, California: Citizens Against Human Rights Abuses, 1997; Beck, Robert. *The Body Electric*, 1985
2. Puharich, M.D., LLD, Andrija, "Successful Treatment of Neoplasms in Mice with Gaseous Suproxide Anion with a Rationale for Effect," Sixth Ozone World Congress of the International Ozone Association, May 22-26, 1983
3. Puharich, Dr. Andrija, "A Way to Peace Through ELF Waves," transcript of a talk delivered at the Understanding Convention of Astara, Upland, California, November 6, 1982. *The Journal of Borderland Research*, March-April 1983
4. Welsh
5. Smith, Jerry, "HAARP—The Beast in the Alaskan Wilderness," *Wake-Up Call America*, May/June 1999; Kent Steadman, at the *Orbit*, http://members.aol.com/phikent/orbit/orbit.html

CHAPTER 25

THE PERSINGER PLAN

D r. Michael Persinger, a psychologist and neuroscientist employed at Laurentian University in Ontario, Canada, lives at the cutting edge of research into the effects of electromagnetics on the mind. Persinger, on the Board of Advisors of the False Memory Syndrome Foundation, has been funded by the Navy and, reportedly, the National Security Agency, and "did research on the effects of electromagnetic radiation on the brain for a pentagon weapons project" according to researcher Daniel Brandt. Persinger says, "My research has not been 'funded by U.S. interests.' All of the money for our human research for the last 30 years has been from my personal income as a professor. The only funding ($10,000) we ever obtained from the U.S. was from the U.S. Navy."

Among Persinger's accomplishments is the ability to cause subjects to think that they have been abducted by aliens, or have had an encounter with angels or God through the use of a modified motorcycle helmet equipped with solenoids to send electromagnetic pulses through the frontal lobes of their brains. "Ultimately," Persinger says, "human experience is determined by what is happening in the brain. And the experience of God can be generated by a process that has nothing to do with whether God exists or not."

In 1993 British journalist Ian Cotton put on the "Persinger helmet" in the course of research on a book on evangelical Christianity. Persinger's team rang temple bells while Cotton's brain was being irradiated and, he said, "I was actually in a line of solemn Tibetan monks, grave-eyed, brown cowls around their heads. I too was a Tibetan monk, and what I realized was that I always had been."[1]

Persinger's article "On the Possibility of Directly Accessing Every Human Brain by Electromagnetic Induction of Fundamental Algorithms," published in *Perceptual and Motor Skills* in June 1995, delves into even more far-reaching mind control possibilities. Concealed within scientific jargon that may be purposefully daunting in its complexity, are keys to understanding just how far mind monitoring and influence has progressed in current years.

The article states that contemporary neuroscience has discovered that there are "fundamental algorithms" and specific codes through which the brain operates. Persinger says that these codes can be stimulated through "contemporary communication networks" and "A process which is coupled to the narrow band of brain temperature could allow all normal human brains to be affected by a subharmonic whose frequency range at about 10 Hz would only vary by 0.1 Hz." These codes "would be determined by the human genome, i.e. be species-specific, and would contribute to or would serve as a substrate upon which all phenomena that affect neurobehavioral measures are superimposed."

Persinger says that "One logical extrapolation to a neurophysical basis of consciousness" is that "random variations of 'noise' within the matrices could potentially differentiate between individual brains." In other words, individuals could be identified by the specific characteristics of their brain output. "Identification of these sequences could also allow direct access to the most complex neurocognitive processes associated with the sense of self, human consciousness and the aggregate of experiential representations (episodic memory) that define the individual within the brain." In other words, using the techniques that Persinger outlines, a person's memory, consciousness, and sense of self can be fully accessed and modified by electromagnetic means. This is essentially the same as saying that a person's personality can be completely shaped by electromagnetic means, in a sentiment that hearkens back to the research and statements of Dr. Ewen Cameron, who employed far more primitive means of erasing consciousness.

Persinger states that he has been studying "Application of weak electromagnetic fields whose intensities are usually less than 10 milligrams (1 microT). The purpose of this research...is to identify the basic codes for the language of the representational systems within the human brain."

Using the information thus obtained, brain processes can be "circumvented by direct introduction of this information within the brain... The basic premise is that synthetic duplication of the neuroelectrical correlates generated by sensors to an actual stimulus should produce identical experiences without the presence of that stimulus."

Persinger is saying that experiences, feelings, memories—virtually any mental state—can be artificially injected into a human brain from an exterior source. The most frightening thing is that the means for doing this already exist in a fully operational form on a worldwide basis.

Persinger says, "The power levels for these amplitudes are similar to those associated with the signals (generated globally by radio and communication systems)... Within the last two decades a potential has emerged which was improbable but which is now marginally feasible. This potential is the technical capability to influence directly the major portion of the approximately six billion brains of the human species...by generating neural information within a physical medium within which all members of the species are immersed."

Within all of the jargon, most of which I have eliminated in this paraphrase, Persinger's message is that the entire human race can be mind controlled through the use of television and radio networks.[2]

Notes:
1. Blackmore, Susan, "Alien Abduction: The Inside Story," *New Scientist*, 11/19/94; Daniel Brandt, Mind Control and the Secret State; Persinger, Michael, letter to Wes Thomas, 1/6/99; Royte, Elizabeth, "The Altered State," *New York Times Magazine*, September 29, 1996; Nichols, Mark, "The God Machine," *MacLean's* magazine, January 22, 1996
2. Persinger, Michael, "On the Possibility of Directly Accessing Every Human Brain by Electromagnetic Induction of Fundamental Algorithms," *Perceptual and Motor Skills*, June 1995

CHAPTER 26

PSI WAR

According to Andrija Puharich, a secret Navy project researching psychic powers was begun in 1948, called Project Penguin. The project was headed by Rexford Daniels; another participant was Army Colonel Jack Cooney, the head of the medical branch of the Armed Forces Special Weapons Project. The well-known psychic Peter Hurkos was among those tested during the course of the Navy program.[1] Possibly as a byproduct of this research, in 1952 Puharich presented a research paper to the Pentagon titled "On the Possible Usefulness of Extrasensory Perception in Psychological Warfare" and, well in advance of the more-touted Soviet research on such matters, lectured the Army, Air Force, and Navy on the possibility of using extrasensory powers for mindwar.[2]

Communist state authorities, the military, and the KGB were engaged in a research program to use ESP in mass mind control as early as the 1960s. Dr. Milan Ryzl said, "Some years ago a project was begun in the USSR to apply telepathy to indoctrinate and 'reeducate anti-social elements.' It was hoped that suggestion at a distance could induce individuals, without their being aware of it, to adopt the officially desired political and social attitudes."[3]

In 1961, according to an in-house report of the CIA, "the chief of CIA's Office of Technical Service (then the Technical Services Division) became interested in the claims of some researchers that ESP was a reality. Technical project officers soon contacted Stephen I. Abrams, the Director of the Parapsychological Laboratory, Oxford University, England. Under the auspices of Project [MK] ULTRA, Abrams prepared a review article which claimed ESP was demonstrated but not understood or controllable. The report was read with interest but produced no further action for another decade."[4]

In 1974 Robert Monroe founded the Monroe Institute, sited near Charlottesville, Virginia, to research remote viewing. Among prominent persons associated with remote viewing who have trained at Monroe—almost all whom have been launched into a degree of prominence by the Art Bell radio show—are Courtney Brown, John Alexander, Albert Stubblebine, and Joseph McMoneagle. Monroe, aside from being the author of a number of books about his out-of-body jaunts, was former vice president of the Mutual Broadcasting System. Journalist Carl Bernstein has indicated that MBS provided cover for CIA agents. According to Andrijah Puharich, Monroe stimulated his ability to go out-of-body by sniffing ether.

Although it has not been confirmed, according to researcher Tom Porter, Robert Monroe is the son of James Monroe, who was the executive director of the Human Ecology Society CIA cutout, a primary agent for MKULTRA financing. Monroe personally supervised the infamous Dr. Ewen Cameron.[5]

In the early 1970s research into what has come to be called 'remote viewing' was begun at Stanford Research Institute. Project Scanate was run by Harold E. "Hal" Puthoff (a former National Security Agency engineer) and Russell Targ. The CIA liason for the funding of the SRI experiments was reportedly former CIA station chief Harold Chipman, alias "Orwell," said to have been in charge of all mind control research being done in the Bay Area at the time. Partial funding came from the Cognitive Sciences department of the defense contractor SAIC, later circumstantially linked to the Heaven's Gate suicide group, and from est guru and former Scientologist Werner Erhard.[6]

Using test subjects Ingo Swann, Pat Price, and others, the purpose of Project Scanate was to determine the ability of subjects to travel out of their bodies and to identify distant locations, in particular the locations and particulars of foreign military targets.[7]

The main participants in Project Scanate, both scientists and psychics, were members of L. Ron Hubbard's Church of Scientology. Some of the funding for SRI remote viewing is also reported to have come from an unnamed Scientologist. Harold Puthoff was an Operating Thetan Class 3 (OT 3) in the lingo of the group, while Ingo Swann was classified in the church hierarchy as an OT Class 7, at the time the highest level of attainment available in the church.

According to church literature, "In this spiritual state it is possible for the thetan [scientologese for "spirit"] to possess complete spiritual ability, freedom, independence and serenity, to be freed from the endless cycle of birth and death, and to have full awareness and ability independent of the body." Pat Price was also ranked as an OT, and Swann has said that fourteen Scientologists ranked "Clear"—a Scientology level below OT—also participated.

Since then Swann is reported to have become disenchanted with Hubbard's church, and is known to have participated in an offshoot group called Avatar.[8]

It is not surprising to note a Scientology connection in remote viewing experiments. Hubbard's church had, according to their own literature, since the early 1950s been involved in "exteriorizing" individuals from their body, and at least believed that they had engaged in out-of-body travel, as can be determined by a perusal of non-introductory Hubbard texts of the sort that are kept away from the newbies.[9]

Remote viewing targets in Project Scanate included locations in Russia and China, and the location of submerged Soviet submarines. One experiment involved Swann and five other SRI subjects descending 2,000 feet in the Pacific in a submersible vehicle to test their ability at locating objects on the ocean floor.

Asked to probe a secret underground military base in Virginia, Pat Price came up with the following information:

Top of desk had papers labeled: Flytrap; Minerva

File cabinet on north wall labeled: Operation Pool—and word unreadable

Folders inside cabinet labeled: Cueball; 14 Ball; 4 Ball; 8 Ball; Rackup; Some of site vaguely seems like Hayfork or Haystack

Personnel: Col. R.J. Hamilton; Maj. Gen. George R. Nash; Major John C. Calhoun??

When a government security officer read Price's results he told Price, "Hell, there's no security left." Intelligence consultant Joseph A. Ball evaluated the results of the psychic testing at SRI and determined that it "produced manifestations of extrasensory perception sufficiently sharp and clearcut to justify serious consideration of possible applications..."

This in fact seems to have been the case, at least judging from Swann's own early descriptions of remote viewing in a book titled *To Kiss Earth Goodbye*.[10]

After Targ's participation in Scanate, he went on to direct the Human Freedom Center in Berkeley, California. Part of Targ's responsibilities at the center were to interview and counsel former cult members, an interesting job for a man who was a physicist. The center had been founded by Elmer and Deanna Mertle—who had changed their names to Al and Jeannie Mills—earlier public relations officers for Jim Jones of the People's Temple. Targ joined the Human Freedom Center four months after the death orgy at Jonestown.

Another Scanate connection to People's Temple is Keith Harary. After a stint as a research associate in psychiatry, Harary moved to San Francisco to counsel former cultists—in particular, ex-members of the Peoples' Temple. A year later Harary joined Puthoff and Targ in the remote viewing research being done at SRI.[11]

Pat Price's ability to remote view may have ultimately brought about his demise. After a meeting with agents of the Office of Naval Intelligence and NSA in July of 1975, Price flew to Salt Lake City for a short, three-hour visit with his son. From there he flew to Las Vegas, where he was met by his friends Frank and Sherry at the airport. Suggesting that he might have believed he was in danger, Price had earlier told his friends that if anything happened to him, that information on the SRI experiments should be given to Hal Puthoff. While registering at the Stardust Hotel, a man bumped into Price. Price soon "began to feel lousy" and retired early. The following day he phoned his friend Frank from his hotel room to tell him that he was sick with stomach cramps, cramps in his back muscles, and impaired breathing. Frank visited Price, who soon seemed to feel better. Frank left, but when he returned later that night, Price was sitting rigidly, staring into space. Price was calm, but his face was deeply flushed. "I think I will be all right now," he told his friend, but then Price's body arched so that only his head and heels were touching the bed. Frank heard what he thought was a "death rattle." Frank attempted CPR and called a doctor, but Price died before the doctor arrived.[12]

SRI was involved in other projects that seemingly had less to do with psychic abilities than with straightforward mind control. In 1975 the scientific assistant to the Secretary of the Navy, Dr. Sam Koslov, was reviewing SRI research projects when he noted a section of SRI work titled *ELF and Mind Control*, the "ELF" referring to "extremely low frequency" electromagnetics. Koslov was upset by this frank admission of mind control research and ordered Navy investigations done by SRI to stop. According to various reports, the experimentation continued to roll on.[13]

After the apparent success of the SRI experiments, funding was increased into remote viewing research. Gondola Wish was an early remote viewing project begun in 1977 and run by Lt. Skip Atwater of the Army Systems Exploitation Detachment (SED). Atwater gained approval to gather a small group of psychics for obtaining remote viewing intelligence. After consultation with SRI, Atwater recruited persons from the Army, Navy, and the private sector. Gondola Wish did not last long, but promising recruits were passed on to SRI for evaluation. After Atwater left the Army in 1987, he became director of research at the Monroe Institute.

At Fort Meade, the home of the National Security Agency, Project Grill Flame ran from 1978 to 1983, operated by Major General Edmund Thompson, with oversight done by the Defense Intelligence Agency. The project was managed by former nuclear physicist Jack Verona, the head of the DIA's Scientific and Technical Intelligence Directorate. Verona also ran Project Sleeping Beauty, dealing with the offensive use of microwave weapons.

Grill Flame included three full time remote viewers: Ken Bell, Joseph McMoneagle, and Mel Riley, with the programs monitored by CIA mind control kingpin Dr. Louis Jolyon "Jolly" West. The remote viewing research program at SRI was merged with Grill Flame in 1979. When Thompson left Grill Flame in 1981, it was taken over by the U.S. Army Intelligence and Security Command (INSCOM).

In 1983 Grill Flame became Center Lane, a designation that would last until 1985. The project was supervised by the head of INSCOM, General Albert Stubblebine, who is married to psychiatrist and UFOlogists Rima Laibow. Additional remote viewers were recruited to the program, including Captain Ed Dames, Captain Bill Ray, Captain Paul Smith, and Charlene Cavanaugh, a civilian analyst employed by INSCOM. These individuals were trained at the Monroe Institute, and had personal training with Ingo Swann. Stubblebine resigned from Grill Flame in 1984, to be replaced by Major General Harry Soyster. Stubblebine later became chairman of the "civilian" remote viewing company Psi-Tech, founded by Ed Dames.

Army funding for Center Lane was discontinued in 1985, and the program was renamed Sun Streak, with control transferred to the DIA's Scientific and Technical Intelligence Directorate. Run by branch chief Fern Gauvin, the program began to emphasize occult methods, including the use of tarot cards and channeling. According to Ed Dames, during a Pentagon evaluation in 1988 three paper shredders burned out while destroying documents.

Around 1991, Sun Streak was renamed Star Gate, and the program moved from Fort Meade to an undisclosed location. Branch chief Dale Graff was in charge of Star Gate until 1993, when he was replaced by an unnamed DIA specialist.

The program was reported to have been terminated after a negative evaluation by the American Institutes for Research, commissioned by the CIA in 1995. Although remote viewer and intelligence specialist Paul Smith has suggested that the program be continued, it was more deeply classified from SAP (Special Access Program) to a LIMDIS (Limited Dissemination) program.

Ed Dames left Sun Streak in 1988, and took on work in INSCOM "strategic deceptions" and an anti-narcotics group termed Team Six. One of his strategic deceptions may be furthered by his current high visibility in the UFO/paranormal research community.[14]

In recent years intelligence agency remote viewing projects have been parlayed into at least a dozen popular books by participants in these projects. Now "experts" can be heard almost any night on talk radio or tabloid TV offering a wacky amalgam made from CIA mind control research and the mostly crackpot beliefs of the psychic and ufological fringe—everything from the "Face on Mars" to an alien hitchhiker tagging along on the Hale-Bopp comet—with little said about the involvement of government in population mind control. Companies have suddenly popped up offering their services to corporations wanting to obtain intelligence through remote viewing, or in teaching others the skills of remote viewing. But then, the CIA and other intelligence agencies have always used the beliefs of occultists, religionists, and UFO hobbyists to further their own agenda.

Interestingly, remote viewer Major Ed Dames, on a recent Art Bell show, stated that he had once lived in Littleton, Colorado, and was familiar with Columbine High School where the 1999 mass shooting took place. Dames announced to Bell that his remote viewing business Psi-Tech was sponsoring Operation Guiding Light, that is, remote viewing classes for the students of Chatfield Senior High School, the school that absorbed the Columbine students after the mass killing took place. It is regrettable that Dames didn't remote view Littleton before the killings took place; or perhaps he did.

Notes:
1. Milner, Terry. Ratting Out Puharich. Excerpt from unpublished book, 1996
2. Constantine, Alex. *Virtual Government*. CIA Mind Control Operations in America. Venice, California: Feral House, 1997; Wilhelm, John, "Psychic Spying?," *Washington Post*, August 7, 1977; McRae, Ron. *Mind Wars*, 1984
3. Ryzl, Dr. Milan, cited in Ostrander and Schroeder. *Psychic Discoveries Behind the Iron Curtain*. New York: Bantam Books, 1970
4. Kress, Dr. Kenneth A., "Parapsychology in Intelligence: A Personal Review and Conclusions," *Studies in Intelligence*, Winter 1977
5. Porter, Tom, "Government Research into ESP & Mind Control"; Brown, Courtney. *Cosmic Voyage*. New York: Dutton, 1996; McMoneagle, Joseph. *Mind Trek*. Charlottesville, Virginia: Hampton Roads, 1993; Schnabel, Jim. *Remote Viewers: The Secret History of America's Psychic Spies*. New York: Dell, 1997
6. Constantine; McRae; Sarfatti, Jack, "In the Thick of it," cited in *Doc Hambone* bio on Werner Erhard at www.io.com/%7Ehambone; Dickson, Paul. *Think Tanks*. New York: Ballentine Books, 1971; SAIC website
7. Wilhelm
8. Wilhelm; *Theology & Practice of a Contemporary Religion: Scientology*. Los Angeles: Bridge Publications: 1998; Constantine
9. Wilhelm
10. ibid.
11. Constantine
12. Milner, Terry. "The Death of Pat Price," *Doc Hambone*, www.io.com/%7Ehambone
13. Wilhelm
14. Constantine; Schnabel, Jim. *Remote Viewers: The Secret History of America's Psychic Spies*. New York: Dell, 1997; Emerson, Steven. *Secret Warriors*. New York: G.P. Putnam's Sons, 1988; Kress; Trull., D., "Operation Star Gate: U.S. Intelligence and Psychic Spies," *Parascope* at www.parascope.com/main.htm; Elliston, Jon, "Parapsychology in Intelligence," *Parascope* at www.parascope.com/main.htm

CHAPTER 27

HARDWIRING HUMANS

Intelligence agencies in league with the scientific establishment are currently in a rush to create the ultimate in control, where a person's entire perception of reality is replaced by another of the controllers' choosing. The means to accomplish this is provided by access and control of the human mind by computer.

The first step in access and control began with mapping the brain. One early experiment was funded by the CIA in 1975 to the tune of $100,000 per year. According to an article in the *San Diego Union* titled "CIA Funds Project At Hospital Here,"

"Children's Hospital and Health Center is conducting experiments under a CIA grant to develop what some say could be a sophisticated lie-detector system that probes the human brain electronically. Experiments on human volunteers, most of them members of the hospital staff, administrators and friends have been conducted for two years. The agency at first asked the hospital not to discuss the project. However, the hospital's medical director and hospital officials later decided it [sic] disliked the idea of secrecy and told the CIA they wanted to be able to talk freely about the work...

"Experiments are being conducted in the health center's Speech, Hearing and Neuromemory Center by its research director, Dr. Albert Lawrence. They involve what are called "visual evoked responses" recorded electronically from brain waves and analyzed by computers. Subjects respond to pictures of faces flashed on screens. Some are familiar, some are unfamiliar. Familiar faces evoke a different brain wave pattern than unfamiliar faces, and the computer can tell the difference even if the subject says nothing."

According to the director of the project, accuracy of identification by computer had reached as high as eighty percent. He also mentioned that the results of the experiments would be combined with clinical trials at the children's hospital.[1]

Apparently San Diego wasn't the only place where brain mapping studies were being done on children. Advanced techniques were patented in 1983 by the Children's Medical Center of Boston for "Brain Electrical Activity Mapping" which in turn would be displayed on detailed present time video "topograpic maps" that could be monitored by technicians.[2]

In a story headed "See Ya Tomorrow!," the *Washington Post* in 1984 reported on a convention of the World Future Society. The author said:

"Perhaps the most exciting stuff came from engineer James B. Beal, who simply told about what already exists that might lead us to mainlining information from one brain to another... He spoke of devices that can be placed in the eyeball to aid sight or behind the ear to stimulate hearing, pacemakers that work from outside the heart, gadgets that can induce all sorts of reaction from vomiting to laughter. The body is, after all, electrochemical and is affected by the low-frequency fields emanating from TV sets, for instance: hyperactive children seem to be made worse by overexposure to TV sets. The fantasy in the film *Brainstorm,* in which a person's mental pictures are literally transferred onto tape to be beamed into someone else's head, will be a reality soon, Beal said..."[3]

This type of research has been on the front burner for intelligence agencies in both the West and East, judging by information released about a mind control device developed by Russians Igor Smirnov and Sergei Kavasovets at the ominously titled Department of Psycho-Correction at the Moscow Medical Academy. "Non-lethal weapons"—including mind control—researchers Janet and Chris Morris watched a demonstration in 1991 of a device that was able to analyze the contents of a person's mind, building up "a picture of the mind" that could be used for subliminal and other forms of "corrective" intervention.

The Smirnov/Kavosovets device was later demonstrated by the Morrises to journalist David Shukman at CIA headquarters in Langley, Virginia, with Shukman videotaping the demonstration. He describes the equipment as being "hardly impressive," simply a few pieces of computer equipment. But the results of the equipment *were* impressive.

Chris Morris acted as a guinea pig, with several electrodes taped to his head. When the equipment was activated a computer screen came to life and displayed a succession of words. Shukman says, "Each letter was at least six letters long; a few made sense but most had the curious characteristic of nearly resembling a recognizable word but not quite doing so: 'Deambutt...Jovotree...Christoph...Ficknell... Borotty...Bainstar...'"

Morris stared at the screen and "The light from the screen flashed across his face, his eyes transfixed by the words. A slight furrow appeared on his brow as he struggled to interpret them in the split-second before they vanished... Yet it turned out that there was another, hidden layer of probing taking place as well. When we replayed our videotape several days later, we discovered that sandwiched between the visible words were other words, caught on a single frame, appearing for as little as one-sixtieth of a second. These had a more sinister tone: 'Armed...attack...defense...weapon.'"

According to the inventors, the words were simply designed to focus the mind and to distract the activity of the conscious mind while the machine delved into the unconscious reactions of the subject. After twenty minutes the Russians downloaded a three-dimensional graph that showed the relationship of ten different factors in Morris' life, including anxiety, health, family, father, and job. Morris found the analysis accurate, so much so that he asked it be kept confidential. Smirnov and Kavosovets remarked that, using the results of the analysis, they could choose "the optimal strategy for treatment."

Smirnov and Kavosovets also talk about analyzing ethnic groups and even countries for problems and vulnerabilities, and then specifically targeting communications with subliminals to handle those problems, or perhaps to exacerbate them.
According to researcher Shukman:
"It is believed in Western intelligence circles that such a technique was applied to certain key Soviet units in Afghanistan. The open scientific literature certainly reveals a highly active research program in this area and, with morale low among the occupying troops, a device for encouraging a robust performance would have proved useful. One former Soviet paratrooper sergeant confirmed as much to me, in an interview in Minsk in February, 1992. He said that before particularly unpleasant missions, such as a search-and-destroy operation, he and his colleagues were sometimes ordered into a dark room to watch swirling colored shapes projected on to a screen and to listen to 'strange noises.'"[4]

In 1990 a device called a "Biomagnetic Analytical System" was patented, consisting of a helmet whose purpose is to minutely map magnetic fields in the brain or any other part of the body through fiber optics. According to the patent, "The output signals...are processed to provide a display or recording exhibiting the pattern or map of magnetic fields resulting from emanations" in the brain or other portion of the body.[5]

A current innovation in the interface between human beings and computers is the creation of a silicon computer chip that stimulates an individual nerve cell without damaging it, with the capability of selectively triggering neuronal response. Designed by Drs. Peter Fromherz and Alfred Stett at the Max Planck Institute of Biochemistry in Munich, the silicon chip triggers neuron impulses and also receives them, using "neuron transistors" that are able to translate those impulses.

Theoretically, these computer chips would have the capability of broadcasting whole complexes of perceptions and thought into the unwitting brain of the hardwired subject, of dumping whole simulations of reality into their minds.[6]

In January 1991, Dr. Stuart Hameroff of the University of Arizona, indicated the possibility that human brain functions could be contained in modules outside of the human body. Hameroff noted that he believed that human consciousness might be dependent upon "computer-like cytoskeletal polymers within living cells," and that, "An idea expressed relevant to life 'beyond 2000,' was that the brain cytoskeletal proteins could be prepared in an artificial environment which may be capable of containing cognitive function." A frankensteinian notion, indeed.

Listings of government spending for 1992 show that the Office of Naval Research (ONR) was funded for research along similar lines that involved the melding of computers and human minds. They were involved in the process of creation of "artificial neural nets," and the emulation of human neurology "within electronic information processing systems" as well as "Multi-Modal Integration": "A final cluster of research includes theoretical and experimental studies of multi-modal perceptual integration, and expression in what appears to be automatic control behavior. The aim of this program is to understand perceptual integration and control processes at a level that permits design guidance for human computer interfaces and supervisory control systems."

Also researched was "Neural Plasticity" in behavior modification. Behind the gobbledygook of jargon is the potential for completely shaping the perceptions of human beings— beyond the kind of shaping that is now done by propaganda and advertising and other less subtle means.[7]

Another startling innovation is the creation of what is called an "intelligence amplifier." In a paper titled "Symbionic Technology and Education" presented in 1983 at the American Educational Research Association annual meeting, Glenn F. Cartwright of the Department of Educational Psychology and Counseling at McGill University reported that "Research findings indicate that major breakthroughs in education will have to occur through direct cortical intervention, using either chemical or electronic means." Cartwright further stated:

"In the future, it will be possible to build more sophisticated intelligence amplifiers that will be internal extensions of our brains. These 'ethnotronic' devices will be significantly more powerful than present day computers and may even be wired directly to the human brain for both input and output. They will amplify and strengthen all the intellectual abilities we now take for granted as comprising intelligent human activity. We may call such devices 'symbionic minds' (symbiotic + bionic), because of the close, interdependent relationships that will almost certainly exist between them and our own brains and because they may make us, to some degree, bionic." Intelligence amplification aside, my concern is that these sorts of devices will be used to delete mind/brain functions that do not conform to the will of the mind control masters.[8]

In 1999 Reuters news service spoke of, "A device that reads brain waves through the skull has enabled paralyzed people to write sentences on a computer screen... Two patients have managed to write messages on a computer screen via electrodes planted in the brain by researchers at Emory University in Atlanta... Now researchers in Germany and the United States have placed small electrodes on top of patients' heads to record signals from the brain. Once patients learn to control the computer cursor in this way, they can begin to write messages."[9]

"Neuroscientists have implanted a device in the motor neocortex of two people that has allowed them to operate a computer display by 'thinking' about it... Dr. Phillip R. Kennedy...at Georgia Institute of Technology and Emory University developed an implant that can by used to detect activity of neurons, and convey these signals to computers for further processing and control operations. The small recording sensor is enclosed in a glass envelope and coated with nerve growth factors that allow neurons in the region of the implant to establish functional connections with the sensor. Surgeries on two patients were performed by Dr. Roy Bakay from Emory... The electrodes were implanted in the motor cortex, near the arm/facial region. Both patients were paralyzed and unable to move their limbs or speak. The first patient, who had the implant for 2.5 months before dying from ayotophic lateral sclerosis, learned to control the signals in an 'on-off' manner for seven days. The second patient who suffered brain stem stroke after a heart attack, has had the implant for 6 months.'[10]

By the 1990s electronic control of human beings was fairly openly mentioned in the literature of the military, as for instance in the the the US Army War College of *The Revolution in Military Affairs and Conflict Short of War*, by Seven Metz and James Kievit, published in 1994. One of the revelations of this book is that "Behavior modification is a key component of peace enforcement," and that such modification will be directed against the American people. This will take place, the authors state, through directed energy systems, whose primary advantage is "deniability." Setting their report sixteen years in the future, Metz and Kievit are straightforward about the unlimited possibilities inherent in "perception molding" through the use of psychotechnolgies. Anyone who objects to this kind of mindwarping will be "identified using comprehensive inter-agency integrated databases," then categorized into "computerized personality simulations," which will be used "to develop, tailor and focus psychological campaigns for each."[11]

The book *New World Vistas* was published in 1996 by the U.S. Air Force Scientific Advisory Board. In this report, under the heading "Biological Process Control," we note that,

"Prior to the mid-21st century, there will be a virtual explosion of knowledge in the field of neuroscience. We will have achieved a clear understanding of how the human brain works, how it really controls the various functions of the body, and how it can be manipulated (both positively and negatively). One can envision the development of electromagnetic energy sources, the output of which can be pulsed, shaped, and focused, that can couple with the human body in a fashion that will allow one to prevent voluntary muscular movements, control emotions (and thus actions), produce sleep, transmit suggestions, interfere with both short-term and long term memory, produce an experience set, and delete an experience set...

"It would also appear possible to create high fidelity speech in the human body, raising the possibility of covert suggestion and psychological direction. When a high power microwave pulse in the gigahertz range strikes the human body, a very small temperature perturbation occurs. This is associated with a sudden expansion of the slightly heated tissue. This expansion is fast enough to produce an acoustic wave. If a pulse stream is used, it should be possible to create an internal acoustic field in the 5-15 kilohertz range, which is audible. Thus, it may be possible to talk to selected adversaries in a fashion that would be most disturbing to them."

Other capabilities mentioned in *New World Vistas* are akin to the creation and broadcasting of artificial realities:

"...The concept of imprinting an experience set is highly speculative, but nonetheless, highly exciting. Modern electromagnetic scattering theory raises the prospect that ultrashort pulse scattering through the human brain can result in reflected signals that can be used to construct a reliable estimate of the degree of central nervous system arousal. The concept behind this 'remote EEG' is to scatter off of action potentials or ensembles of action potentials in major central nervous system tracts. Assuming we will understand how our skills are imprinted and recalled, it might be possible to take this concept one step further and duplicate the experience set in another individual."[12]

Another military paper, titled "Information Operations: A New War-Fighting Capability," published in 1996, "is a study designed to comply with a directive from the chief of staff of the Air Force to examine the concepts, capabilities, and technologies the United States will require to remain the dominant air and space force in the future."

The paper speaks of the primary necessity for the U.S. "for continued success as a superpower" to be "information dominance." Part of this dominance will be the development of a space satellite-linked Information Integration Center, or IIC, which will act as a central processing and control center. The IIC will monitor people who have been implanted with a "microscopic brain chip... [The] chip performs two functions. First, it links the individual to the IIC, creating a seamless interface between the user and the information resources (in-time collection data and archival databases.) In essence, the chip relays the processed information from the IIC to the user. Second, the chip creates a computer-generated mental visualization based upon the user's request...

"One of the techniques to achieve this is "A combination of brain processes and visual imaging [that] has been developed in the laboratory. The California Institute of Technology has developed an energy efficient computer chip which emulates the analog thinking of the human brain... When this capability is fully mature, this chip could provide the baseline for a brain implant hooked to all the sensory segments of the brain, not just the eye."

The paper notes certain concerns. It states:

"Implanting 'things' in people raises ethical and public relations issues. While these concerns may be founded on today's thinking, in 2025 they may not be as alarming. We already are evolving toward technology implanting. For example, the military currently requires its members to receive mandatory injections of biological organisms (i.e. the flu shot). In the civilized world, people receive mechanical hearts and other organs. Society has come to accept most of these implants as a fact of life. By 2025 it is possible medical technology will have nerve chips that allow amputees to control artificial limbs or eye chips that allow the blind to see. The civilian populace will likely accept an implanted microscopic chips [sic] that allow military members to defend vital national interests."[13]

In 1982, Dorothy Burdick wrote a book about her ordeal as an experimental subject of U.S. intelligence agencies. Although this information has not been completely verified, additional information that will be presented in this book leads one to believe that Burdick was not deluded.

She wrote, "Since 1973, the Advanced Research Project Agency of the Defense Department has utilized the combined efforts of the Massachusetts Institute of Technology, New York University, the University of California at Los Angeles and the National Aeronautics and Space Administration, Ames Research Center at Moffett Field in California to read minds at a distance by deciphering the brain's magnetic waves. The

Pentagon denied the project was secret although a reporter was ousted from a meeting on the subject by someone identified as a member of the CIA. "The MEG (magnetoencephalogram) is many times more sensitive than EEG (electroencephalogram). MEG was originally reported in 1968. A computer search of the current literature reveals little published on MEG because it is undoubtedly classified in ARPA's (Advanced Research Projects Agency) computer network."

Another aspect of the technology, Burdick wrote, was "FOCUS (flexible optical control unit simulator) projects hallucinatory images directly on the retina of the eye. When the images are projected the subjects show the same body responses that they would by taking a drug. The subjects cannot tell the machine images from reality. FOCUS was developed at UCLA's Neuropsychiatric Institute by Ron Siegel, an experimental psychologist, who eventually hopes to control retrieval of imagery information at will including that of daydreams, sleep and hallucinations." Although Burdick does not mention it, Siegel was a writing partner with CIA mind control expert Louis Jolyon West.[14]

Evaluating the above information, it is obvious that with the state of the art in computers, electronics, implants, and other forms of manipulation that a threshold has been crossed. We have reached a point where the mind masters can now or very soon will be able to completely control our perception of reality. They will be able to own our reality completely, so much so that we will not know that our thinking, our perceptions, are not our own, but are dictated to us from an exterior source.

As reported in the *New York Times*, in 1998, British Telecommunications is currently at work on a device that they dub the Soul Catcher, a computer chip implanted in the optic nerve behind the eye that, in conjunction with genetic programming, will monitor and record the entirety of a person's thinking, what they see, what they feel. This information, according to Dr. Chris Winter of British Telecommunications, will be stored in a central computer. Information will also be fed to the person from an exterior computerized source, for "extrasensory" experience. Among the other capabilities foreseen for Soul Catcher is the implanting of one person's chip into a newborn baby, thus transplanting the entire experience of one person into another.[15]

Notes:
1. Scarr, Lew, "CIA Funds Project At Hospital Here," *The San Diego Union*, September 24, 1977
2. "Brain Electrical Activity Mapping," U.S. Patent 4,408,616, October 11, 1983
3. Kernan, Michael, "See Ya Tomorrow! At the World Future Society, It's All in the Mind," *The Washington Post*, June 13, 1984
4. Shukman, David. *The Sorcerer's Challenge*; Elliot Dorinda, "A Subliminal Dr. Strangelove"
5. "Biomagnetic Analytical System Using Fiber-Optic Magnetic Sensors," Patent number 4,951,674, August 28, 1990
6. *Physical Science Letters*, August 21, 1995, cited in Constantine, Alex. *Virtual Government: CIA Mind Control Operations in America*. Venice, California: Feral House, 1997
7. U.S. Government Funding for Neural Networks Research, May 1992
8. Cartwright, Glenn F., "Symbionic Technology and Education," research paper presented to the American Educational Research Association at Montreal, Canada, in April. 1983
9. "Computers Now Unlock the Mind," Reuters news service, obtained at the *Millennium Frontier* online discussion group, www.newpower.org
10. "Brain Implants That Allow 'Willful Thinking'," Principles of Psychobiology, *Interactive Study Guide for the Allied Neurosciences*
11. Metz and Kievit. "*The Revolution in Military Affairs and Conflict Short of War*. US Army War College, 1994
12. *New World Vistas*, United States Air Force Scientific Advisory Board, Ancillary Volume, June 1996
13. Osborne, Bethel, Chew, Nostrand, Whitehead, "Information Operations: A New War-Fighting Capability," A Research Paper Presented to Air Force 2025. August 1996
14. Burdick, Dorothy. *Such Things Are Known*. New York: Vantage Press, Inc. 1982; Constantine
15. "The Coming Melding of Mind and Machine," *New York Times*, 8-25-98

Chapter 28

Dreamscape

One of the most fascinating accounts of mind control from the perspective of a victim is provided by a woman named Joanne "JoJo" Carey, a successful 57-year-old artist who lives on a boat docked in Florida. JoJo is an intelligent woman who writes with lucidness and even wit about what has taken place to her and perhaps, according to her count, about a dozen other people in the same vicinity in the last few years. Perhaps significantly, Ms. Carey is an ex-employee of the CIA, who worked on their "French desk" in the United States in 1959-60, and has a 35-year history of supporting human rights movements in print.

For Carey the torture began in 1995.

While in a dispute with her ex-husband and some of his friends, including an ex-Louisiana judge, she began to "hear" threats against her life. The threats, as described by Carey, were like a "holographic sound system—3D, in fact" and seemingly encompassing whole city blocks around her. The threats took on the form of completely scripted scenarios, and were played five or six times during the day, and continuously at night, terrifying her and depriving her of sleep. The voices behind the threats said that they were "DEA and Marine Patrol."

In March of 1995, while feeling as if she was in a strangely drugged state, the voices turned into an interrogation taking place at the level of thought. Another time, four voices in an elaborate scenario demanded that she leave the area in her boat, and threatened her with physical harm if she did not comply. She was told to pack a bag and wait for a Marine Patrol boat to come and pick her up. Later she was told to dive into the water and go under the hull of the boat "to find out where the voices were coming from." Carey comments that another woman had recently drowned in the area. The woman had been hearing voices prior to her "suicide." She also notes that the famous alleged mind control victim Candy Jones almost drowned.

Later she was told that someone would come by with a gun and that "You'll know what to do with it." This continuing assault, along with sleep deprivation, she believes, gradually drove her into a state of shock and dissociation. A friend of hers happened to visit her on her boat, and Carey went unconscious. The friend drove her to a hospital emergency ward, where she woke up in an hysterical state, still overwhelmed with intra-cerebral voices.

Carey was checked into a "Crisis Stabilization Unit," and put on "suicide watch." She says, "I had no idea then this was only the beginning of a three year, 9 1/2 month long nightmare from hell—and that two hundred plus 'near death' trips would follow."

While she was in the CSU facility the intra-cerebral interrogation continued, "asking me to 'give them' people, organizations, events in my life—I didn't know then that meant 'hand over,' tell on—everything I knew about the people involved. They'd mention a person, group or organization, like...a local grass roots civil rights group—then 'prowl' my thought patterns." Among the sounds that she believes were injected into her mind were sounds of cats being tortured. She was told that they were her pet cats. Her friends were also threatened, and she was told that if she did not keep quiet her friends would be killed.

Carey says, "Similar 'scenarios' went on every night for the next 17 days—for hours. This was 'reinforced' about a week into the stay by a 3-D holographic sound 'kidnap' trip— I heard a group of people come into the unit and demand I be handed over to them (did not see the persons—men)—I was told they were going to put me on a boat, take me into the Gulf Stream, handcuff me to an 'inflatable' then sink the inflatable raft with me cuffed to/in it... It scared the hell out of me—it was meant to keep me in the CSU unit—I was told the men were 'DEA agents.'"

After Carey was released from the CSU unit she returned to her boat. She was given a deadline to leave the area, and then for the first time began to be hit by "shocks" to her head, in what she believes was an attempt to drive her from her boat. According to Carey, she was told she was going to be shocked before it happened and that "We'll make it clear... From pin-prick level shocks to 'bee-sting' level shocks would hit my head. I went deeper into shock, my mind running on survive only—memories 'blanking'—being erased—time blurring."

"A lot of interrogation went on about what I had of 'value' anywhere in the world—on 'info' I had on other people and where they kept their valuables."

She says, "There is a specific 'language' to what I hear (at least 2-3 up to 8-12 inputs all at once). Neurolinguistic programming occurs; a lot of 'double-meaning' words or phonetically sounding words with different meanings, somctimes in different languages... A high-pitched ringing always accompanies what is happening—several different pitches at once—also in the background is some sort of sound curtain that echoes like the sound of 18-wheelers driving on an eight lane highway in rain—the audial inputs ride on them and on those sounds. Probably some kind of 'voice changers' are used. Some of the inputs might be linear radio or laser-borne signals—both of which can carry infrasound.

"There's a two-parter to what's going on—the baiting, the scenarios are evidently an external input—the high shrieking voices—these are probably infrasound inputs used here as well in an 'echo' effect...also Radio Hypnotic Intra-Cerebral Control techs, and EDOM, Electronic Dissolution of Memory.

"Hypnosis is used—probably Erickson dual-induction methods—Repetition of negative programming, negative suggestion and elicitation of fear and reaction is also constant and used from dawn 'till sleep all day long. It equates to a high-tech anonymous filthy phone call you can't hang up on anywhere you go...

"What I hear—the baiting—is always vicious, sadistic, threatening, derisive, mocking, hurtful (physically and of course, mentally), sexually aberrant, filthy, in fact; geared to put anyone on edge or over an edge. It is deliberately designed so that when 'repeated' it matches schizophrenic criteria. Anyone with the basic sound equipment and a DMS-IV [psychiatric diagnosis] manual can come up with 'scripts' that match diagnostic symptoms—and aim them at an innocent victim who ends up NUTS resultant."

At one point in the latter part of May, 1995, she sat all night in a chair outside of the hospital drop-in clinic while a "very unfavorable biography" on herself was read to her by a male voice. In the morning, she was told, "You did not do what we told you to—so we're going to give you a heart attack and a stroke." According to Carey, "I fluffed it off and went for coffee. As I stood on the drop-in center porch I felt a sudden pain—as though I'd been shot in the chest." One of the drop-in unit's staff called an ambulance and Carey was taken to the hospital again, "watching my print-out do a Bolshoi Ballet and Martha Graham dance on [the] heartbeat." At the hospital Carey was given an MRI, and then dismissed, told that she had only had an anxiety attack.

Carey characterizes her condition for months after that as being in "shock." "The 'interrogation' by summer took a new twist—the audials began to tell me just as a thought was forming what I was thinking—before I could fully form a thought—then began 'editing' these forming thoughts. That sent me back into deep shock again—from then on in for months I'd be told what I was going to do before I did it.

Carey describes the continuance of perhaps 1,000 different "scenarios" that played out in 3-D sound around her, including an extraterrestrial contact scenario and one scenario where she believes she was "hooked up" to the brain of a dolphin: "One of the few pleasant experiences in all of this— imaged to me inside calm beautiful ocean, endless space, a sense of 'oneness,' with ocean, peace and quiet joy in being there with her (a dolphin named 'Anessa'). She's real—took off from the Dolphin Research Center on Grassy Key before Hurricane Andrew—I learned from other sources. Transplants, implants were tried on her (not on record—no one will go on record with that)...probably associated with the Janus Project research into interspecies communication, an Air Force John Lilly project and DoD 1st Pilot Association project. I looked up the project and talked with people in the know. A lot of the staff were on LSD while 'coming' in to the dolphins... Some of the dolphins in Janus committed suicide after killing other dolphins as a reaction to intra-cerebral access (on record in Lilly's research)."

Carey notes, "About 15 to 20 years ago, a transplanted tribe of Hmong (from Nam) in Texas were dying of nightmares (about two dozen of them...). They probably died as a direct result of the 'dream state' mind control agenda..."

By September of 1995 Carey was discontinuing the use of psychiatric drugs that had been prescribed for her, in an attempt to get at the nature of what was going on. Using the library and a grass roots research team, she read everything that was available on the subject of mind control, as well as a good deal of material that is normally inaccessible.

She says, "I wandered across Delgado's work at Stanford [and] discovered that Delgado was 'translating' brain waves into words in 1977 before his work went 'Classified' context. And that was the concept for the Janus Project—which involved Real Time/Past Time on human thought —which gave me the answer on how anyone could know what I was thinking and edit it before I was fully cognizant of what I was thinking...When neurons fire chemically and interact, a 1.5 to 3 second 'window' exists between cognizing one's own thoughts...and the actual Real Time firing...that chemical firing can and is being computer accessed before a person can cognize, know, think their own thoughts!"

Carey believes that this technology is the basis of current computer-to-pilot interfaces, and says that once she understood this, she realized what was happening to her. She also believes that the technology is probably run through a surveillance satellite system.

Carey says, "The interrogation methodologies have been identified by a former Psy-ops expert at the local American Legion (retired) as 'East German,' definitely KGB origin—classic—and 'beyond his training...scares the hell out of me,' he said."

Carey speculates, "If I were to call this one, I'd almost say the KGB has married the CIA and Italian Mafioso interests and have Chinese thought reform experts on salary in being able to do anything from 'hitting' a head of government (literally) to enacting a New World Order—and somewhere in the middle of this is the Deep Throat equation: 'Follow the money'—and so far that the entire world economy is at risk by so-called non-lethal weapons that could cause war to break out in a Trappist monastery—to WWIII for 50 years into the future. That's a conservative estimate... A Zen master would be clubbing geese to death after this..."

According to Carey, she is not the only one who is "hearing voices" in the area of the country she lives in. "They have conducted extensive interrogation on me on a few 'cult-like' murders down in Big Pine Key, which I know little of except from news reports, but told me the name of a man—'Tom' who was arrested six months later for the murder of a pregnant woman and her husband...so they knew that six months before his arrest...which means they probably used this tech on him, too. I have no idea if he's guilty or innocent.

"A prisoner in Key West was reported to be hearing 'demons' prior to murdering at the Rum Runner Bar, its owner and wounding three other people.

"So was Louise a month ago at Key Colony Beach before her 'suicide' by drowning.

"So was a boy in '89-'90 from the Marathon Housing Projects [hearing demons] and chased out of Key West on a bike and hit by two cars...

"There are a lot more reports of 'voices'...on scene—haunted houseboats in Key West; voices talking from funeral urns; people hearing angels, God the Father, Jesus, devils... All the same source, probably..."[1]

Bill Burke, of Clovis, New Mexico, is another person who believes that he has some insight into the mind control technology that the U.S. government currently possesses. He believes they are using a technology called "Dreamscape" on him.

Burke is a forty-six year old ex-Marine. Twenty years ago Burke checked in to a hospital in the California desert town of Barstow for an ankle problem. He spent three days in the hospital and woke up with someone forcing something into his nose. Later, in recovery at home, he woke up to find four uniformed military men standing by his bed: apparently a holographic or mental projection, but one that carried with it the complete sense of reality.

Burke believes that while he was in the hospital he was implanted with a number of electronic control devices that are capable of projecting computerized images directly into his mind. The mind control projections began three months after he had been operated on in the hospital, and he has been tortured by them on a daily basis ever since.

The mental projections, which he believes are projected through "Dreamscape" technology, vary. He is assaulted by electronic frequencies, by taunting speech, suicidal thoughts, and by "semi-transparent images that are just as real as you and I." He feels constant pressure in his head, popping of the ears, swelling of muscles and other portions of his body, and the sensation of electric shock.

Burke believes that the persons who are monitoring and manipulating him are employed by the Goldstone Tracking Station and the Jet Propulsion Labs—he believes that there is a brain interaction computer at JPL that is used to monitor mind control victims.

How is one to evaluate the plight of a man like Bill Burke? At first glance one would assume that Burke was the victim of delusion rather than government manipulation. But there is evidence that causes one to question that evaluation. To begin with, the kind of technology that Burke describes has been under development for a long time, and since most of this type of research is classified, it is not likely that we are aware of more than the most insignificant portion of this research. But there is more compelling evidence.

Backing up Burke's story is that the implants he speaks of apparently exist. Burke has provided me with medical reports of x-ray examinations performed in 1995 by the Department of Radiology of the Plains Regional Medical Center in Clovis, New Mexico. Among the conclusions in the medical reports is that there are "small metallic type densities seen just posterior to the superior aspect of the of the petrous bone on the right" in the brain. Also, "one can see a very small fleck of what appears to be a metallic object in the area of the AC joint" of the shoulder. In another report analyzing x-rays of his feet is noted: "Impression: retained foreign metallic bodies." A additional medical report, dated May 18, 1998, notes: "there are some questionable foreign body objects in the base of his skull."[2]

Notes:
1. Carey, Joanne, correspondence with the author, December 16-December 20, 1998
2. Burke, Bill. Correspondence with the author, December 18, 1998; Medical report by Michael P. Nachtigal, M.D., November 18, 1995; Medical report by Dr. S.T. Haider, M.D., the Department of Radiology, Plains Regional Medical Center, Clovis, New Mexico, November 9, 1998; Medical report authored by Andrew J. Stansberry, P.A.-C and Doyle B. Hill, D.O., January 1, 1998; Medical report by James B. Moss, M.D., May 18, 1998

CHAPTER 29

ONE-WORLD BRAIN

In the 1930s, British intelligence agent and one-world theoretician H.G. Wells proposed a mind control plan that is apparently coming to fruition now, at the turn of the 21st century, with the creation of the Internet. At a November, 1936 speech before the Royal Institute of International Affairs, Wells laid out his idea for what he called a "World Encyclopaedia." Wells said:

"I want to suggest that something, a new social organization, a new institution—which for a time I shall call World Encyclopaedia... This World Encyclopaedia would be the mental background of every intelligent man in the world... Such an Encyclopaedia would play the role of an undogmatic Bible to world culture. It would do just what our scattered and disoriented intellectual organizations of today fall short of doing. It would hold the world together mentally... It would compel men to come to terms with one another... It is a super university. I am think of a World Brain; no less...Ultimately, if our dream is realized, it must exert a very great influence upon everyone who controls administrations, makes wars, directs mass behavior, feeds, moves, starves and kills populations... You see how such an Encyclopaedia organization could spread like a nervous network, a system of mental control about the globe, knitting all the intellectual workers of the world through a common interest and cooperating unity and a growing sense of their own dignity, informing without pressure or propaganda, directing without tyranny."

Wells was a little more candid in a private memo written in the same month: "The Universities and the associated intellectual organizations throughout the world should function as a police of the mind."[1] Policing of the mind is precisely the danger of the Internet. Although at first blush the possibility of a communications medium that is egalitarian in its ability to accommodate both individuals and media monoliths is exciting, the apparent freedom of the Internet may be transitory...and illusory.

One problem is that along with ability to disseminate information widely and almost instantaneously, due to its technical flexibility the Internet also has the potential for assimilating—for literally devouring—all of the major information sources on the planet. With high-tech linkages and interfaces it is quite probable that worldwide television, radio, computer, and print media will all be sucked into the maw of what is currently called the Internet. All of these information and communication sources are gradually being linked together into a single computerized network, providing an opportunity for unheralded control of what will be broadcast, what will be said, and ultimately what will be thought.

The Internet provides the ability for almost instantaneous monitoring of the content of communications. It is possible that the 'wide open information frontier' of the Internet, as it currently exists, is going to be a temporary thing, and that a program of increased monitoring and regulation—as well as a more aggressive use of mind control, such as foreseen by Dr. Persinger—will emerge.

When NBC and Microsoft launched their joint venture MSNBC, in an attempt to link television and the Internet, newscaster and CFR member Tom Brokaw said, "We can't let that generation and a whole segment of the population just slide away out to the Internet and retrieve what information it wants without being in on it."[2]

In China, they have also not held their tongues about what they see as the necessity of Internet control. Xia Hong, an advocate of government monitoring of the Net has said, "The Internet has been an important technical innovator, but we need to add another element, and that is control. The new generation of information superhighway needs a traffic control center. It needs highway patrols: users will require driver's licenses. These are the basic requirement for any controlled environment."[3]

Is the idea that the Internet can be used for increasing surveillance on the public just paranoia on my part? Then we should examine who currently controls the medium: American intelligence agencies. At this time the major nexus of control of the Internet resides in the monopoly of "domain registration," the keys to the broad Internet landscape. These domain names are registered as Internet Protocol numbers, and until recently were deeded by Network Solutions, Inc., a subsidiary of the government funded National Science Foundation. While Network Solutions registered the I.P. numbers, it was done as a free public service. This is no longer taking place.

Now the long arm of American intelligence agencies has hijacked the free flow of information—registration of domain names now starts at fifty dollars per year—since the purchase of Network Solutions by another company, Scientific Applications International Corp, a group previously mentioned circumstantially in this book in connection with the Heaven's Gate mass suicide—or murder.

SAIC is an arm of the military industrial establishment, with twenty thousand employees and over 90% of its $1.9 billion in 1994 revenues obtained from government contracts. On the twenty-three person board of directors of SAIC are Admiral Bobby Inman, former deputy director of the CIA and head of the National Security Agency; President Nixon's former defense secretary Melvin Laird; General Max Thurman, who commanded the invasion of Panama. Other board members of SAIC have included former CIA director Robert Gates; Secretary of Defense William Perry; and CIA director John Deutch.

Among the projects that Scientific Applications International Corp. has been engaged in recently have been the creation and implementation of technology for the Army Global Command and Control System—the renovation of the Pentagon's computer and communication systems—and the upgrading of national, state, and local law enforcement databases. In other words, SAIC is involved in the upgrading and integration of the computerized infrastructure of the Establishment.

And now SAIC stands at the gate of the Internet.

According to researcher Jesse Hersh:

"The military-industrial complex was the name used to refer to the ruling power elite during the 1950s and 1960s. However, with the wide penetration of television during the '60s, and the further proliferation of electronic media throughout the 1970s and '80s, the complex has dissolved into the inner workings of almost all aspects of our society. The war economy has successfully been transformed into the information economy. Military technology, and military communications systems now control and operate almost all of our political-economic and social relations. This amalgamation of media, and conglomeration of power, is currently being presented to the 'consumer' as the Information Superhighway or 'Internet.'"[4]

If it seems unlikely that Big Brother would concern himself with the communications of ordinary citizens on the Internet, then it should be realized that government is already engaged in monitoring civilian and business communications on an awesome scale. Around the world, electronic messages are intercepted by a collaboration amongst several spy agencies headed by the American NSA, termed ECHELON. Based upon a document known as the UKUSA Agreement, signed in 1948 by the U.S., Great Britain, Australia, Canada, and New Zealand, ECHELON is a system composed of receiving stations in Yakima, Washington; Sugar Grove, West Virginia; Norwenstow in Cornwall, England; Waihopai, New Zealand; and Geraldton, Australia.

The receiving stations of ECHELON sift through the output of the world's electronic media. ECHELON primarily targets non-military domestic and business communications, including email, telephone, fax, and telex networks. This interception is primarily done through monitoring the communications of international phone company telecommunications satellites, civilian communications satellites, and communications as they are sent from undersea cables to microwave transmitters.

ECHELON uses computers that incorporate symbol and voice recognition systems to sift through millions of messages every minute, and to identify keywords and phrases, including business names, e-mail addresses, phone and fax numbers that are of interest to its participating member intelligence groups in the U.S., Britain, Canada, and New Zealand. After these phrases are located and the communications they are embodied in are culled, they are sent to analysts in whatever country requested the intercepts. According to one analyst, Amnesty International and Greenpeace have been among ECHELON's targets.

"Let me put it this way," a former NSA officer said, "Consider that anyone can type a keyword into a Net search engine and get back tens of thousands of hits in a few seconds. Assume that people working on the outer edges have capabilities far in excess of what you do."[5]

The gradual assimilation and control of all communications—and ultimately all transactions entirely, including those of perception and thought—is a long term strategy of the controllers that has in recent years been facilitated through the creation of the interdisciplinary science of cybernetics. Now, with cybernetics, mass control is here, eating up our freedom on a day-to-day basis like a fast-acting viral organism.

The term cybernetics was invented by Norbert Wiener, a professor of mathematics at MIT who was involved with what was termed Operations Research as well as System Dynamics for the U.S. during World War II.

Cybernetics is primarily the science of information theory, and it is currently being applied to the world as a whole. Cybernetics theory was first envisioned as a way of precisely managing wars, but with experience it was seen that the disciplines and projections that were vital in the conduct of war were essentially the same as those utilized by government during peacetime. The cybernetic approach evolved such cross-disciplinary groups as the RAND Corporation, Mitre, and Ramo-Wooldridge (which became TRW), brainstorming the cybernetic approach to controlling society and nature itself. The cybernetics idea also provided the genus for the National Security Agency, which is at this time the largest intelligence agency on the planet. Such is the importance of information, according to the controllers.

According to cybernetic innovator Jay W. Forrester, "The professional field known as system dynamics [or cybernetics] has been developing for the last 35 years and now has a world-wide and growing membership. System dynamics combines the theory, methods, and philosophy needed to analyze the behavior of systems in not only management, but also in environmental change, politics, economic behavior, medicine, engineering, and other fields. System dynamics provides a common foundation that can be applied where we want to understand and influence how things change through time."

One experiment in cybernetics was conducted in 1971 after the Marxist-leaning Dr. Salvador Allende was elected president of Chile. As Castro had done earlier, Allende set about nationalizing the industry, banks, and major companies of Chile. But Allende was no agrarian *primatif*, and therein lay his danger to the Establishment world. He called in the British cyberneticist Stafford Beers to provide the means for micro-managing the country, which is rich in natural resources, but which has always been drained by the major industrial powers with little of its gelt left over for the country itself.

Beer gathered together a highly qualified group of cybernetics-savvy scientists and launched what he called Project Cybersyn, the objective of which was, according to Beers, "To install a preliminary system of information and regulation for the industrial economy that will demonstrate the main features of cybernetic management and begin to help in the task of actual decision-making by March 1, 1972... It was a massive application of cybernetic feedback to help each industry and each factory keep track of itself through a central location. All communications flowed through the central location."

Project Cybersyn utilized three primary components:

—Cybernet, which was something of a precursor to today's Internet, a means by which businessmen and government could communicate and consult with anyone else in the web.

—Cyberstride, the programs necessary for monitoring individual companies as well as the economy as a whole, as well as providing alerts when specific areas needed enhancement or were in trouble.

—Chaco, a computerized model of the Chilean economy that provided effective simulations of potential scenarios.

The purpose of Cybersyn was to monitor, to dissect, and to predict the Chilean economy; to debug it in order to create a functioning machine, in much the same manner that is being done in many countries throughout the world today.

The problem is that Cybersyn may have worked too well and so posed a threat to the capitalist world. As the demonstration project that Allende and Beers foresaw, it might have provided a tremendous public relations coup for the Communist world. Henry Kissigner, it is said, was the one who intervened to put an end to the grand experiment. Salvador Allende was assassinated by Chileans who are reported to have been in the pay of the CIA, and Cybersyn went by the wayside.

The CIA seems to have known precisely what it was doing, since there are indications that the Agency at about the same time was focused on cybernetic concerns of its own. According to Anna Keeler in my *Secret and Suppressed* anthology, "Richard Helms wrote of such a system in the mid-1960s while he was CIA Plans Director. He spoke of 'Sophisticated approaches to the coding of information for transmittal to population targets' in the 'battle for the minds of men' and of 'an approach integrating biological, social and physical-mathematical research in an attempt to control human behavior.' He found particularly notable 'use of modern information theory, automata theory, and feedback concepts...for a technology controlling behavior...using information inputs as causative agents...'"

Elsewhere Helms wrote, "Cybernetics can be used in molding of a child's character, the inculcation of knowledge and techniques, the amassing of experience, the establishment of social behavior patterns...all functions which can be summarized as control of the growth processes of the individual."

Cybernetics and the Internet—otherwise, the one world brain envisioned by H.G. Wells—allows for a regulated, interventionist world, one so fine-tuned that much of the machinations that take place behind the scenes are not observed by the man in the street. Among the control strategies that can be and are employed by the elitists in a cybernetic world are the control of food, the control of the monetary supply, the control of energy, and the control of public opinion. The Clinton administration's close attention to the media and opinion polls, and manipulation of same, are in essence a primitive cybernetic approach that has allowed for the institution in the U.S. of a "soft" cybernetic fascism where violent internal intervention is rarely needed, and then seemingly only for public relations purposes.

The techno-fascists are approaching closure, and may have already achieved it. Not only do governments and intelligence agencies currently have the ability to monitor computer and other media messages, as well as the emotional responses of the electorate via polling and other techniques, they have the ability and the will to use media to brainwash us, to change our opinions when they believe it is warranted, and to sell us on every step on the road to complete utilization. As satirized in works like *Report From Iron Mountain* and *Silent Weapons for Quiet Wars*, the cybernetics approach to world management can yield the ultimate in control. Extrapolating from the accelerating advances of the last century, it is obvious that unless lovers of freedom act, and act fast, within the next twenty years the ruling elite will have effectively realized total control over the minds and bodies of mankind.[6]

Notes:
1. Wells, H.G. Cited in White, Carol. *The New Dark Ages* Conspiracy. New York: The New Benjamin Franklin House, 1980
2. Brokaw, Tom, cited in Pouzzner, Daniel. *The Architecture of Modern Political Power*, http:///www.douzzer.ai.mit.edu:8080/conspiracy.html

3. "The Great Firewall of China" by Geramie R. Barme and Sang Ye, Wired Magazine
4. Hersh, Jesse, "The Internet Complex," *Prevailing Winds*, number 4; King, Bradley J., "Doubleplusungood! The Specter of Telescreening," *Parascope* at www.parascope.com/main.htm
5. Hagar, Nicky, "Exposing the Global Surveillance System," *Covert Action Quarterly* online, www.w2/docs2/c/covertaction.html; "Spies Like Us," *Connected*, 16 December, 1997, at www.telegraph.com.uk; Vest, Jason, "Listening In," *Village Voice*, August 12-18, 1998
6. Helms, Richard, cited in Bowart, Walter. *Operation Mind Control.* New York: Dell Books, 1978/; Friedman, George and Meridith. *The Future of War - Power, Technology, and American World Dominance.* 1996; Beer, Stafford. *Brain of the Firm.* 1986; Wiener, Norbert. *The Human Use of Human Beings—Cybernetics and Society.* 1954; Silent Weapons for Quiet Wars, *Secret and Suppressed*, ed. Jim Keith, Feral House

Jim Keith. 1949-1999.

AFTERWORD

H ere stands the New Man, his mind and body stolen from him, soul reduced to the impulses of the animal he thinks he is. His conception of reality is a dance of electronic images fired into his forebrain, a gossamer construction of his masters, designed so that he will not under any circumstances perceive the actual. His happiness is delivered to him through a tube or an electronic connection. His God lurks behind an electronic curtain; when the curtain is pulled away we find the CIA sorcerer, the media manipulator, the cyberneticist, the weaver of the Dreamscape.

As can be seen in the recitation of horrors in these pages, with the advent of advanced technology for mind control and people control we stand at the edge of an abyss. We are at that moment in history where the controllers can do away with what little freedom the human race still possesses, and chain every aspect of the life of mankind to their own parasitic purposes. We are at the point where it is feasible that the destiny of mankind can be owned, and can be molded and shaped with the ease of shaping clay.

A revolution is taking place in the United States instituted by the controllers, whose agents have learned their materialist, immoral philosophies at the knee of monsters like Cameron and Delgado. They are putting in place mind control technologies, advanced surveillance, computerization, indoctrination, prisons and other people-control technologies, that will render freedom meaningless and obsolete, syllables fallen from the lips of a mind-controlled moron. They are launching new assaults on people's lives every minute.

Using these new and old technologies, dissent and original thought are being ripped from us. Traditions of individual sovereignty and freedom are being expunged from our minds and from the history books. And, due to the multitude of anesthetics we have been shot up with, we don't feel a thing. If we do not succeed in stopping the Controllers, ultimately the only people left will be the marching morons, the gullible, and those so apathetic as to have entirely forgotten that freedom can exist.

I am no technology-hating Luddite of old. I use a computer, I surf the Internet. But I am against the use of technology in the continuing commission of crimes against humanity. As the information in this book must have shown, throughout history new technology has been used in the service of authoritarian control without regard for the presumed—at least in America—rights of individuals. Unless our children are going to be the subjects of a world that makes 1984 look benign, then it is time for us to resist the mutilations that the mind masters are foisting upon us.

People should be reminded that the individual sovereignty of our minds and bodies is our most valuable possession. We must educate the populace about the programs of control that have gone on for at least the latter half of this century. We must expose mind control programs that are currently going on in the military, in religious cults, and in psychiatric experiments, in the media, and see to it that these operations are brought to an end. Mind control fascism should be turned worldwide into a hot button topic so that at the mere mention of new incursions on our freedom, the public uproar will be overwhelming.

We must force government to open all files on mind control and related experimentation. Although much of this information has been destroyed, there is certainly a great deal of such documentation that still exists. We must take back the ownership of our world and ourselves.

Now that you have read this book, it is time to act. As always, I advise against illegality and violence. We must expose the nature of totalitarian control, its technologies, its agents. We must safeguard against further incursions against our freedom, our humanity. We must end the mass control of mankind in our lifetime.

INDEX

CONSPIRACY & HISTORY

MIND CONTROL, WORLD CONTROL
by Jim Keith
Veteran author and investigator Jim Keith uncovers a surprising amount of information on the technology, experimentation and implementation of mind control. Various chapters in this shocking book are on early CIA experiments such as Project Artichoke and Project R.H.I.C.-EDOM, the methodology and technology of implants, mind control assassins and couriers, various famous Mind Control victims such as Sirhan Sirhan and Candy Jones. Also featured in this book are chapters on how mind control technology may be linked to some UFO activity and "UFO abductions."
256 PAGES. 6x9 PAPERBACK. ILLUSTRATED. FOOTNOTES. $14.95. CODE: MCWC

MASS CONTROL
Engineering Human Consciousness
by Jim Keith
Conspiracy expert Keith's final book on mind control, Project Monarch, and mass manipulation presents chilling evidence that we are indeed spinning a Matrix. Keith describes the New Man, where conception of reality is a dance of electronic images fired into his forebrain, a gossamer construction of his masters, designed so that he will not—under any circumstances—perceive the actual. His happiness is delivered to him through a tube or an electronic connection. His God lurks behind an electronic curtain; when the curtain is pulled away we find the CIA sorcerer, the media manipulatorÖ Chapters on the CIA, Tavistock, Jolly West and the Violence Center, Guerrilla Mindwar, Brice Taylor, other recent "victims," more.
256 PAGES. 6x9 PAPERBACK. ILLUSTRATED. INDEX. $16.95. CODE: MASC

LIQUID CONSPIRACY
JFK, LSD, the CIA, Area 51 & UFOs
by George Piccard
Underground author George Piccard on the politics of LSD, mind control, and Kennedy's involvement with Area 51 and UFOs. Reveals JFK's LSD experiences with Mary Pinchot-Meyer. The plot thickens with an ever expanding web of CIA involvement, from underground bases with UFOs seen by JFK and Marilyn Monroe (among others) to a vaster conspiracy that affects every government agency from NASA to the Justice Department. This may have been the reason that Marilyn Monroe and actress-columnist Dorothy Kilgallen were both murdered. Focusing on the bizarre side of history, *Liquid Conspiracy* takes the reader on a psychedelic tour de force. This is your government on drugs!
264 PAGES. 6x9 PAPERBACK. ILLUSTRATED. $14.95. CODE: LIQC

INSIDE THE GEMSTONE FILE
Howard Hughes, Onassis & JFK
by Kenn Thomas & David Hatcher Childress

Steamshovel Press editor Thomas takes on the Gemstone File in this run-up and run-down of the most famous underground document ever circulated. Photocopied and distributed for over 20 years, the Gemstone File is the story of Bruce Roberts, the inventor of the synthetic ruby widely used in laser technology today, and his relationship with the Howard Hughes Company and ultimately with Aristotle Onassis, the Mafia, and the CIA. Hughes kidnapped and held a drugged-up prisoner for 10 years; Onassis and his role in the Kennedy Assassination; how the Mafia ran corporate America in the 1960s; the death of Onassis' son in the crash of a small private plane in Greece; Onassis as Ian Fleming's archvillain Ernst Stavro Blofeld; more.
320 PAGES. 6x9 PAPERBACK. ILLUSTRATED. $16.00. CODE: IGF

NASA, NAZIS & JFK:
The Torbitt Document & the JFK Assassination
introduction by Kenn Thomas
This book emphasizes the links between "Operation Paper Clip" Nazi scientists working for NASA, the assassination of JFK, and the secret Nevada air base Area 51. The Torbitt Document also talks about the roles played in the assassination by Division Five of the FBI, the Defense Industrial Security Command (DISC), the Las Vegas mob, and the shadow corporate entities Permindex and Centro-Mondiale Commerciale. The Torbitt Document claims that the same players planned the 1962 assassination attempt on Charles de Gaul, who ultimately pulled out of NATO because he traced the "Assassination Cabal" to Permindex in Switzerland and to NATO headquarters in Brussels. The Torbitt Document paints a dark picture of NASA, the military industrial complex, and the connections to Mercury, Nevada which headquarters the "secret space program."
258 PAGES. 5x8. PAPERBACK. ILLUSTRATED. $16.00. CODE: NNJ

MIND CONTROL, OSWALD & JFK:
Were We Controlled?
introduction by Kenn Thomas
Steamshovel Press editor Kenn Thomas examines the little-known book *Were We Controlled?*, first published in 1968. The book's author, the mysterious Lincoln Lawrence, maintained that Lee Harvey Oswald was a special agent who was a mind control subject, having received an implant in 1960 at a Russian hospital. Thomas examines the evidence for implant technology and the role it could have played in the Kennedy Assassination. Thomas also looks at the mind control aspects of the RFK assassination and details the history of implant technology. Looks at the case that the reporter Damon Runyon, Jr. was murdered because of this book.
256 PAGES. 6x9 PAPERBACK. ILLUSTRATED. NOTES. $16.00. CODE: MCOJ

SAUCERS OF THE ILLUMINATI
by Jim Keith, Foreword by Kenn Thomas

Seeking the truth behind stories of alien invasion, secret underground bases, and the secret plans of the New World Order, *Saucers of the Illuminati* offers ground breaking research, uncovering clues to the nature of UFOs and to forces even more sinister: the secret cabal behind planetary control! Includes mind control, saucer abductions, the MJ-12 documents, cattle mutilations, government anti-gravity testing, the Sirius Connection, science fiction author Philip K. Dick and his efforts to expose the Illuminati, plus more from veteran conspiracy and UFO author Keith. Conspiracy expert Keith's final book on UFOs and the highly secret group that manufactures them and uses them for their own purposes: the control and manipulation of the population of planet Earth.

148 PAGES. 6X9 PAPERBACK. ILLUSTRATED. $12.95. CODE: SOIL

THE SHADOW GOVERNMENT
9-11 and State Terror
by Len Bracken, introduction by Kenn Thomas

Bracken presents the alarming yet convincing theory that nation-states engage in or allow terror to be visited upon their citizens. It is not just liberation movements and radical groups that deploy terroristic tactics for offensive ends. States use terror defensively to directly intimidate their citizens and to indirectly attack themselves or harm their citizens under a false flag. Their motives? To provide pretexts for war or for increased police powers or both. This stratagem of indirectly using terrorism has been executed by statesmen in various ways but tends to involve the pretense of blind eyes, misdirection, and cover-ups that give statesmen plausible deniability. Lusitiania, Pearl Harbor, October Surprise, the first World Trade Center bombing, the Oklahoma City bombing and other well-known incidents suggest that terrorism is often and successfully used by states in an indirectly defensive way to take the offensive against enemies at home and abroad. Was 9-11 such an indirect defensive attack?

288 PAGES. 6X9 PAPERBACK. ILLUSTRATED. $16.00. CODE: SGOV

ARKTOS
The Myth of the Pole in Science, Symbolism, and Nazi Survival
by Joscelyn Godwin

A scholarly treatment of catastrophes, ancient myths and the Nazi Occult beliefs. Explored are the many tales of an ancient race said to have lived in the Arctic regions, such as Thule and Hyperborea. Progressing onward, the book looks at modern polar legends including the survival of Hitler, German bases in Antarctica, UFOs, the hollow earth, Agartha and Shambala, more.

220 PAGES. 6X9 PAPERBACK. ILLUSTRATED. $16.95. CODE: ARK

THE LUCID VIEW
Investigations in Occultism, Ufology & Paranoid Awareness
by Aeolus Kephas

An unorthodox analysis of conspiracy theory, ufology, extraterrestrialism and occultism. *The Lucid View* takes us on an impartial journey through secret history, including the Gnostics and Templars; Crowley and Hitler's occult alliance; the sorcery wars of Freemasonry and the Illuminati; "Alternative Three" covert space colonization; the JFK assassination; the Manson murders; Jonestown and 9/11. Also delves into UFOs and alien abductions, their relations to mind control technology and sorcery practices, with reference to inorganic beings and Kundalini energy. The book offers a balanced overview on religious, magical and paranoid beliefs pertaining to the 21st century, and their social, psychological, and spiritual implications for humanity, the leading game player in the grand mythic drama of Armageddon.

298 PAGES. 6X9 PAPERBACK. ILLUSTRATED. $16.95. CODE: LVEW

POPULAR PARANOIA
The Best of Steamshovel Press
edited by Kenn Thomas

The anthology exposes the biologocal warfare origins of AIDS; the Nazi/Nation of Islam link; the cult of Elizabeth Clare Prophet; the Oklahoma City bombing writings of the late Jim Keith, as well as an article on Keith's own strange death; the conspiratorial mind of John Judge; Marion Pettie and the shadowy Finders group in Washington, DC; demonic iconography; the death of Princess Diana, its connection to the Octopus and the Saudi aerospace contracts; spies among the Rajneeshis; scholarship on the historic Illuminati; and many other parapolitical topics. The book also includes the Steamshovel's last-ever interviews with the great Beat writers Allen Ginsberg and William S. Burroughs, and neuronaut Timothy Leary, and new views of the master Beat, Neal Cassady and Jack Kerouac's science fiction.

308 PAGES. 8X10 PAPERBACK. ILLUSTRATED. $19.95. CODE: POPA

DARK MOON
Apollo and the Whistleblowers
by Mary Bennett and David Percy

•Did you know a second craft was going to the Moon at the same time as Apollo 11?
•Do you know there are serious discrepancies in the account of the Apollo 13 'accident'?
•Did you know that 'live' color TV from the Moon was not actually live at all?
•Did you know that the Lunar Surface Camera had no viewfinder?
•Do you know that lighting was used in the Apollo photographs—yet no lighting equipment was taken to the Moon? All these questions, and more, are discussed in great detail by British researchers Bennett and Percy in *Dark Moon*, the definitive book (nearly 600 pages) on the possible faking of the Apollo Moon missions. Bennett and Percy delve into every possible aspect of this beguiling theory, one that rocks the very foundation of our beliefs concerning NASA and the space program. Tons of NASA photos analyzed for possible deceptions.

568 PAGES. 6X9 PAPERBACK. ILLUSTRATED. BIBLIOGRAPHY. INDEX. $25.00. CODE: DMO

24 hour credit card orders—call: 815-253-6390 fax: 815-253-6300
email: auphq@frontiernet.net   www.adventuresunlimitedpress.com   www.wexclub.com

ORDER FORM

**10% Discoun
When You Ord
3 or More Item**

One Adventure Place
P.O. Box 74
Kempton, Illinois 60946
United States of America
Tel.: 815-253-6390 • Fax: 815-253-6300
Email: auphq@frontiernet.net
http://www.adventuresunlimitedpress.com

ORDERING INSTRUCTIONS

✓ Remit by USD$ Check, Money Order or Credit Card
✓ Visa, Master Card, Discover & AmEx Accepted
✓ Paypal Payments Can Be Made To:
    info@wexclub.com
✓ Prices May Change Without Notice
✓ 10% Discount for 3 or more Items

SHIPPING CHARGES

United States

✓ Postal Book Rate { $4.00 First Item / 50¢ Each Additional Item
✓ POSTAL BOOK RATE Cannot Be Tracked!
✓ Priority Mail { $5.00 First Item / $2.00 Each Additional Item
✓ UPS { $6.00 First Item / $1.50 Each Additional Item
  NOTE: UPS Delivery Available to Mainland USA Only

Canada

✓ Postal Air Mail { $10.00 First Item / $2.50 Each Additional Item
✓ Personal Checks or Bank Drafts MUST BE
  US$ and Drawn on a US Bank
✓ Canadian Postal Money Orders OK
✓ Payment MUST BE US$

All Other Countries

✓ Sorry, No Surface Delivery!
✓ Postal Air Mail { $16.00 First Item / $6.00 Each Additional Item
✓ Checks and Money Orders MUST BE US$
  and Drawn on a US Bank or branch.
✓ Paypal Payments Can Be Made in US$ To:
  info@wexclub.com

SPECIAL NOTES

✓ RETAILERS: Standard Discounts Available
✓ BACKORDERS: We Backorder all Out-of-
  Stock Items Unless Otherwise Requested
✓ PRO FORMA INVOICES: Available on Request

ORDER ONLINE AT: www.adventuresunlimitedpress.com

Please check: ✓

☐ This is my first order   ☐ I have ordered before

Name
Address
City
State/Province   Postal Code
Country
Phone day   Evening
Fax   Email

Item Code	Item Description	Qty	Total

Please check: ✓

☐ Postal-Surface
☐ Postal-Air Mail (Priority in USA)
☐ UPS (Mainland USA only)
☐ Visa/MasterCard/Discover/American Express

Subtotal ▶
Less Discount-10% for 3 or more items ▶
Balance ▶
Illinois Residents 6.25% Sales Tax ▶
Previous Credit ▶
Shipping ▶
Total (check/MO in USD$ only) ▶

Card Number
Expiration Date

10% Discount When You Order 3 or More Items!